Tibetans in Nepal

STUDIES IN FORCED MIGRATION

General Editors: Stephen Castles and Dawn Chatty

TIBETANS IN NEPAL

The Dynamics of International Assistance
among a Community in Exile

―――――――

Ann Frechette

Berghahn Books
NEW YORK • OXFORD

First published in hardback in 2002 by

Berghahn Books

www.berghahnbooks.com

First paperback edition published in 2004

Library of Congress Cataloging-in-Publication Data

Frechette, Ann.
    Tibetans in Nepal : the dynamics of international assistance among a
community in exile / Ann Frechette.
        p. cm.
    Includes bibliographical references and index.
    ISBN 1-57181-157-5 (cl. : alk. paper) – ISBN 1-57181-686-0 (pbk. : alk. paper)
    1. Tibetans–Nepal. 2. Exiles–Nepal. 3. Tibetans–Ethnic identity. I. Title

DS493.9.T53 F74 2002
305.895'405496–dc21

                                                                2002025432

British Library Cataloguing in Publication Data

A catalogue record for this book is available from the British Library.

Printed in Canada on acid-free paper

Cover photo: Atisha student in Tibetan opera costume

Photo credit: Ann Frechette

Contents

List of Illustrations

MAPS

TABLES

Preface

This book is about relationships between international assistance organizations and local communities. It argues that relationships of international assistance involve normative dynamics that influence the way in which local communities define their collective norms and values. It focuses specifically on the Tibetan exiles in Nepal. It explores the ways in which Tibetan exiles in Nepal negotiate their norms and values as they interact with the many international organizations that assist them. It argues that their negotiations complicate the Tibetans' efforts to define themselves as a community.

The book is based on eighteen months of field research I conducted in the Kathmandu Valley of Nepal between 1989 and 1995. Supplemental research included three months in 1994 in Dharamsala India, the seat of the Dalai Lama's exile administration, and two months in 1995 in Lhasa, the capital of Tibet. The initial question I sought to answer through my research is how the Tibetan exiles were able to develop and maintain control over Nepal's largest industry, the manufacture and export of hand-made woolen carpets, given that upon their arrival in Nepal, the Tibetans were poor, landless, stateless, inexperienced in international business, and without rights to own land or register export businesses in Nepal. The answer, I found, is that international patrons helped the Tibetans to secure rights to land and business ownership and provided them with the resources they needed—including investment capital, education and training, material goods, and diplomatic connections—to develop and control the carpet industry. International patrons continue to assist the Tibetans in Nepal. The relationship between the Tibetans and their international patrons has persisted for more than forty years and is critical to the ability of the Tibetans to maintain their economic and political influence not just over the carpet industry but also over Tibetan settlement camps, monasteries, and schools in Nepal.

International assistance to the Tibetan exiles has, indeed, helped them to achieve economic and political influence in Nepal, yet it has also had broader, more far-reaching effects. It is the effects of international assistance that is the topic of this book. It analyzes the way in which international assistance to the Tibetan exiles in Nepal affects how the Tibetans define and discuss the Tibetan identity. As the Tibetans interact with each of the many international organizations that assist them, they negotiate what it means to be Tibetan to accommodate their patrons' expectations. Sometimes their patrons' expectations are communicated clearly and unambiguously, as when they constitute conditions upon which the continuation of assistance is contingent. An example is U.S. intergovernmental assistance to the Dalai Lama's exile administration contingent upon its democratic transformation. At other times, Tibetans infer what their patrons expect of them and accommodate their expectations without explicit negotiation. The headmaster at the Tibetan school where I taught, for example, sent Christmas cards to all of the school's sponsors not because he himself celebrates Christmas (as a Buddhist, he does not), but because he thought they, as Christians, would expect to hear from him at that time of year. As the Tibetans accommodate their patrons' expectations, they take on values and behaviors that were never before part of being Tibetan. These values and behaviors complicate the Tibetans' efforts to define themselves as a community.

My argument here–that international assistance to the Tibetan exiles complicates their efforts to define themselves as a community–is intended to counterbalance the existent literature on the Tibetan exiles, most of which documents in a relatively uncritical manner the ways in which the Tibetan exiles preserve and protect what is presumed to be a traditional Tibetan identity. Such literature portrays the Tibetan exile communities as a kind of living museum–a place where Tibetan traditions can be preserved and protected, documented and observed, until they can be reintroduced into Tibet. It portrays international assistance to the Tibetan exiles, similarly, as a kind of benign philanthropy, a financial resource that serves merely to support the Tibetans' own efforts to preserve and protect their culture, values, and traditions. My argument is that international assistance to the Tibetan exiles is not value-free–a resource that serves merely to support the Tibetans' own efforts–as portrayed in the existent literature. Relationships of international assistance have their own normative dynamics. They shape the ways in which the Tibetan exiles define and discuss what it means to be Tibetan. They are one of the means through which what it means to be Tibetan is defined and transformed. The interpretation of the Tibetan exile communities that I advance here, therefore, is that of a set of interconnected and highly politicized sites where Tibetan identities are continually constructed and contested. The social actors involved include Tibetans, members of the Tibetans' host communities, and various international patrons who support the Tibetans. As they interact with each other, all of these groups negotiate what it means to be Tibetan in a manner that is no less dynamic than that which occurs in Tibet. What is means to be Tibetan is changing just as much outside Tibet–within the exile communities–as within Tibet. There is no traditional Tibetan identity in exile.

The relationships the Tibetan exiles maintain with the many international organizations that assist them complicate more than just the Tibetan identity as well. They complicate the sovereignty of Nepal as a host state to Tibetans, the authority of the Dalai Lama's exile administration over the Tibetans, and the loyalty of the Tibetans to Tibetan national goals. They complicate all of these issues—sovereignty, authority, loyalty, and identity—as they create incentives for the Tibetans to identify, affiliate, and act in concert with groups alternative to their local and national communities. Relationships of international assistance constitute a type of international community through which new norms, values, and rules for interaction are negotiated. My interest is in how such relationships influence everyday interactions at the local level.

This book is not only about the effects that international assistance has in the specific case of the Tibetan exiles. It is also, on a more general level, about how to analyze the effects that international assistance has on any local community. The Tibetan case may be unusual in the number of international organizations involved and in the duration of their involvement, yet it is not unusual in the dynamics of their involvement. It is, in fact, precisely because of the intensive and long-term nature of the Tibetan case that it illustrates the dynamics of international assistance so clearly. This book therefore uses the Tibetan case to outline a framework for the analysis of international assistance that accounts for its normative dynamics and analyzes its effects on local communities. The framework, which I call the entitlement model of global-local relations, recognizes that international assistance is rarely, if ever, a free gift; it comes with the expectation that local communities will transform in some way so as to accommodate their patrons' norms and values. It asks how accommodation to their norms and values affects issues of sovereignty, authority, loyalty, and identity.

The Tibetan exiles among whom I conducted my research discussed the process of accommodating the norms and values of those who assist them in terms of the metaphor of a bat, a creature they describe as neither bird nor rat yet with the capacity to imitate both. The bat metaphor depicts the Tibetans as very much in control of the process of accommodation. It portrays them as people with a solid identity at the core who accommodate the expectations of others only on the surface, only to the extent that it helps them to pass as acceptable. When they describe themselves as bats, Tibetans assert their capacity to maintain their core identity as Tibetan (as bats) and at the same time imitate others (as birds and rats) without complication, without actual accommodation to others' norms and values. Through the bat metaphor, in other words, the Tibetans claim a high degree of agency in the process of negotiating international assistance. Tibetans talk about themselves as actively controlling the impression they make on others, so that others perceive them as similar and therefore worthy of acceptance and assistance.

What I found through my research, however, is that the bat metaphor overstates the Tibetans' capacity to control the process of accommodating the

norms and values of others. Tibetans do not merely pretend to accommodate others' expectations. They instead struggle with what they experience
as conflicting expectations and conceptualizations of themselves and their
goals. The efforts of the Tibetan exiles to accommodate the values of
democracy provide an example. The Dalai Lama's exile administration, in
response to U.S. intergovernmental assistance, developed a plan for governing the Tibetan exile communities in a democratic manner, with elected
representation and a system of checks and balances among three branches
of government. One could interpret the plan as mere instrumentalism, as
something the Tibetan exiles put together only to ensure that U.S. intergovernmental assistance continues. That interpretation accords with the
Tibetans' description of themselves as bats, as people who accommodate
others' expectations only on the surface while maintaining their identity as
Tibetan at the core. What that interpretation does not capture, however, are
all the debates that occur among Tibetan exiles about democracy and its
role in Tibetan society. Some Tibetan exiles, it would seem, believe quite
sincerely in the values of democracy. They argue that it is not only a good
way in which to govern Tibetan society but that it also reflects values that
Tibetans have always held dear. They struggle then to reconcile their commitment to democracy with their belief in the righteousness of government
by the Dalai Lamas. Their efforts to reconcile the two belief systems—one of
which entrusts government to the will of the people, the other of which
entrusts it to a supreme enlightened being—engage the very fundamentals of
the Tibetan identity. They reflect a process of accommodating the norms
and values of others that is far more than skin deep.

The values of democracy are not the only values the Tibetans have been
challenged to accommodate. The Tibetans' international patrons have challenged them to accommodate also the values of human rights, liberalism,
humanism, multiculturalism, environmentalism, and even, ironically, self-
sufficiency. As the Tibetans struggle with all of these expectations, they
argue about what it means to be Tibetan, what is important to pass on to the
next generation as part of the Tibetan identity. Is democracy essential to the
Tibetan identity? Is Buddhism? Is commitment to the Dalai Lama? Is the
Tibetan language? Is the Tibetan independence cause? What about the
intent to return to Tibet? As Tibetans construct their own answers to these
many questions, they challenge the efforts of the Dalai Lama's exile administration to define the content of the Tibetan identity so as to make claims
to national self-determination and to educate the next generation as
Tibetans. What it means to be Tibetan is a highly contested issue, as a result,
both within the Tibetan exile community and between the Tibetan exiles
and their compatriots in Tibet.

Discussions I had with many Tibetans over many years in Nepal, India,
Tibet, and the United States led me to the understanding that I present in this
book. Research for the book consisted of life history interviews, event-based

interviews, surveys of Tibetan businesses and residential communities, day-to-day site observations in three separate Tibetan settlement camps (Jawalakhel, Boudha, and Jorpati), and archival research in a number of Tibetan exile organizations. I conducted most of the research in the Kathmandu Valley of Nepal in 1995. Throughout 1995, I lived just outside of the Tibetan settlement camp in Jawalakhel. I taught at Jawalakhel's Tibetan school and conducted a number of projects for both the Tibet Office (the representative of the Dalai Lama's exile administration in Nepal) and the Snow Lion Foundation (a non-profit organization founded by Swiss inter-governmental officials to provide assistance to Tibetans in Nepal).

I first became aware of the extent of the role that international organizations play in the lives of the Tibetan exiles in Nepal through the life history interviews I conducted. Tibetans I met in the camp, at the school, and through the survey projects I conducted agreed to be interviewed and recommended others who would be good to interview to provide me with an understanding of a variety of life experiences. I conducted more than fifty life history interviews. My interviewees were a fairly even mix of males and females. They lived in various neighborhoods dispersed throughout the Kathmandu Valley (see Map 0.2). All were in their thirties or older. They included carpet factory owners, hotel and restaurant owners, trekking company owners, shop keepers, monks, teachers, employees of the Dalai Lama's exile administration, and former guerrilla fighters living out their days in retirement. Interviews were in both Tibetan and English. I discussed all of my interviews with my Tibetan language teachers as well as with other Tibetan and Nepali people with whom I interacted on a regular basis to solicit further information and commentary on what I had learned. All of my informants were, in one way or another, influenced by international assistance organizations. Even when they did not personally interact with them, their major life choices were shaped by the resources international organizations provide.

That led to the question of why international organizations were providing assistance to the Tibetan exiles in the first place. To answer that question, I collected information on the relevant international organizations as well. In Nepal, I conducted interviews with representatives from the Swiss Development Corporation, USAID, and UNHCR; I conducted research in the Tibet Office and Snow Lion Foundation archives on the history of their assistance relationships; and I observed the day-to-day interactions between Tibetan exiles and representatives from international assistance organizations at the Tibet Office, the Tibetan settlement camp in Jawalakhel, and the reception center for newly arrived Tibetans in Nepal. In the United States, I collected U.S. government records on the Tibetan exiles, including declassified CIA documents and minutes from U.S. congressional meetings. I read the brochures, web sites, and fundraising materials published by various friends of Tibet organizations. Several recently published memoirs were also of great assistance: Hagen's (1994) recounts his role in establishing a program for Swiss intergovernmental assistance to Tibetans in Nepal; Knaus's (1999) and McCarthy's (1997) document the role of the U.S. CIA in the Tibetan guerrilla war.

I have organized the book, in part, around the Tibetans' assistance relationships. Chapters 1 through 3 examine the Swiss-Tibetan, U.S.-Tibetan, and friends of Tibet relationships respectively. Each includes a history of the assistance relationship and a discussion of its normative dynamics. I ask how the relationship affects the Tibetans' efforts to define themselves as a community. Chapters 4 through 6 analyze the other effects of the Tibetans' assistance relationships. Chapter 4 uses the relationship between the Tibet Office, the UNHCR, and the Nepal government to analyze how international assistance to the Tibetans complicates Nepal state sovereignty. Chapter 5 uses interactions between the Dalai Lama's exile administration and other Tibetan exile organizations supported through international assistance to analyze the issue of authority. Chapter 6 uses details on Tibetan families, mutual aid societies, and other local-level organizations to analyze issues of loyalty and identity. The introduction and conclusion use the Tibetan case to outline the framework I propose for the analysis of international assistance, the entitlement model of global-local relations, and to situate it within the literature on entitlements; migrant and refugee studies; and the anthropological study of international, transnational, and global organizations.

Acknowledgments

There are many people who helped to make this book possible and to guide me to its completion. First are the many people, Tibetan and Nepali, who welcomed me into their lives and shared their stories with me. Norlha and Tamding, Kunsang and Chösang, and Mudukar and Greta also graciously provided me, at various times, with a home away from home. To all of the Tibetans who agreed to be interviewed, I extend my sincere appreciation. Tamding, Tsering, and Tensang, in addition to teaching me Tibetan, also provided friendship, advice, and invaluable insight. I thank also Nabina, Kamala, Nawang, and Tenzin for teaching me Nepali and Tibetan. The teachers and students at the Atisha School, Karma and Dechen, Upendra, and the staff of the Tibet Office provided assistance and gracious hospitality. I am grateful to them all.

For the means with which to travel and conduct research, I thank Harvard University's Department of Anthropology, the Mellon Foundation, the Blakemore Foundation, the Fulbright Foundation, and the MacArthur Foundation. For the means with which to write up my research, I thank the Cora DuBois Foundation and the Mellon Foundation. For permission to conduct research in their countries, I thank the governments and people of Nepal, India, and China.

Dan Martin, Elliot Sperling, and Michael Aris taught me how to read and translate Tibetan. Barbara Harrell-Bond, Tsering Shakya, and the staff at the Refugee Studies Programme provided advice, assistance, and the chance to present my work. Dawa Norbu, Amrita Rangasami, and the staff of the Library of Tibetan Works and Archives provided advice and assistance in the earlier stages of the project. I am grateful also to Myron Weiner, Michael Herzfeld, Ken George, Andreas Glaeser, Komatra Chuengsatiansup, Levent Soysal, Don Seeman, and Thomas Malaby for their critical comments and moral support. I thank Fredrik Barth, Stanley Tambiah, and the anonymous reviewer enlisted by Dawn Chatty and Marion Berghahn for their very helpful comments on various drafts of the manuscript. I thank Lee McBride for her editorial assistance. To Sally Falk Moore, my principal advisor, role model, and an exceptional teacher, I am most grateful for advice, criticism, guidance, and support.

To Jane and Sytze van Heteren, Maris Gillette, Caroline Reeves, Elizabeth Remick, Elanah Uretsky, and Susan Ferguson I am grateful for advice and friendship throughout the research and writing process. To my husband, Andrew Haber, who shared my research in Nepal with me as with every-thing, I am most grateful and I thank him by dedicating this book to him.

List of Abbreviations

CDO   Chief District Officer
CIA   Central Intelligence Agency
CTC   Carpet Trading Company, Continental Trading Company
DIIR   Department of Information and International Relations
FNCCI   Federation of Nepalese Chambers of Commerce
           and Industry
FPMT   Foundation for the Preservation of the Mahayana Tradition
HIMCAR   Himalayan Carpet Exporters
HIMS   Himalayan International Mountain School
ICRC   International Committee of the Red Cross
ICVA   International Council for Voluntary Associations
JHC   Jawalakhel Handicraft Center
MTAC   Mongolian and Tibetan Affairs Commission
NTIRRC   Nepalese Tibetan International Refugee Relief Committee
OCM   Oriental Carpet Manufacturers
PLA   People's Liberation Army
PRC   People's Republic of China
SATA   Swiss Association for Technical Assistance
SDC   Swiss Development Corporation
SLF   Snow Lion Foundation
TIN   Tibet Information Network
TWA   Tibetan Women's Association
TYC   Tibetan Youth Congress
UML   United Marxist-Leninist party
UN   United Nations
UNDP   United Nations Development Program
UNESCO   United Nations Educational, Scientific and
           Cultural Organization
UNHCR   United Nations High Commissioner for Refugees
UNICEF   United Nations Children's Fund

UNPO	Unrepresented Nations and Peoples Organization
U.S.	United States
USAID	United States Agency for International Development
USIA	United States Information Agency
VDC	Village Development Committee
WHO	World Health Organization

A Note on Tibetan Translations and Transliterations

Tibetan words in the following account are represented, in the body of the text, as pronounced, preceded by their nearest English equivalent. They are then listed in the glossary at the back, followed by transliterations from the Tibetan script, in accordance with the system developed by Wylie (1959). For example, when I discuss mutual aid societies among the Tibetans, in the body of the text, I write: mutual aid society (*kyiduk*). In the glossary at the back, I write: kyiduk, skyid-sdugs, mutual aid society. Occasionally, very common Tibetan or Nepali words appear in the main text without their English equivalents. They are italicized to mark them as foreign, yet they are modified grammatically as if they were English words. For example, Tibetans eat *tsampa* and wear *chubas*. Nepali people pay for their goods in *rupees*.

TABLE 0.1: International Organizations Assisting Tibetans in Nepal, 1960–1995

1960–1962
British Council of Churches
USAID
Swiss Red Cross
American Red Cross
British Red Cross
Red Cross of Liechtenstein
Indo-German Social Service
Thyssen Concern
Oxford Committee for Famine Relief
Nepalese Tibetan International Refugee
 Relief Committee (NTIRRC)
American Emergency Committee for
 Tibetan Refugees
Australian National Committee for
 World Refugee Year

Source: Data derive from Holborn
(1975); Hagen (1994).

1962–1966
USAID
SATA
Swiss Red Cross
Swiss Aid to Tibetans
Australian Refugee Committee
Norwegian Refugee Council
American Emergency Committee for
 Tibetan Refugees
Nepal International Tibetan Refugee
 Relief Committee (NITRRC)
UNHCR
Nepal Red Cross Society
Save the Children Fund–UK
Save the Children Fund–Sweden
Catholic Relief Services
The United Protestant Mission in Nepal
U.N. Food and Agriculture Organization
World Health Organization (WHO)
UNICEF

Source: Data derive from Information
Office of the Dalai Lama (1969); Holborn (1975).

1975–1995
U.S. Congress
U.S. Department of State
USAID
U.S. CIA
Taiwan's MTAC
Swiss Development Corporation (SDC)
ICRC
UNHCR
Minority Rights Group
Asia Watch
International Campaign for Tibet
Campaign Free Tibet
Swiss Aid to Tibetans
Friends of Tibet Switzerland
Norwegian Refugee Council
Tibet Development Foundation
 Belgium
Tibet Development Fund Holland
SOIR-IM, Rajpur
UMCOR
German-Nepal Help Association
German Aid to Tibetans
Tibet Fund USA
Tibet Health and Development Fund
Tibet Cultural Institute USA
MISEREOR
Save the Children British Columbia
Tibet Society UK
Tibet Foundation UK
Help the Aged International–UK
Help Tibet Trust UK
Friends of Tibet–UK
Tibet Relief Fund London
Tibetan Refugee Aid Society Canada
Canadian Teachers Federation
SOS International
Dana International Centre Japan
TRCS Japan
Aide à l'enfance Tibetaine
Fiona Fund
Association Tibet Libre
American Himalayan Foundation
Association Tibet Freand
REDD BARNA
Nepal Red Cross Society

Source: Data derive from Snow Lion
Foundation Annual Reports, 1975–1995.

MAP 0.1: Location of Tibetan Settlement Camps in Nepal

TABLE 0.2: Distribution in the Kathmandu Valley of Tibetans Who Claim Refugee Status (Index for Map 0.2)

Map Location		Number of Tibetans	Map Location		Number of Tibetans
1	Budanalikantha	51	36	Nagpokari	9
2	Toykal	13	37	Kamal Pokhari	20
3	Bansbari	160	38	Chabahil	133
4	Baluwatar	1	39	Gaushala	4
5	Sundarijaal	1	40	Nagarkot	0
6	Vajrayogini	0	41	Ganesthan, Nar Devi	12
7	Ichangu, Sitapaila,Ramkhot	28	42	Asan Tole	10
8	Balaju	14	43	Bhotahity	7
9	Gongabu	23	44	Rani Pokari	5
10	Dapasi	22	45	Bagh Bazaar	11
11	Maharaj Ganj, Chaksal	52	46	New Road	8
12	Gorkana	7	47	Tundikhel	0
13	Swayambhu	167	48	Sundhara	20
14	Kal Dhara	16	49	Baneswar	1
15	Paknajol	28	50	Babar Mahal	8
16	Naya Bazaar	18	51	Besigaun	19
17	Lazimpat	171	52	Nakhu	4
18	Bhatbhateni	2	53	Langankhel	15
19	Handigaon, Tangal	5	54	Pulchowk	6
20	Bishalnagar	10	55	Kupontole, Lalitpur	14
21	Thinchuli	182	56	Patan	140
22	Boudha	2381	57	Koteswore	3
23	Kopan	97	58	Jawalakhel	141
24	Tusal	305	59	Bhaktapur	8
25	Jorpati	687	60	Sunakoti	13
26	Sankhu	5	61	Sanogaun	8
27	Kimdole	22	62	Pharping	57
28	Chauni	5	63	Chapagaun	15
29	Dalu	207	64	Godavari	3
30	Bijeswari	26			
31	Chettrapati	174			
32	Thamel, Jhoche	169			
33	Thahity	113			
34	Jyatha Tole	86			
35	Kathmandu	62			

Source: Data derive from Nepal Home Ministry Tibetan Refugee Identity Book Applications, 1994–1995.

MAP 0.3: Development of the Jawalakhel Settlement Camp

TABLE 0.3: Development of the Jawalakhel Settlement Camp (Index for Map 0.3)

1   Cooperative Society restaurant.
2   Tibetan monastery built on public land.
3   Privately owned Nepali houses. Rented to Tibetans.
4   Privately owned Nepali houses built on private land. Tibetans argue it is camp land.
5   Nepali school. Built by SATA for Tibetans but nationalized by Nepal government in 1971.
6   Medical Dispensary. Site of new staff quarters.
7   Private Nepali house. Built on land that was once part of the Tibetan camp.
8   Tibetan old person's home.
9   Tibetan nursery.
10 Circle of houses built for Tibetans by SATA in 1967.
11 Private Tibetan factory built on several garden plots.
12 Private Newar farmhouse on privately owned land.
13 Small one-room shacks built on factory land for Tibetans in 1975.
14 Poultry farm house built on factory land. Now used as staff quarters.
15 Atisha School built on factory land with factory money. Serves as elementary school.
16 Factory spinning hall. Built on factory land in 1967.
17 Cooperative Society sales shop. Built on public land that once housed a Shiva temple.
18 Tibetan temple (chorten).
19 New factory building. Serves as weaving hall, sales shop, and administrative offices.
20 New factory storeroom. Also serves as a meeting hall.

Source: Base map derives from SATA's Tibetan Resettlement in Jawalakhel, Kathmandu, 1967. Revisions are my own, based on my own field survey, 1995.

Introduction

Entitlement Systems and Identity Politics

―――――――――――

"We are like bats," Tashi said to me with a sly smile. "If we open our wings and soar in the sky, birds think we are birds. If we lie crouched on the ground and bare our teeth, rats think we are rats."

It seldom happens that I understand Tibetans when they express themselves through such short, somewhat-cryptic sayings. This time, however, I understood immediately. I had just watched Tashi, one of many wealthy, successful Tibetan carpet factory owners in Boudha, an urban neighborhood northeast of Kathmandu, finish his carpet factory work for the day. Tashi had just bundled together his Nepali citizenship papers, business registration papers, and a statement of his accounts, and was handing them to his Nepali business advisor to take to the Department of Cottage Industries to renew Tashi's business license for the year. As Tashi signed the papers with his Nepali name, I asked his business advisor where he is from. "I am a true Nepali," he said, and I thought, at first, he was teasing Tashi for being Tibetan, but he soon explained that he is a Newar born just outside of Kasthamandap in Kathmandu's Darbar Square. Of all people in Nepal, a Newar (people from whom the word Nepal is believed to be derived) born at Kasthamandap (a place from where the word Kathmandu is believed to be derived) is one person who can most unarguably make such a claim.[1] As Tashi handed his advisor the business documents, bound in a clear plastic binder, he paused to point to his photograph that showed through the cover. "Look at how young I looked then," he said. And we all laughed.

There are many Tibetans in Nepal like Tashi, the self-proclaimed bats of Tibetan exile society. Skilled at strategies of identity negotiation, they link themselves into multiple local, national, and (most importantly) international networks to access the resources they need to build their business and social organizations. In Tashi's case, he acquired Nepali citizenship, and along with it, the right to buy land, to register a business, to travel outside the country, and to vote for people to represent his interests. He secured various sources of international assistance. He attended a two-year administrative training course organized by Swiss intergovernmental officials for Tibetans in Nepal and then later met a sponsor who sent him to business school in the United States. Tashi used his connections to build a successful carpet business in Nepal; to found a social welfare organization; and, along with a number of other Tibetans in similar positions of influence, to build a hospital in his home village in Tibet. He owes his success, he claimed, to the many people and organizations who assist him.

"Sometimes we feel guilty," Tashi said, "The younger generation, they do not have this guilt, but we know what it is like to live in Tibet. We have seen Tibet and we know. We know what it is like to live in Nepal, too. We have lived here for so long." Tashi's guilt, he explained, comes from being wealthy and successful when many other Tibetans, and most Nepalese, are poor. Nepal is home to some of the poorest people in the world, and as a country, Nepal ranks consistently in World Bank statistics among the poorest in the world. With an economy based on subsistence agriculture, Nepal has an average per capita income of only $200 per year. Fifty to 60 percent of its population lives at or below the absolute poverty level, and some 30 percent is chronically indebted.[2] Just how Tashi, and other Tibetans like him, went from being poor, landless, and stateless to being wealthy, well connected, and politically influential is what I went to Nepal to learn.

What I learned, however, involves more than just how a particular group of Tibetans became economically successful and politically influential within a host country that struggles to support its own population. Far more important is what I learned about the limitations of existent approaches to the analysis of migrant and refugee people to account for the causes and consequences of Tibetan success. Existent approaches rarely discuss international assistance organizations and the role they play in refugee success. This book focuses specifically on the role that international assistance organizations play in the lives of Tibetan exiles in Nepal. It asks how international assistance contributes to the economic success of the Tibetan exiles, yet more importantly, it asks what other effects derive from the assistance relationship. It is intended as a study of the Tibetans as well as a model for the analysis of other populations, migrant or indigenous, who regularly receive international assistance.

The book has three principal arguments. It argues that the relationships the Tibetan exiles maintain with the many international organizations that assist them play a critical role in their economic success. It argues further that identity negotiation on the part of the Tibetan exiles is necessary to maintain their economic success. Finally, it argues that the Tibetans' identity negotiations complicate issues of sovereignty, authority, loyalty, and identity. The book uses the case of the Tibetan exiles to propose a framework for the analysis of international assistance that accounts for what I refer to as its normative dynamics. I analyze international assistance as a type of entitlement system, comparable to the entitlement systems of welfare states, in order to emphasize its role in promoting alternative norms and values among local communities worldwide.

International assistance to the Tibetan exiles has helped them in many ways. It has helped them to build an economic base, to build international awareness for their political cause, to reconstruct their monastic institutions, and to educate their children. The benefits have been numerous. International assistance has also had other effects, however, that are critical to the ways in which the Tibetan exiles define and discuss the Tibetan identity. International assistance to the Tibetan exiles complicates their efforts to define the Tibetan identity. It does so by promoting alternative norms and values among them. The challenge for the Tibetan exiles is to accommodate the norms and values of the organizations that assist them without losing sense of what it means to themselves to be distinctly Tibetan.

"We are like bats," Tashi's self-characterization, is one way of conceptualizing what it means to be Tibetan in a context of conflicting normative expectations. It is one way of making sense of the process of identity negotiation. Being a bat means being able to accommodate others' expectations on the surface while maintaining a consistent sense of oneself at the core. It is an empowering concept that enables Tibetans, at an individual level, to manage the process of identity negotiation. The process of identity negotiation involves more than just the individual transaction of norms and values, however. It involves also the cultivation and maintenance of collective norms and values. Identity negotiation is generative as well as transactional (Barth 1969: 10); it is a collective process as well as an individual process. More than just the negotiation of the individual self, it involves also the reproduction of the collective self over time and across generations.

The relationships the Tibetan exiles maintain with the many international organizations that assist them challenge their efforts to reproduce a collective sense of Tibetanness over time and across generations. They do so by providing incentives for the Tibetans to identify, affiliate, and act in concert with groups alternative to their local and national communities. Such relationships, far from acting to preserve the Tibetan identity (Devoe 1983; Klieger 1992), act to transform it.[3] They introduce alternative norms and values that influence how the Tibetan exiles define and discuss their identities and goals. Relationships of international assistance, although critical to the Tibetans' economic success, are thus best viewed not as a value-free source of financial support for Tibetan cultural continuity, but rather as a mechanism of change. It is the goal of this book to understand how they function as a mechanism of change at the local level and to analyze their specific effects on issues of sovereignty, authority, loyalty, and identity.

Tibetan Success: Definitions, Explanations, and the Role of International Organizations

The existent literature on the Tibetan exiles is in general agreement that the Tibetans are, indeed, successful.[4] The Tibetans have integrated economically into their host countries (Goldstein 1978; Devoe 1983; Saklani 1984; Gombo 1985; Forbes 1989; Chhetri 1990). They interact constructively with their host communities (Gombo 1985; Forbes 1989; von Fürer-Haimendorf 1990; Hagen 1994). They display little evidence of psychological trauma associated with other exile communities worldwide (Goldstein 1978; Miller 1978; Nowak 1984; Norbu 1994). Some authors discuss the role that international organizations play in the social and psychological aspects of this process (Devoe 1983; Klieger 1992). The role that international organizations play in the economic aspects of Tibetan success, however, has thus far received little attention.

This study began as an inquiry into the factors that led to the economic success of the Tibetan exiles. It defines success in terms of income level and property ownership. It focuses on the Tibetan exiles in Nepal, in particular, as they are, in economic terms, exemplars of success, even among Tibetans. The Tibetan exiles are a group who arrived in Nepal with few marketable skills, little capital, and little experience with international business.[5] They were further disadvantaged by Nepali laws and policies restricting land and business ownership to Nepali citizens only.[6] And yet, within a single generation, the Tibetan exiles went on to introduce, establish, and control what is now one of the largest and most important industries in the country, the manufacture and export of hand-woven woolen carpets. Nepal had no carpet industry whatsoever before the Tibetans arrived as exiles in the 1960s.[7] By 1993, the carpet industry, then at its peak, comprised more than five percent of Nepal's gross domestic product and more than half of its total annual export earnings (FNCCI 1995: 29, 66).[8] Total annual sales, from 1989–1993, amounted to more than $150 million, as compared with about $80 million for garment manufacture and $70 million for tourism (FNCCI 1995: 66, 116).[9] With more than 250,000 workers, the industry employs more people than any other in the country (Shrestha 1992: 15). It is a driving force in Nepal's industrialization.[10]

The economic success of the Tibetan exiles in Nepal involves more than just their control over the carpet industry as well. Tibetans also own and manage hotels, jewelry shops, and trekking equipment shops. They have built dozens of monasteries to serve as religious centers for all Buddhists and dozens of schools to educate children of Tibetan exiles as well as of other ethnic Tibetans in Nepal. Tibetan exile carpet factories, shops, monasteries, and schools serve as the most visible evidence of Tibetan success. Observers speak of a "renaissance of Tibetan civilization" in Nepal (von Fürer-Haimendorf 1990).

The relationships the Tibetan exiles maintain with the many international organizations that assist them play a critical role in their economic success. Explanations proposed in the past, however, have tended to obscure that role. Explanations proposed in the past tend to follow either of two approaches that dominate the more general literature on migrants and refugees. The first explains economic success in terms of the structural conditions of the host country. It asks such questions as: Are local labor markets relatively open or closed? At what level can migrants participate economically, given their particular skill sets? Do host government policies facilitate, or hinder, migrant entrepreneurship? Soysal's (1994) analysis of guestworker policies in Europe provides an example of this approach on a general, comparative level. She proposes a typology of incorporation regimes to analyze how states govern the migrants that enter and remain in their territory (1994: 37).[11] The second approach explains economic success in terms of particular cultural characteristics thought to predominate within the group. It asks such questions as: Does the culture of the migrant group emphasize entrepreneurship? Does it place a high value on educational achievement? Does it glorify risk takers? Sowell's (1996) analysis of German, Japanese, Chinese, Italian, Indian, and Jewish migrants is the most recent use of this approach on a general level. He argues that the reason all of these groups have succeeded economically is that their cultures emphasize such values as education, skill, industriousness, risk, social cohesion, and a concern for the future of their children.[12]

The economic success of the Tibetan exiles has been explained in the past in terms of either cultural characteristics or structural conditions. Saklani (1984: 219), for example, argues that Tibetan success is due to cultural characteristics, such as the Tibetans' penchant for trade, their willingness to work hard, and the willingness of Tibetan women to work as hard (outside the home) as Tibetan men.[13] Goldstein (1978) and Norbu (1994), based particularly on the experience of the Tibetan exiles in India, argue that two basic structural conditions are involved: The generous and very liberal policies of the host government, including the donation of land on which the Tibetans could resettle (Goldstein 1978: 397–398; Norbu 1994: 15–16); and the structure of the government of the settlements, headed by the Dalai Lama's exile administration (Goldstein 1978: 406–409; Norbu 1994: 19–29).

The economic success of the Tibetan exiles in Nepal can indeed be explained, in part, by these two approaches. The Tibetans' cultural characteristics, such as their willingness to work hard, certainly played a role. Certain structural conditions in Nepal, such as a surplus of labor, lowering the costs of carpet manufacture, and a lack of competition, at least initially, from Nepali carpet businesses, helped as well. These explanations are incomplete, however, as they cannot explain individual differences among the Tibetan exiles, as attested, for example, by Jha (1992). They also cannot explain why other ethnic Tibetans in Nepal–such as the Gurung, the Manangi, the Thakali, and the Lopa–do not share in the same economic success. All share the same cultural characteristics and structural conditions. If either factor alone, or in combination, were determinative, we should expect all ethnic Tibetans in Nepal to be equally successful, yet they clearly are not.[14]

The success of the Tibetan exiles was, and is, greatly facilitated, as well, by the relationships the Tibetan exiles maintain with a multitude of international patrons, some of whom have been assisting the Tibetan exiles for more than forty years. The Tibetans' international patrons include a broad variety of organizations, both intergovernmental and non-governmental. They include development organizations, Buddhist organizations, refugee assistance and human rights organizations. They facilitate Tibetan success in two ways. They provide the Tibetans with capital and other resources unavailable to other peoples in Nepal, and they serve as guarantors in a series of legal arrangements that enables the Tibetans to circumvent Nepal's restrictions on land and business ownership.[15] The relationships the Tibetan exiles maintain with their international patrons differentiate them from other ethnic Tibetans in Nepal. They are the factor that enabled the Tibetans to acquire the resources they needed to establish and maintain their carpet factories, shops, monasteries, and schools.

The Tibetan Exiles and Their International Patrons

At least five major networks of international assistance contribute to the success of the Tibetan exiles in Nepal. The first revolves around Swiss intergovernmental organizations. They helped the Tibetans establish the first carpet factories and export companies in Nepal. Many of the Tibetans who now control the carpet industry in Nepal started their careers in the Swiss-Tibetan factories or otherwise under the direction of Swiss intergovernmental officials.

A second revolves around U.S. intergovernmental organizations. They helped the Tibetans launch a guerrilla war against China, at times from bases in Nepal. Their efforts included instruction in such skills as operations management and public relations, skills that would later benefit Tibetan managers and entrepreneurs. U.S. officials also helped the Tibetan exiles to establish a separate network of carpet factories and export companies as well as the Dalai Lama's exile administration, represented in Nepal by the Tibet Office.

A third patronage network revolves around a more disparate group of non-governmental organizations I refer to as "friends of Tibet organizations." They helped the Tibetans construct and finance numerous schools and monasteries in Nepal. They also sponsor educational and resettlement opportunities to enable Tibetans to study in, and migrate to, India, the United States, and Europe.

A fourth patronage network revolves around Taiwan's Mongolian and Tibetan Affairs Commission (hereafter the MTAC). The MTAC provides financial support to some Tibetan individuals, monasteries, and schools.[16] Which ones are involved is difficult to discern, however, as few Tibetans admit to accepting its patronage themselves. The reason is that, in contrast with the Tibetans' other patrons, the MTAC carries a moral stigma among the Tibetan exiles due to Taiwan's position that Tibet has always been a part of China. Tibetans describe accepting patronage from the MTAC as "licking honey off the edge of a razor," that is, sweet but dangerous, as it could be interpreted as a sign of support for Taiwan's claims over Tibet.[17] Many of my informants accused other Tibetans of accepting MTAC assistance. Only two implied, indirectly, that they themselves accept it. Both did so by defending their right to accept financial assistance from anyone who offered it.

A fifth patronage network involves the office of the United Nations High Commissioner for Refugees (UNHCR). Its role differs from that of the Tibetans' other patrons. Whereas other patrons help long-term Tibetan exiles establish and maintain their organizations, UNHCR helps newly arrived Tibetan exiles in Nepal. UNHCR provides funds and legal assistance to the Tibetan Refugee Welfare Office to facilitate the transit of Tibetan exiles through Nepal and into resettlement communities in India. Its assistance also serves as a form of moral support to the Tibetan exiles, and particularly to the Dalai Lama's exile administration, which views UNHCR support as legitimation of its claims over Tibet.

These international patrons, taken together, provide the Tibetan exiles with three basic types of resources. The first constitute what may be called human resources. They include English language education and skills training in accounting, business management, and public relations, all of which helped the Tibetans not just to start their businesses but more importantly to be able to operate them on an international scale. The second are material resources, such as direct grants, loans, and computer equipment. The third are what may be called symbolic resources, such as personal recommendations, public statements of support, and marketing assistance. They help the Tibetans maintain an international reputation for spirituality, vulnerability, non-violence, and humility, a reputation that has helped the Tibetans expand their network of patrons, secure protection in their host countries, and market their goods.

Differential access to the resources that international patrons provide is one reason why some Tibetan exiles in Nepal are more successful than others.

Some Tibetan exiles in Nepal, whether because of their personal histories or their organizational abilities, have direct access to international patronage. For them it is comparatively easy to secure the resources they need to start and maintain their business and social organizations. Most Tibetans have only indirect access, however. They work with Tibetan intermediary organizations to secure the resources they need. Control over the resources that international patrons provide has thus become a form of political power among the Tibetan exiles in Nepal. It constitutes one basis for the system of hierarchical relations that governs Tibetan exile society.

Tibetan exile society functions as a stratified system of patron-client relations with international patrons, the source for critical resources, at the top, and with various strata of Tibetan intermediary organizations underneath. The second stratum consists of formal well-organized Tibetan organizations, such as the Snow Lion Foundation and the Dalai Lama's exile administration,

FIGURE I.1 The System of Patron-Client Relations that Structures Tibetan Exile Society

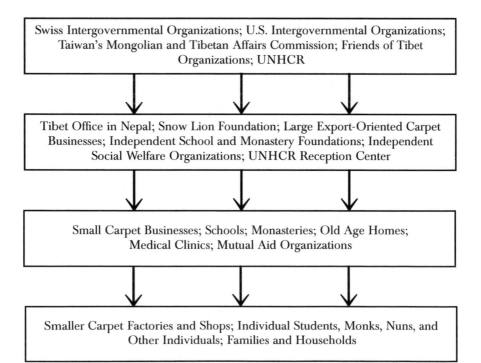

which mediate access to international patrons, and in the process, influence how other Tibetans behave. The third consists of smaller Tibetan organizations, such as Tibetan exile schools, which mediate access to larger Tibetan organizations, and also use their positions to influence how other Tibetans behave. The fourth consists of individuals and less well-organized groups whose access to the resources international patrons provide is limited and highly mediated by other Tibetans' interests. In this system, the ability to mediate access to international resources is a form of political power as well as a factor in economic success.

The Normative Dynamics of International Assistance

The relationships the Tibetan exiles maintain with the many international organizations that assist them involve the transaction of critical resources. Equally important, however, they also involve the transaction of norms and values. These norms and values influence the ways in which the Tibetan exiles define and discuss their identities and their goals. All of the many international organizations that assist the Tibetan exiles maintain their own narratives about who the Tibetans are, why they should be assisted, and who they should become by means of assistance. These narratives are the basis for what I refer to as the normative dynamics of international assistance.

Swiss intergovernmental organizations provide an example. They maintain a narrative about the Tibetans as a humanitarian concern. They promote market mechanisms as a means for resettling the Tibetans. Their goal is Tibetan self-sufficiency through the production of goods for the market, particularly the international carpet market. Toward that end, they seek to promote certain values among the Tibetans that will help them to compete in international markets; they include cleanliness, efficiency, and an international orientation.

U.S. intergovernmental organizations, in contrast, maintain two interrelated narratives about the Tibetans. For them, the Tibetans are fellow anti-Communists as well as advocates for global democracy. U.S. intergovernmental organizations promote democratic governance among the Tibetans. Their goal is the development of a democratic system not just within the exile communities but also in a future Tibet. Toward that end, U.S. officials seek to promote certain values among Tibetans that will help them to develop a democracy; they include a belief in representative government and a commitment to equality of opportunity.

Friends of Tibet organizations maintain a variety of narratives about who the Tibetans are and who they should become by means of assistance. Some maintain a narrative about the Tibetans as a human rights concern. Others portray the Tibetans as an issue of cultural survival. Still others maintain a narrative about the preservation of Tibetan Buddhism as a system of knowledge with potential benefits for all humankind. What all of these groups have in common is a liberal humanist worldview that celebrates and supports the rights of individuals to maintain their own cultural heritage. They promote such values among the Tibetans as humanism, multiculturalism, environmentalism, and legal activism.

As the Tibetan exiles interact with each of these many international organizations, they learn to define themselves and their goals in terms of the appropriate narratives. They adopt the same language and normative frameworks. In the process, they reinterpret their own values, culture, and tradition in terms of their patrons' worldviews. With repeated interactions over time, they come to entertain their patrons' worldviews as alternatives to their own.[18] It is in this manner that the normative dynamics of international assistance function as a mechanism for change. It is my contention that these dynamics occur not only among the Tibetan exiles yet among all local communities that regularly receive international assistance.

The Entitlement Model of Global-Local Relations

This book therefore proposes a model not just for the analysis of the Tibetan exiles yet for all local communities that regularly receive international assistance. The model is intended to facilitate the analysis of the normative dynamics of international assistance. It analyzes relationships of international assistance as a type of entitlement system, similar in some respects to the entitlement systems organized and maintained by welfare states. The central process around which the model is constructed is the process of legitimation. I ask how international organizations legitimate the assistance they provide. (How do they portray certain communities as more entitled to assistance than others?) And I ask how recipient communities legitimate their claims to assistance. (Why do they portray themselves as more entitled to assistance than others?) Recipient communities, I argue, learn over time how to legitimate their claims in terms of the same norms and values as the international organizations that assist them. That process is what I refer to as the normative dynamics of international assistance.

Existent models used to analyze international assistance do not account for its normative dynamics, as they do not account for the ways in which recipient communities legitimate their claims to assistance. Existent models analyze international assistance in terms of either charity or humanitarianism on one hand or political instrumentalism on the other. Both of these models take the point of view of the international organization involved, and what we assume to be its intentions, rather than the point of view of the recipients and their efforts to legitimate their claims. The humanitarianism model is used most often to analyze multilateral intergovernmental assistance (as provided, for example, by the United Nations Development Program) or non-governmental assistance (as provided, for example, by Save the Children). By the conventions of the literature, we assume their intentions to be benevolent, apolitical, and concerned only for human well-being (Shawcross 1984; Harrell-Bond 1986; Hancock 1989; and Baintenmann 1990; among others, challenge these assumptions). The instrumentalist model, in contrast, is used most often to analyze bilateral intergovernmental assistance (as provided, for example, by the United States Agency for International Development). By the conventions of the literature, we assume their intentions to be politicized, instrumentalist, and also often neo-imperialist (Zolberg et al.'s 1989: 277 analysis of refugee warrior communities, for example, takes this perspective, as does Reynell 1989). Both of these models assume the intentions of the international organizations involved, yet even more problematic, both ignore the point of view of the recipient communities.

The model I propose, and that I call the entitlement model of global-local relations, takes into account the points of view of both the international organizations involved and the recipient communities. I ask how international organizations legitimate the assistance they provide and how recipient communities legitimate their claims to assistance. I refer to the model as the entitlement model of global-local relations in order to emphasize the central role that processes of legitimation play in these normative dynamics.

I take Sen (1981) as my starting point in the discussion of entitlements and their legitimation. Sen (1981: 1) describes entitlement relations as recursive rules of legitimacy that connect the claims that people make to resources to each other. In so doing, he highlights the fundamental relationship between entitlements and frameworks of legitimacy. He proposes the following example:

> Consider a private ownership market economy. I own this loaf of bread. Why is this ownership accepted? Because I got it by exchange through paying some money I owned. Why is my ownership of that money accepted? Because I got it by selling a bamboo umbrella owned by me. Why is my ownership of the bamboo umbrella accepted? Because I made it with my own labour using some bamboo from my land. Why is my ownership of the land accepted? Because I inherited it from my father. Why is his ownership of the land accepted? And so on. Each link in this chain of entitlement relations "legitimizes" one set of ownership by reference to another, or to some basic entitlement in the form of enjoying the fruits of one's own labour. (1981: 1–2)

Following Sen (1981), I begin with a very broad concept of entitlements centered on the issue of legitimation. I ask how international organizations decide who should receive their assistance and how they legitimate those decisions. I ask further why recipient communities consider themselves legitimate recipients of assistance. Central to this process is a transaction of norms and values. A particular international organization may decide that a group is worthy of assistance, for example, because they are developing democratic governance or open markets, or because they have some particular characteristic considered worthy of promoting. The transfer of resources, on both sides, is legitimated with reference to those values. Possessing and enacting those values is what makes one entitled to a claim.

I characterize international assistance as a type of transfer entitlement–a resource one is entitled to because it is willingly given by another who legitimately owns it (Sen 1981: 3). Transfer entitlements may be distinguished from trade-based entitlements (resources one obtains by trading something one owns with a willing party); production-based entitlements (resources one obtains by arranging production using one's own resources); and own-labor entitlements (resources one obtains through one's own labor power). Transfer entitlements are willingly given in a context of shared values. Why is the transfer considered legitimate? Because the recipients are presumed to be part of the same moral community.

Transfer entitlements are normally discussed only with reference to state welfare programs. Numerous scholars characterize state welfare as a type of entitlement transferred from the state to its citizens (Marshall 1950, 1965; Offe 1972; Freeman 1986; Mann 1987; Young 1995). It is my contention that the concept of entitlements can be applied also beyond the level of the state to discuss resources transferred from international assistance organizations to recipient communities worldwide. What state welfare and international assistance have in common is that, in addition to being a transaction of resources, they are also both a transaction of values. Both serve to promote particular norms and values, not the least of which is the value of community. State welfare promotes the idea of a national community; international assistance promotes the idea of an international community. It promotes the idea that we, as human beings, all share a basic common humanity and that we are all entitled to a minimal standard of life and livelihood. This idea of an international community is enshrined in such documents as the Declaration of Human Rights and the Covenant on Economic, Social, and Cultural Rights. International assistance is intended, at least in part, to reinforce this basic idea through a transfer of resources aimed at its achievement.

State welfare programs and international assistance programs are also both intended to promote certain other norms and values as well. Consider Goodin et al.'s (1999: 22) list of six moral values state welfare is intended to achieve:

1. Promoting economic efficiency
2. Reducing poverty
3. Promoting social equality
4. Promoting social integration and avoiding social exclusion
5. Promoting social stability
6. Promoting autonomy

Goodin et al.'s (1999: 125–236) concern is the degree to which three types of social welfare regimes achieve any or all of these goals. They compare liberal welfare regimes (exemplified by the United States), corporatist welfare regimes (exemplified by Germany), and social democratic welfare regimes (exemplified by the Netherlands) for their achievements in this regard.[19]

My concern is the extent to which any or all of these goals are promoted by international assistance programs. The same language employed at the level of the state, I argue, is also used at the international level. The means (resource transfers), too, are the same. The principal difference between the two types of relationships involves the larger system within which they are embedded. Welfare states are constructed on the logic of a closed system. They are characterized by a closed and bounded membership (their citizenry) that contributes to the system through a sense of affiliation, solidarity, and a willingness to share resources with each other (Walzer 1983). International assistance relationships, in contrast, are constructed on the logic of an open system. Such relationships may develop between any international assistance organization and any local community. I refer to the resources transferred in both types of relationships as entitlements to emphasize the role they play in promoting shared norms and values. We may refer to the

FIGURE I.2 The Normative Dynamics of International Assistance

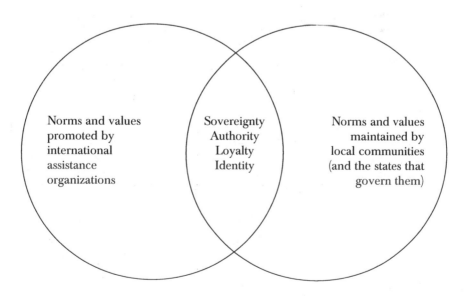

Norms and values promoted by international assistance organizations

Sovereignty
Authority
Loyalty
Identity

Norms and values maintained by local communities (and the states that govern them)

first type as membership entitlements to acknowledge the boundedness of the larger system within which they are transacted; we may refer to the second as non-member entitlements to acknowledge the openness of the larger system. International assistance has long served as a means through which organizations of all types promote their norms and values worldwide. Missionary religious organizations, for example, have for centuries used assistance relationships to promote their values. What is new is the extent to which other types of organizations—whether governmental or non-governmental, whether organized to promote human rights, development, or refugee assistance—use international assistance as a means to promote their norms and values among others.[20] My interest is in the effects that relationships of international assistance have on recipient communities. I argue that relationships of international assistance, due to their normative dynamics (that is, due to the role they play in promoting alternative norms and values), complicate four related issues for recipient communities and the states in which they live. They are sovereignty, authority, loyalty, and identity.

Sovereignty

There are as many different definitions of the concept of sovereignty as there are answers to the questions where, within a state, does it reside, what are its limits, and how is it affected by changing international norms (Fowler and Bunck 1995). Sovereignty is defined here as the rights, powers, and privileges a state possesses over its membership and territory. States negotiate the limits of their sovereign rights in their interactions both with other states (Thomas et al. 1987; Lyons and Mastanduno 1995; Onuf 1995; Rosenau 1995; Donnelly 1995) and with their own citizenry (Philpott 1997: 20). In general, the sovereign rights of states include the right to control the passage of both people and goods into and out of state territory, the right to decide who may become a citizen or non-citizen member of the state polity, and the right to control state domestic affairs, including the right to collect taxes, define and prosecute crimes, and provide for the general welfare of the citizenry.

Relationships between international assistance organizations and the recipients of their assistance complicate the issue of sovereignty, for they involve their own normative dynamics that may at times conflict with the norms and values promoted by the state. International assistance organizations may promote the values of democracy, for example, within a state that is decidedly undemocratic. They may promote women's empowerment within a state that defines women's roles as subordinate to men. They may promote rights to religious expression within a state that considers certain forms of religious expression a threat to national interests. States evoke the issue of sovereignty when the international organizations that assist their people promote values that conflict with their own.

Issues of state sovereignty become even more complex when international organizations intervene in a state to assist people they consider refugees. Many of the organizations that assist Tibetan exiles in Nepal, for example, consider them to be refugees; UNHCR considers them to be "persons of concern." International organizations that assist refugees, referred to elsewhere as the "international refugee regime" (McLean 1983: 175; Zolberg et al. 1989: 258; Malkki 1995a: 504), promote a special set of norms and values that concern how refugees ought to be treated. These norms and values have been institutionalized in a set of international agreements, including the 1951 Convention Relating to the Status of Refugees, and its 1967 Protocol, signed by one hundred forty states worldwide.[21] These international norms for the treatment of refugees do, at times, conflict with the norms and values promoted by states themselves (Weiner 1998: 433). Four issues regularly arise.

The first is the issue of who can or cannot enter state territory. States regard this decision as a fundamental symbol of state sovereignty (Weiner 1995: 9; Brubaker 1989: 14; Hammar 1990: 16); they resist pressure from international organizations to admit certain groups as refugees when they themselves do not consider the situation to warrant refugee status. The second involves assistance to refugees that, intentionally or not, supports armed resistance movements within state territory. International assistance organizations may unintentionally support armed resistance movements when the camps they maintain become recruitment centers, sources of supplies, or safe havens for the combatants and their dependents (Zolberg et al. 1989: 277; Weiner 1998: 438). The third issue involves the level of assistance international organizations provide to refugees. International assistance organizations do, at times, provide assistance to refugees at a level far more generous than that which the state provides its own citizens (Chambers 1986; Harrell-Bond 1986). Assistance that exceeds state welfare provisions sets new, at times unfeasible, standards for the state itself. A fourth issue involves when states may ask refugees to leave state territory. International refugee agreements stipulate that refugees cannot be made to return unwillingly to their home country, a provision that has been referred to as the principle of non-refoulement.[22] UNHCR is obligated to enforce the principle of non-refoulement, yet at times, that principle conflicts with the norms of state sovereignty, and in particular, the state's sovereign right to control its own borders (Weiner 1998: 438).

The relationship between international assistance organizations and the Tibetan exiles in Nepal has led Nepali officials to raise the issue of state sovereignty a number of times. The most striking involves U.S. intergovernmental assistance to a Tibetan resistance movement that used Nepal's Mustang region as a base from which to engage in guerrilla activities against China (Andrugtsang 1973; Avedon 1984; McCarthy 1997; Knaus 1999). The Nepal government never openly acknowledged the guerrilla movement. It is questionable that Nepal ever granted permission for it to operate in its territory. When the Nepal army disbanded the movement in the 1970s, government newspapers carried stories about how shocked Nepal's officials were to discover what had occurred in their territory. They accused the U.S. of violating the norm of state sovereignty.

UNHCR assistance to the Tibetan exiles in Nepal involves a different sort of normative conflict involving control over Nepal's borders. The UNHCR reception center system in Nepal finances the transit of approximately 2,500 Tibetans from Tibet through Nepal and into India each year. Some of those Tibetans find their way back into Nepal, as Nepal provides Tibetans better economic opportunities than India. UNHCR's agreement with the Nepal government specifies that Nepal will not accept any new Tibetan exiles, and that all Tibetans who arrive after December 31, 1989 must proceed out of Nepal state territory. Some Nepali officials consider the re-entrance of these new Tibetan exiles as a violation of state sovereignty that justifies deportation.

International assistance organizations are also in a position to help support state norms and values, as when they provide assistance to the state itself, or to projects that the state also supports. It is only when the norms and values promoted by international assistance organizations come into conflict with state norms and values that the issue of state sovereignty is evoked.

Authority

Authority is defined here as the legitimate ability to command thought or behavior and to be obeyed. Authority may be legitimated through personal charisma, traditional procedures, or rational-legal procedures (Weber 1968: 212–245). It may be exercised through control over economic resources or through control over the coercive apparatus of the state–the military, the police, the prisons, and the courts (Weber 1968: 941–948). Relationships between international assistance organizations and the recipients of their assistance complicate the issue of authority in two ways. They involve the transaction of resources that could be used either to support or to challenge existent sources of authority within a state. They could, in other words, be channeled through existent leadership structures or through emergent leaders whom international officials seek to promote.[23] Either way, the international organization involved introduces a new set of norms and values through which positions of authority are legitimated. Either intentionally or not, international assistance introduces a new framework for legitimation.

The Tibetan exiles provide an example. At least some of the assistance that international organizations provide the Tibetan exiles–including much of the assistance that U.S. intergovernmental organizations provide–is channeled through the Dalai Lama's exile administration. That assistance serves, in part, to support the authority of the Dalai Lama's exile administration. In doing so, however, it introduces a new set of norms and values through which its authority is legitimated. U.S. intergovernmental assistance, in particular, introduced the values of democracy as a framework for legitimation. Thus, the authority of the Dalai Lama's exile administration becomes legitimated not only through its association with the Dalai Lama, the traditional spiritual and political leader of the Tibetan people, yet also through its promotion of democratic ideals (Norbu 1990; Thinley 1990; Bhattacharjea 1994). Just how democratic the Dalai Lama's exile administration is becomes a criterion for assessing the legitimacy of its authority.

The issue of authority becomes even more complex when international assistance is channeled through middlemen who lack traditional sources of support. In that case, international assistance serves to establish an alternative leadership structure, legitimated in terms of norms and values initially not shared by the local community. Over time, those norms and values could come to be shared by the local community, and the new leaders could be accepted, yet that process involves a struggle between existent and emergent leaders; it involves a struggle for legitimacy. Again, the Tibetans provide an example. The initial leader of the Tibetan guerrilla movement in Nepal was a monk, Baba Yeshe. He helped resettle the guerrillas in northern Nepal and oversaw their activities for nearly a decade. Fellow guerrilla fighters accepted him as a leader in part because he was involved with the guerrilla movement from its inception but also in part because of his status as a monk. Over time, the U.S. intergovernmental organizations that supported the guerrilla movement in Nepal sought to replace Baba Yeshe with a leader they trained themselves. They wanted someone younger, and who could speak English, in that leadership position. They sent Wangdu Gyatsotsang, a young charismatic CIA-trained Tibetan, to replace Baba Yeshe, who refused to leave. The two leaders fought for control over the guerrilla movement until it was disbanded in the early 1970s. Many young guerrilla fighters supported Wangdu Gyatsotsang; they supported him not only because of his considerable personal charisma but also because he represented a new style of leadership unassociated with the monastic tradition yet legitimated through U.S. support.

Loyalty

Loyalty is defined here as a feeling of allegiance or commitment to a person, institution, ideal, product, or cause. States are one institution around which loyalty is constructed. States command the primary loyalty of their citizens. Relationships between international assistance organizations and the recipients of their assistance complicate the issue of loyalty. They provide a locus for the development of allegiances alternative to the state, that transcend the state, and that involve an alternative set of norms and values through which loyalty may be constructed.

Loyalty to a state is constructed through the association of many complex ideals, such as nationality, citizenship, kinship, common history, and a commitment to the same norms and values. It is often expressed through a commitment to die for the state and its ideals, as through enrollment in the military. It is also often expressed through cooperation with state decisions, even when they conflict with individual interests, provided that the decisions are made through a process deemed legitimate (Hammar 1989: 88). Within democratic states, loyalty can be expressed through the exercise of the right to vote. Finally, loyalty to all states can be expressed through contribution to the state, whether in the form of taxes or voluntary service (Harris 1987).[24]

Welfare programs are one way in which states reinforce state loyalty. They are one way in which states reinforce the idea that all members of the state are part of the same community, with the same norms and values, and entitled to the same opportunities for participation in state activities. State welfare is intended, in part, to help all members of the state achieve an economic level at which participation in the basic social life of state is possible (Marshall 1950; Offe 1972; Freeman 1986). Participation in the basic social life of the state reinforces state loyalty.

Many different types of relationships may complicate loyalty to a state. Loyalty to a religion, for example, may complicate loyalty to a state, as when state decisions conflict with religious norms and values.[25] Dual citizens (Hammar 1989), political exiles (Shain 1989), and diaspora communities (Sheffer 1993) may also complicate the issue of loyalty, for they all involve people with potential loyalties to two separate states.

Relationships between international assistance organizations and the recipients of their assistance complicate loyalty as well, for they provide another structure, entitlement system, and system of norms and values within which loyalties may be constructed. Again, the Tibetan exiles in Nepal provide an example. The relationship between Swiss intergovernmental organizations and the Tibetans of the four Swiss-Tibetan settlement camps in Nepal involves a fundamental conflict between economic self-sufficiency and political loyalty. Swiss intergovernmental organizations established the four Swiss-Tibetan settlement camps, and their affiliated carpet businesses, to enable the Tibetan exiles to become self-sufficient. Tibetan exile leaders use them, however, to promote loyalty to themselves and the independence cause through efforts that undermine the goal of self-sufficiency. Tibetan exiles face a normative conflict in the administration of the camp businesses, whether to use them to maintain self-sufficiency, as Swiss officials initially intended, or to cultivate loyalty, as Tibetan exile leaders would like.

The relationship between Taiwan's Mongolian and Tibetan Affairs Commission (MTAC) and the Tibetans it assists involves a conflict of loyalties as well. The MTAC provides assistance to Tibetan exiles in Nepal with the understanding of them as overseas Taiwanese citizens. Tibetan exiles who accept assistance from the MTAC may or may not consider themselves Taiwanese. They may or may not feel any particular loyalty to Taiwan. Fellow Tibetan exiles consider accepting assistance from the MTAC to be an expression of loyalty to Taiwan and disloyalty to the Dalai Lama's exile administration, however. In the words of one young Tibetan exile, a student in a school supported, in part, by the Dalai Lama's exile administration:

> It is known and seen to all that there are lots of Tibetan factories, monasteries, schools, [and] organizations in Nepal financed and backed by irrelevant foreign associations.... Be it monasteries or schools, uneducated short sighted Tibetans [have] made themselves parasites and [have] never realized the significance of ones country and culture. Days were gone when Tibetans needed food, clothing, and shelter. Now we have a set of Tibetan traitors, terrorists who don't realize their people, citizen, and nation are on the verge of destruction. Solely because they are made crazy by money.[26]

The normative dynamics of MTAC assistance, in this case, involves a conflict between loyalty to Taiwan and loyalty to the Dalai Lama's exile administration and the independence cause.

Identity

Identity is defined here as the contextualization of oneself among others. It consists of two interrelated processes. The first, which may be called processes of internal identity formation, involves the continuously negotiated narrative we tell ourselves about ourselves. The second, which may be called processes of external identity formation, involves the myths, images, symbols, and metaphors others use to make sense of us. Processes of internal and external identity formation work together to construct a sense of self. They work at both the individual and the collective level.

Many theorists discuss identity as the central problematic of late twentieth-century industrial society, a society in which the speed of change outpaces our ability to adapt to it (Habermas 1987, 1995; Harvey 1990; Giddens 1991; Glick-Schiller 1992; Beiner 1995; Ong 1999). Within such a society, national identity formation, in particular, faces simultaneous challenges from two sides, from globalizing pressures and localizing pressures (Beiner 1995). Globalizing pressures derive from the global expansion of capital, labor, and credit markets; the development of new transnational migration networks; and the development of global media markets; all enabled by the invention of new transportation and telecommunications technologies. Localizing pressures derive from the revaluation of subnational forms of identity in a global context that promotes multiculturalism. How do individuals and communities conceptualize national identity when both globalizing and localizing pressures challenge their efforts?

Some people respond in an active and reflexive manner; they respond "flu-idly and opportunistically to changing political-economic conditions" (Ong 1999: 6); they experiment with a variety of lifestyle options (Giddens 1991: 225) to enrich themselves materially and experientially. We may consider this response a model of empowerment. We see this response among some Tibetan exiles in Nepal, wealthy carpet factory owners, in particular, who travel relatively unproblematically between China, Nepal, India, Switzerland, and the United States on many different passports. When Tibetan exiles describe themselves with the phrase "we are like bats," they convey the idea that they are empowered by global change, that they respond actively and reflexively to the challenges of identity formation in a global context.

Other people respond in an anxious and defensive manner to the challenges of identity formation. They feel victimized by the characterizations others use to make sense of them. They criticize the ways in which these characterizations marginalize them and their views. We may consider this response a model of disempowerment. We see this response in the way in which Gómez-Peña (1988: 132), for example, writes about the myths the American media, in particular, promotes about Mexican-Americans like himself:

> We lack ontological existence and anthropological concreteness. We are perceived indistinctly as magic creatures with shamanistic powers, happy bohemians with pre-technological sensibilities, or as romantic revolutionaries born in a Cuban poster from the 1970s. All this without mentioning the more ordinary myths, with link us with drugs, supersexuality, gratuitous violence, and terrorism, myths that serve to justify racism and disguise the fear of cultural otherness [that] obstructs true intercultural dialogue [and] homogenizes true cultural diversity.

We see this response, as well, in the ways in which some Tibetan exiles criticize the myths international patrons use to make sense of them. Tsering Shakya, for example, argues that the myth of Tibet as Shangri-La, in particular, has "influenced the Western perception of the Tibetan political struggle, and has obscured and confused [its] real nature" (1992: 15), that it has reduced Tibetans to an endangered species (1992: 16) and rendered Tibet "a lost cause" (1992: 16). "If the Tibetan issue is to be taken seriously," he writes, "Tibet must be liberated from both the Western imagination and the myth of Shangri-La" (1992: 16).

Within the context of late twentieth-century industrial society—whether we consider it modern (Appadurai 1996), late modern (Ong 1999), or postmodern (Harvey 1990)—states provide one center for the continuous reconstruction of the self toward identification with a national community. Within states, welfare entitlements provide one mechanism for promoting the idea of a national identity. States are continuously challenged, however, by other organizations that encourage alternative identifications of the self with other communities. International assistance organizations are one example. They provide incentives for people to identify, affiliate, and act in concert with groups alternative to their local and national communities. Individuals and communities that receive assistance from international organizations often find themselves in a situation that encourages identification with multiple repertoires of identity. Collective answers to the questions "Who are we?" and "What are our interests?" become more difficult to construct.

The entitlement model of global-local relations may be used to analyze the relationship between international assistance organizations and the recipients of their assistance. We may expect the same issues—sovereignty, authority, loyalty, and identity—to emerge no matter which states or international organizations are involved. Examples of organizations that may be involved include development organizations, such as the World Bank or UNDP; refugee assistance organizations, such as UNHCR or ICVA; human rights organizations, such as Amnesty International or Human Rights Watch; bilateral intergovernmental organizations, such as USAID or SDC; or single-interest non-governmental organizations, such as the International Campaign for Tibet or the Free Romania Fund. The entitlement model of global-local relations helps us to analyze the normative dynamics of the relationship between any of these organizations and the recipients of their assistance. It helps us to analyze the role that international organizations play in promoting alternative norms and values worldwide.

The Anthropology of the International, the Transnational, and the Global

The entitlement model of global-local relations can be situated within a more general field of inquiry within anthropology described elsewhere as the anthropology of globalization and transnationalism (Kearney 1995: 547). The general question addressed in this literature is how can anthropologists analyze processes that transcend local communities when intensive local research is the basis for anthropology as a discipline. What are the research methods that enable anthropologists to access data beyond the local level? What are the theoretical frameworks that enable anthropologists to contextualize localized data within larger social fields, whether characterized as international (between nations), transnational (across many nations), or global (beyond the context of the nation)? How can anthropologists analyze the effects that international, transnational, and global social processes have on the local communities that are the basis for anthropological research? Many solutions have been proposed, which I discuss under the categories of economic, cultural, and institutional approaches to global-local relations. The institutional approach to global-local relations is the closest to the entitlement model I propose, as it asks how organized social action and the transaction of global norms and values interrelate. Economic approaches to global-local relations overemphasize organized social action to the detriment of the analysis of global norms and values. Cultural approaches overemphasize the transaction of global norms and values to the detriment of the analysis of organized social action. The analysis of the relationship between international assistance organizations and the recipients of their assistance, I argue, requires the analysis of how organized social action and the transaction in global norms and values interrelate. That is what I seek to analyze through the entitlement model of global-local relations.

Economic Approaches

Economic approaches to the study of global-local relations overemphasize the analysis of organized social action to the detriment of the analysis of global norms and values. We may take Wallerstein (1975, 1982) as our example. His model, world system theory, is very useful for analyzing organized social action, and in particular, the organization of production and exchange. He proposes the existence of a single economic system, global in scope, whose component parts (core, periphery, and semi-periphery) are bound in continuous ever-shifting relationships of capitalist accumulation and unequal exchange (Hopkins and Wallerstein 1982: 42–47). Core regions work continuously to accumulate capital through unequal exchange (valuing their manufactured products more than the agricultural and mineral products exported by peripheral regions) and to use their accumulated capital to expand their exchange relationships further, to encompass the globe. Peripheral regions find themselves continuously bound to core regions through the organization and reorganization of their production processes, always in service to the core (Hopkins and Wallerstein 1982: 50). Semi-peripheral regions act in some ways as core regions, in some ways as peripheral regions (Hopkins and Wallerstein 1982: 47). Together, these three regions constitute a world system that may change in terms of the products and production processes involved, that may expand and contract in scope, yet that remains continually bound together through exchange relations (Hopkins and Wallerstein 1982: 43).

Anthropologists have found world system theory very useful for analyzing such processes as the organization of production for world markets (Nash 1981: 397); the organization of immigrant labor markets (Nash 1981: 406); and the establishment of mines, factories, and consumer goods stores where once there were none.[27] What world system theory has been less useful for is analyzing how these forms of organized social action relate in any way to the negotiation of global norms and values. World system theory does not accommodate the discussion of how global norms and values are constructed and contested, as it rests fundamentally, yet implicitly, on the idea that all human beings act based on rational self-interest, irrespective of whatever other norms and values we may uphold.[28]

If we apply world system theory to the analysis of the relationship between international assistance organizations and the recipients of their assistance, what we see are self-interested forms of international assistance and self-interested aspects of the assistance relationship. We see, for example, the ways in which certain forms of international assistance encourage recipient communities to become dependent on foreign aid or foreign exports (thereby contributing to capital accumulation through unequal exchange). We see inappropriate forms of assistance sent only to dispose of overstock and to secure tax write-offs (Hancock 1989: 12). Not all forms of international assistance are grounded in this way in rational self-interest, however, and even for those that are, to analyze international assistance as if rational self-interest were the only normative framework involved, misses out on the ways in which international assistance is legitimated. The analysis of the relationship between international assistance organizations and the recipients of their assistance requires a model that combines how global norms and values and organized social action interrelate. Only then can we understand why and how recipient communities accommodate the norms and values of those who assist them.

Cultural Approaches

Cultural approaches to global-local relations fare no better for analyzing how global norms and values and organized social action relate. They overemphasize the analysis of global norms and values to the detriment of the analysis of how those norms and values lead to organized action. They are largely concerned with the question of how individuals, and the communities they construct, create meaning in a world characterized by intensive global interaction. We may use them to identify what ideas are transacted at the global level and how people respond to, and interpret, those ideas. What they are less useful for is analyzing how those ideas influence action. Three distinct models may be discerned. Malkki (1994) proposes that global-local relations are constructed around a single idea–the idea of a family of nations (1994: 42). She locates the idea of a family of nations in such forms as national flags, the Olympic Games, Disneyland's "It's a Small World" ride, the Miss World and Miss Universe pageants, and UNICEF's people of the world dolls (1994: 49–52). All of these forms, she argues, help us to imagine ourselves not just as members of particular nations but also as members of a family of nations. The idea of a family of nations, she argues, underlies the global moral order (1994: 42). Malkki (1994: 61) uses the idea of a family of nations to speculate on how relationships of international assistance operate; she argues that the idea of a family of nations renders migrants, refugees, and other stateless peoples liminal; and that therefore there is a danger that people who administer refugee assistance may interpret the refugees' liminality as a sign of their lesser humanity. The analysis raises only the potential that anyone would or could use the idea of the family of nations in this manner, however. As a cultural approach to global-local relations, it does not engage organized social action.

Appadurai (1996), likewise, proposes a cultural model of global-local relations that does not engage organized action. His focus is on the work of the individual imagination in the construction of the subjective self (1996: 3). He argues that the imagination is the key component of the self in this new global order (1996: 31). He outlines five global cultural flows that serve in the construction of the self (1996: 33); they are ethnoscapes (people with whom we have social relationships), technoscapes (the technology we use), financescapes (configurations of global capital), mediascapes (newspapers, magazines, television, film), and ideoscapes (freedom, welfare, rights, sovereignty). Appadurai (1996: 31) proposes an infinite variety of ways in which individuals may use these "-scapes" to configure their sense of self. He sees these individual configurations as "subversive micronarratives" that undermine the power of the state (1996: 10). Appadurai's (1996) analysis alerts us to the potential that individual acts of imagination could combine in such a way as to undermine the power of the state, yet it provides no way in which to understand how that could happen. His analysis proceeds only on the level of ideas; it does not engage organized action.

Hannerz's (1987, 1992) model of global-local relations comes closer to engaging the analysis of organized action, yet it, too, is essentially a cultural model. His model (1987: 555), based simultaneously on Wallerstein's (1975) world system, on the linguistic model of creolization, and on the metaphor of a river or stream, proposes the existence of multiple communities of ideas that intersect in different ways in different places throughout the world:

> The world system, rather than creating massive cultural homogeneity on a global scale, is replacing one diversity with another.... Along the entire creolising spectrum, from the First World metropolis to Third World village, through education and popular culture, by way of missionaries, consultants, critical intellectuals and small town storytellers, a conversation between cultures goes on.... [This] creolist view of contemporary Third World cultural organization ... suggests that different cultural streams engaging one another in creolisation may all be actively involved in shaping the resultant forms.

Hannerz (1987, 1992) analyzes the role that all participants in the global system play in the construction not just of their own individual imagined worlds yet also in shared worlds of meaning. He proposes a "distributive view of culture" (1992: 37) to accommodate the role that "a multiplicity of perspectives and voices" plays in the construction of global meaning (1992: 34). He (1992: 37) locates four sites through which we negotiate meaning—they are form of life (relations of everyday working and living), the market, the state, and social movements—and as such, he leads us closer to the analysis of the ways in which norms and values relate to organized action. The analysis of the relationship between international assistance organizations and the recipients of their assistance, however, requires a model that combines even further the ways in which global norms and values and organized social action relate.

Institutional Approaches

The institutional approach to global-local relations is the closest to the entitlement model I propose, as it analyzes how global norms and values and organized social action relate. Meyer et al. (1987), Boli (1987), and Ramirez (1987), the authors of the institutional approach, focus on how global norms and values (progress and justice, in particular) become institutionalized (Ramirez 1987: 317; Meyer et al. 1987: 12). They define institutionalization as "the process by which a given set of units and a pattern of activities come to be normatively and cognitively held in place, and practically taken for granted as lawful" (Meyer et al. 1987: 13); and as "the building of relationships that organize action, on one hand, and locate action in expanding cultural theories and ideologies, on the other" (Meyer et al., 1987: 37). Their focus is on how states, through their relationships with each other (as through their participation in international organizations and transnational treaty-making processes) promote the values of progress and justice; and on how states, through their relationships with their citizens, institutionalize progress and justice in such instruments as state constitutions, citizenship legislation, educational policies, and state welfare policies (Meyer et al. 1987: 33–35; Ramirez 1987: 326).

What I take from Meyer et al. (1987), Boli (1987) and Ramirez (1987) is the idea of institutionalization and its application at the global level. What I do differently is to apply the idea of institutionalization to the relationship between international assistance organizations and the recipients of their assistance rather than to relationships states maintain both with each other and with their citizens. I argue that international assistance constitutes an institutional mechanism for the negotiation of global norms and values.

The Entitlement Model

The entitlement model of global-local relations analyzes the normative dynamics of the relationship between international assistance organizations and the recipients of their assistance. It analyzes how international organizations legitimate the assistance they provide and how recipient communities legitimate their claims to assistance. It argues that recipient communities learn to legitimate their claims to assistance through the same norms and values as the international organizations that assist them. That is one way in which global norms and values are constructed and contested not just on an individual level, yet on a collective level so that they serve to organize social action.

Norms and values transacted through relationships of international assistance have the potential to conflict with norms and values transacted at other social levels, such as at the level of the state or even among local communities. When that happens, we may expect sovereignty, authority, loyalty, and identity to emerge as issues for negotiation. The entitlement model of global-local relations analyzes the ways in which international assistance organizations promote global norms and values and the ways in which those global norms and values influence the negotiation of issues of sovereignty, authority, loyalty, and identity.

Identity, Community, and Entitlement among Tibetan Exiles in Nepal

The Tibetan exiles in Nepal maintain relationships with a multiplicity of international assistance organizations. They include Swiss intergovernmental organizations, U.S. intergovernmental organizations, and friends of Tibet organizations, among others. Each of these many organizations promotes its own set of norms and values that legitimates the assistance it provides to the Tibetans. Swiss intergovernmental organizations, for example, promote self-sufficiency; U.S. intergovernmental organizations promote global democracy; friends of Tibet organizations promote liberal humanism. The challenge for the Tibetan exiles is to accommodate these norms and values without losing sense of what it means for themselves to be distinctly Tibetan.

The Tibetan exiles discuss their approach to the challenge in terms of the metaphor of a bat. Being a bat means accommodating the norms and values of others only on the surface–to gain access to resources–while maintaining one's own norms and values at the core.[29] The bat metaphor overstates the degree to which the Tibetan exiles in Nepal can control the process of accommodating the norms and values of the international organizations that assist them, however. It may be an apt metaphor for the way in which some Tibetan exiles in Nepal negotiate the transaction of norms and values at the individual level. What it obscures are the challenges of negotiating norms and values at the collective level. The normative dynamics of the relationship between the Tibetan exiles in Nepal and the international organizations that assist them challenge their efforts to define themselves as a community; they challenge their efforts to reproduce a collective sense of Tibetanness over time and across generations. They do so by providing incentives for the Tibetans to identify, affiliate, and act in concert with groups alternative to their local and national communities.

We see this dynamic most in the challenges that relationships of international assistance pose to the efforts of the Dalai Lama's exile administration to construct and maintain a Tibetan exile community. Exile officials promote the idea of a unified and distinct Tibetan exile community in a number of ways. They publish books, pamphlets and posters that emphasize the unity of the Tibetan exiles and the role of the Dalai Lama's exile administration in governing them. They convene public meetings in all Tibetan exile settlements to discuss their activities. They sponsor public events, such as the Dalai Lama's birthday celebration, Tibetan National Day, and the Tibetan New Year. They issue a type of identity booklet, called green books in English, due to the color of their covers, or freedom passes (*rangzen lagteb*) in Tibetan, because of the office that issues them, that identifies their owners as Tibetan citizens (*yulmi*) who are entitled to apply for the scholarship and resettlement opportunities that international assistance organizations make available through their offices.[30]

International assistance organizations, in some ways, help the Dalai Lama's exile administration in its efforts to maintain a unified and distinct Tibetan exile community. They provide the scholarship and resettlement opportunities, for example, that the exile administration makes available to members of the Tibetan exile community. They also, as in the case of U.S. intergovernmental assistance, provide the funds that maintain the exile administration itself. At the same time, however, these relationships challenge the Dalai Lama's exile administration to accommodate alternative norms and values. They challenge them to accommodate their own view of what it means to be Tibetan. Nawang Dorjee, director of education for the Tibetan Children's Village Schools in India, for example, explains. He criticizes his fellow Tibetan exiles for mistaking the goals of the international organizations that assist them for their own:

> [W]e have done really well in creating a community in exile with the infrastructure and programmes to care for our people and preserve our culture and identity. But can we honestly say that they are getting the job done? We pride ourselves [in] establishing one of the most successful resettlement programmes in modern history, as if the final goal were to live as "proud refugees." Our goal is to regain freedom for Tibet. Or have we changed our course? Surely our goal is not to be "model citizens of the world" … We are so drunk with being the "best refugees" in the world that we are delirious. As long as we are able to do our petty business, get our salaries [on] time, and generally go about eking out the pleasures of life at the individual level, we don't seem to care. Over time, we seem to have lost the collective psychology, and the sense of urgency, to get our freedom. We have become model settlers and resettlers!–as pliant and flexible as rubber without the steel in it. (1992: 11)

Maintaining a Tibetan identity, focused on the independence cause, is important to many Tibetan exiles. For Tibetan exile officials, in particular, the Tibetan identity and the independence cause are of critical importance. They maintain their position as representatives of the Tibetan people and as dominant intermediaries in the provision of international assistance to Tibetans. Not all Tibetan exiles agree that the Tibetan identity and the independence cause are of critical importance, however. Some Tibetan exiles, successful carpet factory owners, in particular, explained to me that being good at business is more important. We see in their comments a certain accommodation of the norms and values Swiss officials sought to promote among Tibetan exiles, such as the value of self-sufficiency. One Tibetan carpet factory owner, for example, explained to me that "maintaining an identity as a Tibetan is not as important as how you feel inside," for "If you can do something, you should do it and not waste your time just sitting in camps.... You can always continue to work hard and always continue to find something to do.... There is no limit to progress, no limit to hard work, and no limit to ambition" (personal communication, July 30, 1995). Another Tibetan businessman who conducts trade in many different countries, with claims to many different identities, likewise, reasoned to me that "When you have no country of your own ... going from one country to the next is all the same more or less" (personal communication, May 7, 1995).

Other Tibetan exiles expressed disillusion with the exile administration and the values they believe exile leaders promote through the language of the independence cause. One Tibetan exile explained to me, for example, that he was once enthusiastic about the Tibetan cause, but "found that in order to do politics you have to be dishonest or you will not go anywhere" for "people in politics are like wolves in sheep's clothing who are trying to destroy the Tibetan society while they pretend to work for it" (personal communication, August 30, 1995). We can see in his life how he accommodated the values of the international patrons who assisted him. He founded a number of social welfare projects, funded by international assistance organizations, to provide health care to Nepali people as well as Tibetans. Another Tibetan exile, in a similar situation, founded a social welfare organization specifically to assist women.

The relationships the Tibetan exiles maintain with the many international organizations that assist them challenge their efforts to reproduce a collective sense of Tibetanness over time and across generations. They challenge the efforts of the Dalai Lama's exile administration, in particular, to define the content of the Tibetan identity so as to make claims to national self-determination and to educate the next generation as Tibetans. They do so by challenging the exile administration to accommodate their own view of what it means to be Tibetan. For the estimated 130,000 Tibetans today dispersed throughout India, Nepal, Bhutan, Taiwan, Switzerland, Canada, and the United States, what it means to be Tibetan has become increasingly complex. As birds, rats, and bats, being Tibetan has taken on multiple meanings including multiplicity itself.

Notes

1. Tashi's business advisor, by claiming status as a "true Nepali," was on one level express-ing sentiments held generally by the Newar people. The Newar claim descent from the original inhabitants of the Kathmandu Valley (Gellner 1986: 103) and, as such, consider all other residents to be interlopers on their territory (Gellner 1986: 137). By telling me further that he was born at Kasthamandap, he was making a claim to special status even among the Newar. Kasthamandap is the site on which a public rest house once stood on the old east-west trade route through Kathmandu. The word Kathmandu is believed to derive from the word Kasthamandap (Slusser 1982: 88).

2. The U.S. Department of State (1995) estimates a per capita income of $200 for Nepal. Guru-Gharana (1994: 15) estimates it to be below $180 per year. Those who live at absolute poverty level, as defined by Guru-Gharana (1995: 1–2), are those who spend most of their income on food alone, who use a small amount for clothes and fuel, and who have almost nothing left for health and education.

3. Klieger's (1992) project, like Devoe's (1983), is to understand the role that international patrons play in the persistence of the Tibetan identity. Klieger (1992: 16), like Devoe (1983: 65, 75–76, 114), argues that the Tibetans have been successful in maintaining a separate identity due to their interpretation of international patronage through the indigenous cul-tural frameworks of priest/patron (*chö-yön*) and patron (*jindag*). Klieger (1992: 18) observes, however, that although the separateness of the Tibetan identity has remained the same, its content has changed: "But the ideology of the patron/client relationship has not merely reproduced itself in history, substituting one category of people for another. Rather, with each attempt at systematic reproduction, people's differential assessment of meaning has tended to change the outcome. In action, other aspects of culture may in turn change, often unintentionally." My project is to understand the dynamics of this change.

4. Some of the many accounts that document the successful resettlement of the Tibetan exiles include Holborn (1975: 753), Goldstein (1978), Devoe (1983) Saklani (1984), Nowak (1984), Gombo (1985), Forbes (1989), Chhetri (1990), von Fürer-Haimendorf (1990), French (1991), Klieger (1992), Hagen (1994), and Norbu (1994).

5. Some Tibetans in Tibet–the Pandatsangs, for example–did have experience with large-scale international trade, yet few Tibetans had any experience with the organization of manufacturing for trade. Tibetan exiles in Nepal had to learn how to manufacture carpets for international markets (Hagen 1994: 297). Carpets, in pre-1950 Tibet, were woven pri-marily by local craftsmen for local consumption; few pieces ever even left the country (Worcester 1992: 45).

6. The 1961 Industrial Enterprises Act restricted ownership of export businesses to Nepali citizens; the 1964 Land Reform and Ukhada Land Tenure Acts restricted land ownership to Nepali citizens.

7. Swiss intergovernmental organizations helped the Tibetans start the first carpet factory in Nepal in 1961 (Hagen 1994: 267).

8. Carpets accounted for 4.8 percent of Nepal's gross domestic product (GDP) in 1991–1992; 5.6 percent in 1992–1993; and 4.8 percent in 1993–1994 (FNCCI 1995: 29, 66). To provide a sense of what that means in terms of their overall importance to the economy, it may be worth considering that the automobile manufacturing industry in the U.S. comprises only about 1.1 percent of U.S. GDP; only construction (4.1 percent), bank-ing (5.3 percent), and health services (5.7 percent) in the U.S. compare with carpets in Nepal (www.bea.doc.gov/bea/dn2/gposhr.htm). Comparison with the U.S. only goes so far, however, as the U.S. economy is much larger and more diverse than Nepal's. Agri-culture in Nepal continues to comprise the largest component, more than 40 percent, of GDP (FNCCI 1995: 30).

9. Statistics from 1994–1998 show an overall decline in carpet sales of about 11 percent since 1993 (www.fncci.org/fncci/text/carpet.txt), yet the industry continues to maintain its overall importance.

10. Few other exile communities—that is, people who were forced to flee their homelands for political reasons—have contributed as much to their host communities as the Tibetan exiles. Fermi (1968), Harris (1979), and Heilbut (1983) analyze the considerable contributions that exiles fleeing from Nazi Europe from the 1930s onward made to economic, cultural, and educational institutions in the United States. Zetter (1992) discusses the contributions that Greeks displaced from Turkish- to Greek-controlled Cyprus made. He analyzes, specifically, how a housing program established for displaced Greeks contributed to post-war economic growth in Cyprus (Zetter 1992: 14). Chambers (1986) argues for more attention to the effects that exiles and other displaced communities have on their hosts. He argues that international assistance programs should be designed so as to assist host communities as well (Chambers 1986). The Tibetan exiles provide an example in which at least some of the international assistance programs initiated to help them did indeed also take into account their hosts (Hagen 1994).

11. Soysal (1994: 32) defines an incorporation regime as the set of legal rules, discursive practices, and organizational structures that define the status of foreigners vis-à-vis the host state. In accordance with her typology, we may characterize Nepal as a fragmental incorporation regime, meaning that the state, although it holds sovereign rule, is organizationally weak, so that it is ineffective in managing the incorporation of migrants into its territory (1994: 39).

12. Sowell's (1996) study makes a strong argument for the cultural approach to economic success, as it analyzes migrant groups who seem to succeed economically wherever they settle. His argument, that their success is due to "the varying kinds and amounts of their cultural capital," is aimed specifically to counteract structural models of migrant performance (1996: 382). The argument, compelling as it is, has two major shortcomings, however. The first is that it relies on somewhat of a black box conceptualization of culture, that is, it defines culture so broadly as to be of little explanatory value. Culture, for Sowell, includes very specific skills such as clock-making, piano-building, and beer-brewing (1996: 2); more general attitudes toward work and risk-taking (1996: 3); and very general ideas about time, noise, safety, cleanliness, violence, thrift, intellect, sex, and art (1996: 379). Which of these many factors, either alone or in combination, influences economic performance is unclear, and is ultimately, I think, impossible to define in a general way that has any real comparative value. The second major shortcoming of Sowell's (1996) argument is that it overstates just how much culture can explain. Culture cannot explain variation within migrant groups. It cannot explain, for example, why Arabs and Turks perform better in the United States than they do in France or Germany (Weiner 1996: 131). Host country structures (labor markets, immigrant policies, educational opportunities) must play some role. Culture also cannot explain variation between the migrant group and those who remain at home. Indians and Chinese abroad, for example, are far more successful than Indians and Chinese at home (Weiner 1996: 131). Structural differences between host and home countries could also play a role, or alternatively, a principle of self-selection could be involved (Weiner 1996: 131). Those who choose to migrate may be higher risk-takers, for example, than those who stay at home.

13. Saklani's (1984) book is more about issues of cultural continuity and change than about Tibetan success *per se*. In her chapter on economic change, however, she argues that Tibetans, when asked, indicate three reasons for how well they have done economically— that they are hardworking; that their women work as hard as their men, if not more; and that they have a natural instinct for trade (1984: 219). Saklani also mentions "a flow of foreign money too, coming from foreigners who visit the place [Dharamsala] and also from the foreign aid and sponsorship programmes" (1984: 219). My interest is in the role that foreign aid and sponsorship plays in Tibetan economic success.

14. Sherpa are the exception. Sherpa, too, have become economically successful in Nepal through their role in the development of the tourist industry. The reasons for Sherpa success, it would seem, parallel those for Tibetan exile success. Sherpa, too, have long-term patrons who provide them with capital and other resources unavailable in Nepal. A recent ethnography of the Sherpa reports: "Sherpas recruit Western Others to become their sponsors, 'lifelong' friends, and supporters who provide them with gifts, money, advice, employment, and more, in response to Western desires to become part of 'the Sherpa world'" (Adams 1996: 9).

15. Informants within the Nepal government and the Swiss organization responsible for helping the Tibetans circumvent Nepal's legal restrictions both emphasized to me that Nepal's legal restrictions on land and business ownership were intended primarily to prevent Indian entrepreneurs, in particular, from dominating Nepal's economy. Nepali officials helped the Tibetans circumvent the laws, as they did not consider the Tibetans to be as much of a threat to Nepali entrepreneurs as the much more numerous Indian community in Nepal.

16. The MTAC was established in China under the Kuomintang government in 1928 (Goldstein 1989: 215) and re-established in Taiwan after the Kuomintang exile (*Tibetan Review* 1976: 18). According to the *Tibetan Review* (1990: 8), the MTAC, in 1990, allocated four million U.S. dollars, out of a ten million dollar budget, as assistance to Tibetan exile organizations. Correspondence I conducted with a former official of the MTAC confirms MTAC assistance to some Tibetan exile educational and social welfare organizations in Nepal (personal communication, April 6, 1996).

17. The phrase in Tibetan is *pu-ti kha-yi drang-tsi dag.* For an example of its use in context, see Tsering (1994: 1).

18. I take here, as a starting point, the proposal put forth by Handelman and Leyton (1978: 6) that to analyze any bureaucratic organization, it is necessary to take into account at least two different worldviews: "the ways in which supralocal institutions conceive of administrative territories and the ways in which territorially based populations conceive of themselves as communities." How, they ask (1978: 6), do the social actors involved negotiate the differing definitions of their overlapping situation, "with each definition supported by a different world of experience, institutional frameworks, resources, and goals?" Scott (1998) provides an example of the type of analysis they propose. What I add to the discussion is first, an illustration of what happens when the bureaucratic organizations involved are international in scope, and second, what happens when many different bureaucratic organizations, each with their own worldviews, are involved. What effects, I ask, do any or all of the international organizations involved have on issues of sovereignty, authority, loyalty, and identity?

19. Goodin et al. (1999) borrow their typology of welfare regimes from Esping-Andersen (1990), who uses the United States, Germany, and Sweden as examples of liberalist, corporatist, and social democratic regimes.

20. The number of international organizations worldwide, according to the Union of International Associations, has increased more than ten-fold in the past thirty years, from 3,547 in 1968 to 28,942 in 1988 to 44,128 in 1996 (www.uia.org/uiastats/stybv296.htm). That number includes intergovernmental, international non-governmental, and international religious organizations.

21. International agreements that outline how refugees ought to be treated include the 1951 Convention Relating to the Status of Refugees, along with its 1967 Protocol; the 1966 Asian-African Legal Consultative Committee's Principles Concerning the Treatment of Refugees; the 1969 OAU Convention Governing the Specific Aspects of Refugee Problems in Africa; and the 1984 Cartegena Declaration on Refugees. The 1951 Convention Relating to the Status of Refugees defines a refugee as "any person ... who, owing to a well-founded fear of being persecuted for reasons of race, religion, nationality, membership of a particular social group or political opinion, is outside the country of his nationality and

is unable or, owing to such fear, is unwilling to avail himself of the protection of that country; or who, not having a nationality and being outside the country of his former habitual residence as a result of such events, is unable or, owing to such fear, is unwilling to return to it." The 1951 Convention restricted the definition of a refugee to people who had a well-founded fear of being persecuted owing to events occurring in Europe before 1 January 1951. The 1967 Protocol removed those restrictions.

22. Article 33 of the 1951 Convention Relating to the Status of Refugees states that "No contracting state shall expel or return (*refouler*) a refugee in any manner whatsoever to the frontiers of territories where his life or freedom would be threatened on account of his race, religion, nationality, membership of a particular social group or political opinion" except on national security grounds. UNHCR empowers refugees themselves to decide when it is safe to return; for UNHCR, the principle of voluntariness is "the cornerstone of international protection with respect to the return of refugees" (UNHCR 1997: 90, cited in Weiner 1998: 438).

23. The situation described here resembles, in many ways, the position of middleman minorities (Bonacich 1973). Middlemen minorities are immigrants who derive their power in society from a dominant position in some sphere of intermediary economic activity (banking for example); lacking the traditional means through which to legitimate their power, they become the objects of host-state hostility.

24. Hirschman (1970) argues that loyalty to a state is most clearly seen in times of societal dysfunction; it involves either an evaluation of the ability of the state to get back on track or a belief in the state's inherent superiority over others.

25. The sanctuary movement in the United States provides an example. Members of the sanctuary movement support the right to sanctuary as a religious right; they help refugees to remain within the United States, even when the U.S. Immigration and Naturalization Service rules in favor of their deportation. Some parties view the actions of sanctuary movement members as expressions of disloyalty; the members of the movement themselves view them as efforts to hold the state accountable to its own norms and values (Coutin 1993; Cunningham 1995).

26. In May 1995, I sponsored an essay contest for students in the seventh grade in schools affiliated with the Dalai Lama's exile administration in Nepal. The essay question involved whether or not, in their opinion, Tibetan exiles should accept citizenship in Nepal. Some students strayed from the topic. This is an excerpt from one of those essays.

27. Nash (1981) summarizes some of the criticisms that have emerged as anthropologists have tried to use Wallerstein's (1975) framework in the analysis of their own field materials. World systems theory, Nash (1981) argues, fails on a number of accounts: It inaccurately depicts core and periphery as homogenous in their modes of production (1981: 396); inaccurately depicts the periphery as passive (1981: 398); overemphasizes exchange relations as the mechanism for dependency relationships (1981: 401–403); and pessimistically depicts the expansion of the world capitalist system as inevitable (1981: 408).

28. The world system framework does contain the seeds for the discussion of the relationship between global norms and values and organized social action. Wallerstein (1975: 347–348) does characterize the world system as, in essence, a "social system" with "rules of legitimization and coherence." He does discuss, in passing, such values as economic efficiency, private ownership, technological progress, global integration, and temporal homogenization (Wallerstein and Hopkins 1982: 54). His discussion of values is only tangential, however; the world system framework does not accommodate other explanations, besides rational self-interest, for organized social action.

29. The way in which the Tibetan exiles discuss this process is very similar to what Goffman (1959) referred to as impression management. Impression management uses the metaphor of a stage performance to analyze the ways in which people reinvent themselves differently in different contexts in order to influence others. It is an instrumentalist way in which to conceptualize the process of identity negotiation. The Goffman (1959)

approach does indeed carry a certain amount of explanatory value in the analysis of the relationship between the Tibetan exiles and the international organizations that assist them. Tibetan exiles in Nepal do indeed, at times, quite literally stage performances for the international patrons with whom they interact. As a teacher in a Tibetan exile school in Nepal, I participated in a number of these staged performances. I describe one of these performances in chapter 3. Devoe (1983) discusses a similar process of impression management in her analysis of the relationship between Tibetan exiles in India and their long-term patrons, although she uses the term "intentional strategizing" instead. She writes: "Most donors are invited as special guests to all important Tibetan social functions such as Tibetan New Years (Losar) and the children's annual school picnics. If the donor plans a visit in nonholiday times, Tibetan children are asked to perform Tibetan dances, dramas, or singouts for him.... The community, then, was prompted ... to even literally stage shows for donors" (1983: 142). At these events: "The process of showcasing begins by emphasizing one of two separate identities—Tibetan or refugee—whichever is most instrumental in swaying the donor's heart. Refugee identity is typically used to promote Tibetans as 'needy'; Tibetan identity usually serves as a back-up to the aid request, a 'character reference' persuading donors they will be worth it, as clients" (1983: 140).

30. There are three terms the Tibetan exiles use for citizen. The first, *yulmi*, means quite simply a person from a particular area, a native. The second, *nga-wang*, is an adaptation of a term used in Tibet before the exile to refer to subjects of the Dalai Lama who held estate lands in Tibet. The third, *mi-ser*, is an adaptation of a term used in Tibet before the exile for tenant laborers on estate lands in Tibet.

1

Swiss Assistance and Self-Sufficiency

Swiss intergovernmental organizations were among the first to extend assistance to the Tibetan exiles in Nepal. They first became involved with the Tibetan exiles in the 1960s. They were still actively assisting them in the 1990s, throughout the period of my research. Swiss intergovernmental organizations were instrumental in helping the Tibetan exiles to resettle in Nepal. They built the first four Tibetan settlement camps (setting the model on which other settlement camps were based). They started the first Tibetan carpet factories and carpet export companies in Nepal. They trained the first generation of Tibetan carpet factory managers. Many of the Tibetans who now control Nepal's carpet industry started their careers in the Swiss-Tibetan factories or otherwise under the direction of Swiss intergovernmental officials. Throughout the period of their involvement, Swiss officials have transferred responsibility for assisting the Tibetan exiles from one Swiss intergovernmental organization to another, yet they all have maintained the same narrative about the Tibetan exiles. They discuss the Tibetan exiles as a humanitarian concern. They promote market mechanisms as a means for resettling them. Their goal is Tibetan self-sufficiency through the production of carpets for the international carpet market.

Swiss intergovernmental organizations were successful in helping the Tibetan exiles to achieve economic self-sufficiency. Swiss officials, as far back as 1975, considered the Tibetan exiles to be self-sufficient. They started then to try to withdraw from their involvement in the Tibetan project. The Tibetan exiles have argued successfully to maintain Swiss involvement, however. They argue that they remain entitled to Swiss assistance due to a lack of their own government to represent them. At the same time that they seek to maintain Swiss involvement, however, the Tibetan exiles seek to contain it as well. They seek to use the resources Swiss intergovernmental organizations provide them to promote their own norms and values and to resist the norms and values promoted by the Swiss. We see this behavior most in representatives of the Dalai Lama's exile administration who, in the 1970s, took control over the management of the Swiss-Tibetan settlement camps and businesses. They now use the settlement camps and carpet businesses more to cultivate loyalty to the exile administration and the independence cause than to remain self-sufficient.

The normative dynamics of the relationship between Swiss intergovernmental organizations and the Tibetan exiles thus involve a fundamental conflict between the goals of economic self-sufficiency and political loyalty. We see this conflict most clearly in the Jawalakhel settlement camp. Jawalakhel is the site most associated with Swiss intergovernmental assistance to the Tibetan exiles in Nepal. Located just south of Kathmandu city, it is within a stone's throw of the Swiss Development Corporation compound. It is also only about an hour by taxi from Kathmandu's international airport, making it the most accessible (to international visitors) of the four Swiss-Tibetan settlement camps in Nepal (see Map 0.2). We see in the Jawalakhel settlement camp many signs of Swiss intergovernmental involvement. Its initial buildings, designed to mimic the shape of a Swiss village (see Map 0.3), bear such signs as "Dirt Makes Sickness" and "Please Keep Clean." They reflect the efforts on the part of Swiss officials to help the Tibetan exiles develop certain values they thought they would need to compete in international markets and achieve self-sufficiency. They include cleanliness, efficiency, and an international orientation.

At the same time, we see in the Jawalakhel settlement camp attempts on the part of the Dalai Lama's exile administration to promote their own values, most notably, loyalty to the exile administration and the independence cause. Since the 1970s, when exile administration officials took control over the camp, they have built a meeting hall where they can address the camp population. They have written textbooks, with their own version of Tibetan history, for use in the camp school. They have allowed for the development of nearly triple the number of houses so as to keep as many Tibetans as possible in residence at the camp. The Jawalakhel camp, initially constructed for only about four hundred Tibetans, now houses more than seventeen hundred Tibetans of all ages, both those who fled Tibet in the 1960s and their descendants, born in Nepal (see Map 0.3). Representatives of the Dalai Lama's exile administration administer the Jawalakhel camp and its affiliated carpet businesses. They use them as "technologies of power" for promoting their own version of Tibetan national consciousness (Malkki 1989, 1995b). They use them to promote and maintain the idea of a unified and distinct Tibetan community in exile, loyal to the Dalai Lama and his administration, and poised to return to Tibet upon Tibetan independence from China. Their efforts, and particularly those intended to keep Tibetans in the camp, undermine the goal of self-sufficiency. They undermine the norms and values that Swiss officials seek to promote.

This chapter analyzes the normative dynamics of the relationship between the Tibetan exiles and the Swiss intergovernmental organizations that assist them. It proceeds in four parts. The first discusses the context in which the relationship first developed, the arrival of the Tibetan exiles in Nepal. The second analyzes how Swiss officials discuss the relationship, as intended to promote self-sufficiency. The third analyzes how Swiss assistance helped the Tibetan exiles in Nepal become economically self-sufficient. It demonstrates the role that Swiss officials played in incorporating the Tibetan exiles both into the Nepal state and into the international carpet market.[1] It argues that throughout the process of incorporation, a conflict between the goals Swiss officials seek to promote and the goals Tibetan exile leaders seek to promote emerged. The final section analyzes how representatives of the Dalai Lama's exile administration now use the resources that Swiss intergovernmental organizations provide to promote loyalty to themselves and the independence cause. It argues that their efforts undermine the goal of self-sufficiency and render the Swiss-Tibetan businesses unable to compete with the many privately owned Tibetan and Nepali carpet businesses that have emerged in Nepal. The Swiss-Tibetan businesses, unable to compete, now rely on sympathy for the independence cause to remain in business.

The Arrival of the Tibetan Exiles in Nepal

Nepal is a small, independent nation-state located in the central Himalayas (see Map 0.1). Commonly described as comprising three regions—the mountains in the north; the hills in the middle; and the plains in the south—Nepal is the site of some of the highest mountains, deepest gorges, and most varied terrain in the world. Bordered by India on the west, south, and east and by the Tibetan region of China in the north, Nepal is a landlocked country with few marketable resources.[2] Agriculture is the primary means of subsistence for 90 percent of the population, who work the limited arable land, located principally in the plains.[3] The remainder of the population engages in trade, small business, tourism, and government service.

Kathmandu, the capital of Nepal, sits in the middle of a valley surrounded by high hills. Once a principal market for transhimalayan trade, the Kathmandu Valley served as the seat of the Licchavi dynasty in the seventh century; the kingdom of the Newars from the thirteenth to the eighteenth centuries; and the political center of the Shah dynasty, Rana oligarchy, and Nepal nation-state from the eighteenth century until today.[4] Once the principal inhabitants, the Newars continue to comprise the majority of the people of the Valley, although military conquest; economic development; and the travel, carpet, and garment industries have brought increasing numbers of Brahman, Chhetri, Tamang, Sherpa, and other peoples to the Valley as well. Today, the Kathmandu Valley is a multi-ethnic urban and cosmopolitan center linked via its airport, satellite television, and a variety of telecommunications services, to the rest of the world.

People from Tibet have been traveling to Nepal for purposes of pilgrimage and trade for centuries. Starting in the 1950s, however, an estimated twenty to thirty thousand Tibetans started to arrive in Nepal for a different purpose, to escape the ill-effects of the incorporation of their homelands into the People's Republic of China (PRC).[5] The Tibetan exiles settled at first in the borderlands—in Mustang, Manang, Khumbu, Walung, and Trisuli—where fellow ethnic Tibetans live (see Map 0.1). From there, they could monitor the situation in Tibet and determine when it would be safe to return. Many did return; others migrated back and forth across the border in response to conflicting stories; still others moved on to India, where Tibet's spiritual and political leader, the Dalai Lama, had settled. An estimated eight thousand Tibetans remained in Nepal.[6] About half gathered in sites where international organizations were providing aid. The others survived by selling their jewelry, animals, and other movable property and by establishing relationships with local people to secure land, food, and fuel.[7]

These initial years were full of insecurity for the Tibetan exiles. They had to decide whether to remain in Nepal, return to Tibet, or move on to India. Often the decision was predicated on the ability to find food. We see the role food plays in the way in which one Tibetan exile remembers his life from that time:

> When we [the speaker, his father, mother, and one sister] came over the border, we stayed in Thangto in Solu Khumbu at first. There were many Tibetans there. We formed a tent community on the open land. My father started a small school for the children. After a few years, some foreigners arrived and they distributed vitamins and salt and what we called yellow *tsampa* [*tsampa* is the Tibetan word for barley flour]. It was very rich tasting. We did not know how to cook with it and so we tried to make it just like *tsampa* but it did not taste the same. Then a lot of Tibetans started to arrive and there was a shortage of food. Many went back to Tibet. My other two sisters came out of Tibet with my grandmother and grandfather. They stayed for five or six months until they went back. They went back because we had to eat a lot of potatoes and they missed their food and their life in Tibet. At this time, we regularly heard news about what was going on in Tibet from the many newcomers to the camp. That was all in 1961 and 1962. (personal communication, August 30, 1995)

In the Kathmandu Valley, the Tibetan exiles gathered at three principal sites—the two monumental stupa at Boudha and Swayambhu, sites long familiar to Tibetan pilgrims, and the Tundikhel, a large open field in the center of the city that once served as a tent site for Tibetan traders (see Map 0.2).[8] At these sites, the Tibetan exiles could beg for food from traders and pilgrims. The Tamang people of Boudha, the Newars of Swayambhu, and the Newar, Brahman, and Chhetri people of Kathmandu city, however, soon found themselves unwilling hosts to a large and expanding group of people they refer to as "bhote," a derogatory term that connotes uncleanliness, immorality, and criminality.

In Kathmandu city, hospitality was soon exhausted, and all the stereotypes local Nepali people have of bhote began to find support. Nepali people took to throwing stones at the Tibetans, while the Tibetans, exhausted of the property they had brought with them, had nothing on which to live. It was then that the small expatriate community in Kathmandu formed the Nepalese Tibetan International Refugee Relief Committee (NTIRRC), also called the Father Moran Committee for the Jesuit leader of the group, to solicit funds for the Tibetans and to distribute blankets, clothing, and food to them (Forbes 1989: 25). Father Moran describes the conditions the Tibetans faced when he became involved:

> There was no Red Cross or any other group helping the Tibetans. They were arriving by the hundreds and were under a tree here, under a tree there. They gravitated to Boudha and Swayambhu, with their dirty black tents. They had never lived in a house in their lives, ninety percent were nomads. They were a menace to Kathmandu, diseased people and dirty and they were dying. In the morning they would be found dead by the road. (quoted in Forbes 1989: 25)

Starvation and disease were the principal problems, at first. The Tibetans had no food and nothing with which to purchase food. Equally devastating, they were unaccustomed to life at lower altitudes where they became susceptible to diseases unheard of in Tibet. The Tibetans:

> continued to live as they had in Tibet. They slept and cooked in tents made to withstand the bitter winters of the Tibetan plateau. They wore heavy black wool robes that looked and smelled like the yaks from whose hair they were woven; they rarely bathed, and they ate meat that was rotten, hanging it raw from strings in their tents to dry. The altitude and cold of Tibet had protected them from the health hazards of such customs. The tropical 90-degree temperatures of Kathmandu in the summer had the opposite effect: latent germs suddenly came to life, people contracted illnesses for which they had no immunities, and disease ran rampant. (Forbes 1989: 29)

The NTIRRC secured food from the U.S. Agency for International Development for the Tibetans. They distributed it once, sometimes twice, daily. They tried to teach the Tibetans the importance of keeping clean. They made them cotton clothes more appropriate to the climate and helped them to build grass huts. The NTIRRC, dependent entirely on local fundraising efforts, lacked the means to launch a more extensive assistance program, however (Forbes 1989: 26–30). For that, the Tibetans would rely on the Swiss government, which was just then founding its first intergovernmental organizations in Nepal. Swiss intergovernmental officials, initially reluctant to become involved, began to take interest.[9] They initiated an assistance relationship that continues today.

Swiss Assistance to the Tibetans: The Tibetans as a Humanitarian Concern

Swiss intergovernmental assistance to the Tibetan exiles began in 1960 with the activities of Toni Hagen, a Swiss geologist and development official, who had been working in Nepal for the United Nations Food and Agriculture Organization. Hagen, upon learning about the situation of the Tibetans, took interest in them and used his government connections to help them. "I was deeply impressed by the Tibetan culture," he writes of his involvement, "in which religion based on a philosophy of tolerance, non-violence, and respect for all living creatures is woven into the fabric of daily life ... [and] I recalled, knowing it for the outrage it was, the infamous slogan 'the boat is full,' with which Switzerland justified sending back thousands of Jews to certain death in Hitler's Germany during the last war" (Hagen 1994: 204–206). It was through the activities of Toni Hagen that the narrative Swiss intergovernmental organizations maintain about the Tibetan exiles in Nepal first developed. That narrative defines the Tibetans as a humanitarian concern and promotes market mechanisms as a means for resettling them. It was Hagen who argued that Swiss intergovernmental assistance to the Tibetan exiles should promote economic self-sufficiency. It was his plan that promoted self-sufficiency through the production of carpets for the international carpet market.

Hagen's plan involved Tibetan exiles in four areas of Nepal–Chialsa in Solukhumbu; Dhorpatan in Baglung; Pokhara in Syangja; and Jawalakhel, just south of Kathmandu city (see Map 0.1). These were areas in which Tibetan exiles had gathered in significant numbers; they were to become the first four Tibetan settlement camps. With permission from Nepal's government to implement his plan, Hagen flew to Switzerland to solicit international support.[10] The United Nations, having declared the Tibetan situation to be China's internal affair, refused UNHCR permission to coordinate his plan, so Hagen arranged for himself to be assigned to the International Committee of the Red Cross (ICRC), a Swiss-based multilateral intergovernmental organization, to pursue his plan through them instead.

According to Hagen, both he and the ICRC interpreted his plan to be in accordance with the humanitarian reputation of the Swiss:

> I [had] been working for Switzerland's good name continuously ... particularly for its positive neutrality, its exceptional status, and its humanitarian mission in the world. It is for this reason that the International Committee of the Red Cross was

the sole organization entrusted with aiding the refugees in Nepal. The refugee programme is sailing solely under the Swiss flag.[11]

Hagen and the ICRC disagreed over what it means to be humanitarian, however. For the ICRC, being humanitarian meant only the distribution of emergency assistance, such as food, blankets, and clothing. For Hagen, it meant longer-term development activities to enable the Tibetans to become self-sufficient. For Hagen, "the first matter of business was to stop the distribution of free food that had begun," for "nothing is more harmful for development than well-intentioned charities that require nothing from their beneficiaries" (1994: 214).

Hagen's plan involved a cash-for-work program that enabled the Tibetans to build houses, medical dispensaries, and factories; make clothing more appropriate to the climate; and start the production of woolen belts, jackets, bags, sweaters, and carpets. The Tibetans purchased wool, through a Sherpa trader, from the Chinese state-owned Sino-Tibetan trading corporation and sold their woolen goods on the local tourist market. The Nepal government approved of their efforts. King Mahendra even inaugurated the first Tibetan sales shop in Jawalakhel on August 26, 1961 (Hagen 1994: 267).[12] When representatives from the ICRC visited the Jawalakhel camp that November, however, they were not pleased; they informed Hagen that "schooling, training, production, and sales are against the rules of the ICRC" (Hagen 1994: 267). Hagen argued for the continuation of the project nevertheless; various factors combined to enable responsibility for the project to be transferred to the Swiss Red Cross, Switzerland's first bilateral intergovernmental organization in Nepal, in 1963 (Hagen 1994: 279). The project was then, quite literally, sailing solely under the Swiss flag. Tibetans recall from that time seeing a Swiss flag flying above the buildings in which they worked (Forbes 1989: 23).

Once the Swiss Red Cross took control, the project expanded to involve not only the establishment of factories, schools, and cooperative societies, but also the more permanent incorporation of the Tibetan exiles into the Nepal state. Swiss officials sought to incorporate the Tibetan exiles into Nepal through the mechanism of the market, a strategy the Swiss use to incorporate migrants into their own country.[13] Swiss officials identified the hand-woven woolen carpet market as the most logical choice for the Tibetans, given the availability of wool and the lack of competition in the market from Nepali entrepreneurs. Nepal had no carpet industry whatsoever at the time (Hagen 1994: 267). Swiss officials recruited the few Tibetan exiles they could identify who knew anything at all about carpet production to help them. They were local craftsmen who, in Tibet, had woven carpets for local consumption, for use as saddles, seats, wall hangings, and bed covers (Forbes 1989: 49; Worcester 1992: 45). Swiss officials helped to disseminate their knowledge among the rest of the camp residents and to organize them to produce first for local markets and then for international markets. Forbes (1989: 49–50) describes how it all began:

> Heidi Schultess, a professional Swiss weaver whose husband was a member of the Swiss mission in Kathmandu... while wandering through the Kathmandu bazaar... discovered Ming Ma, a Tibetan carpet master weaving carpets with wool dyed in gaudy colors from Indian chemical dyes. She convinced him to return with her to Jawalakhel, where she helped him set up several looms in a small room... Ming Ma's daughter and two other Tibetan women were recruited as weavers, and dozens of women were hired to spin the wool brought down from Tibet... Under Ming Ma's direction, five looms were built, wool was purchased, and 20 young women were trained in weaving. Older Tibetans were put to work spinning the wool... and a local Nepalese was hired to teach teenage boys not interested in weaving how to wash and dye the wool.

Swiss officials went on to help the Tibetans of the four Swiss-Tibetan settlement camps to transform what started as a local enterprise into a large-scale export-oriented industry. They did so in a number of ways. They helped the Tibetans to build carpet factories within each of the Swiss-Tibetan settlement camps and to register an export company, based in Kathmandu, to get their carpets to market. They provided the export company with loans from Swiss banks. They located the first international buyers for their carpets. And they trained the first generation of Tibetan carpet factory managers.[14] Their efforts enabled the Tibetans of the Swiss-Tibetan settlement camps to become economically self-sufficient, yet more importantly, they established a model for economic self-sufficiency. Tibetan exiles trained in the Swiss-Tibetan factories and otherwise under the supervision of Swiss officials went on to establish their own private factories and to grow the carpet business into the largest industry in Nepal.

Responsibility for the Tibetan project was transferred a number of times from one Swiss intergovernmental organization to another, from the Swiss Red Cross in 1963, to the Swiss Association for Technical Assistance in 1972, to the Swiss Development Corporation in 1988. Swiss officials continued, throughout their involvement, to legitimate their assistance to the Tibetan exiles through the language of humanitarianism. Swiss officials I interviewed in 1995 stressed repeatedly that they were involved in the project for humanitarian reasons and that being humanitarian means promoting self-sufficiency rather than providing subsistence goods.[15] In 1975, Swiss officials determined the Tibetan exiles to be self-sufficient. They started then to try to withdraw from their involvement in the project.[16] The Tibetan exiles have argued successfully to maintain Swiss involvement, however. Swiss officials remain involved in the project in their role as guarantors of the Swiss-Tibetan settlement camp lands and as shareholders in the camp businesses. Their role is institutionalized in a frame agreement signed in 1972 between the Swiss and Nepal governments to enable Swiss intergovernmental organizations to remain in Nepal indefinitely. That agreement includes provisions that protect the Tibetan project.[17]

Incorporation of the Tibetan Exiles into Nepal

Swiss intergovernmental organizations effectively enabled the Tibetan exiles of the four Swiss-Tibetan settlement camps to become economically self-sufficient through the production of carpets for international markets. Swiss officials enabled the Tibetans to become self-sufficient by incorporating them into the Nepal state and into the international carpet market. For their incorporation into the Nepal state, ownership of the camp lands and ownership of the shares of the camp businesses were the most important issues to negotiate, as the Tibetan exiles, as non-citizens, were not entitled to ownership themselves. For their incorporation into the international carpet market, the management of the camp businesses was the most important issue to negotiate. Swiss officials trained the Tibetan exiles in the values and skills they believed they needed to be able to compete in international markets. We see throughout the process of incorporation the emergence of a conflict between the values Swiss officials sought to promote (toward the goal of self-sufficiency) and the values Tibetan exile leaders sought to promote (loyalty to the exile administration and the independence cause). Representatives of the Dalai Lama's exile administration, since they secured control over the management of the Swiss-Tibetan settlement camps and carpet businesses in the 1970s, have used them more to cultivate loyalty than to remain self-sufficient.

Ownership of the Camp Lands

Ownership of the settlement camp lands was one of the most important issues Swiss officials helped the Tibetan exiles to negotiate. Land ownership was, and is, considered important to provide the Tibetan exiles a certain amount of political and economic security in Nepal. Land serves not just as a physical base for the Tibetan exiles' houses, factories, and schools; it serves also as a symbol of membership in the Nepal state (Regmi 1965; Sever 1993). The Swiss Red Cross, in 1964, effectively incorporated the Tibetan exiles of the four Swiss-Tibetan settlement camps as landholders, if not landowners, into the Nepal state. Since that time, however, the agreement through which they did so has threatened to unravel. We see in the negotiation of an alternative the emergence of the conflict between the efforts of Swiss officials to promote self-sufficiency and the efforts of Tibetan exile leaders to use Swiss assistance to promote the independence cause instead.

The lands for the four Swiss-Tibetan settlement camps—in Chialsa, Pokhara, Dhorpatan, and Jawalakhel—were initially found and purchased by the

Nepal Home Ministry with funds provided by the Swiss government in 1963.[18] Who would own the land, however, was initially unclear. Under Nepali law, non-citizens cannot own land, so both the Swiss and the Tibetans, few of whom had Nepali citizenship at the time, were excluded.[19] For the security of the Tibetan exiles, Swiss officials did not trust the Nepal government to the land. The Nepal government had demanded the removal of the Tibetan exiles once before from land they had donated.[20] The compromise involved a 1964 agreement between Swiss intergovernmental organizations and the Nepal government to establish the Nepal Red Cross Society, a non-governmental organization, and to entrust it with the land until the Tibetans could become eligible for ownership themselves.[21]

Since the 1964 compromise, however, politics internal to the Nepal Red Cross Society have emerged that threaten the Tibetans' status as landholders in Nepal. The executive director, the only Nepal Red Cross official involved with the Tibetans for years, intends to retire soon. He worries about what might happen to the Swiss-Tibetan settlement camp lands when he transfers their management to younger officials who, he explains, tend to view the Tibetans only as wealthy factory owners. He explains, "When I first started working on the Tibetan project, I read everything I could find about the Tibetans, and that helped me to understand them.... It is very difficult to find anyone else in the Nepal Red Cross who is sympathetic to the Tibetans. None of the people who work here today were around when the Tibetans first arrived."[22]

The executive director is concerned that younger officials may want the land for themselves. Both the amount and the value of the land held in trust by the Nepal Red Cross on behalf of the Tibetan exiles has increased dramatically. In 1966 and 1971, two additional Tibetan settlements, one just outside of Pokhara and one in Rasuwa (see Map 0.1), were entrusted to the Nepal Red Cross. Over the years, the land in all six settlements has been developed with both residential and commercial properties. The value of the land in Jawalakhel is especially high, now that it is part of Kathmandu's expanding urban complex. A Tibetan administrator explains: "Most of the settlement land is held by the Nepal Red Cross ... although up to now, the authorities have been very helpful, there may be some oversights.... The value of the land is very high."[23]

One way in which the Tibetan exiles could maintain their status as landholders is to become Nepali citizens. Tibetan exiles discuss a provision of the 1964 agreement that would transfer control over the lands from the Nepal Red Cross to them, as a community, if they accepted Nepali citizenship en masse, all at the same time. The executive director of the Snow Lion Foundation explains:

> If the Tibetans wanted to take citizenship *en masse*, the Nepal government would welcome that and would easily give it to everyone.... Then they could say to the

Chinese that there is no longer a Tibetan refugee problem in Nepal, that there are only Nepali citizens in Nepal…. What they are against is Tibetans taking citizenship as individuals, one by one, like a dripping faucet, because that does not help them…. That still leaves them with a Tibetan refugee problem.[24]

If the Tibetan exiles were to take Nepali citizenship, en masse, to enable the land to belong to them, they would no longer be dependent on Swiss support for the 1964 agreement to protect the status of their lands. Tibetan exile leaders have argued against the idea of taking Nepali citizenship en masse, however, as they believe it would signify a renunciation of the Tibetan independence cause. A Swiss official in Nepal explains:

Even though many, many Tibetans have acquired citizenship as individuals, as a community, they would never apply. To do so would mean renouncing the independence cause, and the Tibetan government [the Dalai Lama's exile administration] forbids it. Only recently has the Tibetan government [sic] agreed to allow Tibetans to become Nepali citizens individually.[25]

We thus see in the issue of the camp lands the first signs of the conflict between the goals of self-sufficiency and political loyalty. The Tibetan exiles could become owners of the camp lands, in their own right, without the need for Swiss support. Tibetan exile leaders refuse to allow the Tibetan exiles to become eligible for ownership, however, so as not to threaten their political cause. Tibetan exile leaders have argued successfully to maintain Swiss support nevertheless. They argue that they remain entitled to it due to a lack of their own government to represent them. Swiss intergovernmental organizations thus remain committed to their relationship with the Tibetan exiles until at least the issue of the camp lands is resolved.

Ownership of the Shares of the Camp Businesses

Ownership of the shares of the settlement camp businesses was the other major issue Swiss officials helped the Tibetan exiles to negotiate. According to Nepali law, non-citizens cannot hold shares in small-scale village and cottage industries in Nepal, yet in accordance with both the 1964 and 1972 Swiss-Nepal agreements, Swiss intergovernmental organizations were allowed to hold shares in the camp businesses on behalf of the Tibetans.[26] Swiss ownership of the shares enabled the businesses to register with the Nepal government, purchase land, import raw materials, export finished products, maintain bank accounts, and accept foreign currencies. Swiss ownership also enabled them to establish, in the early years of Nepal's carpet industry, a dominant share of the export market. Swiss ownership of the shares effectively incorporated the Tibetan exiles as business owners into Nepal and enabled their economic self-sufficiency.

In 1975, Swiss intergovernmental organizations initiated their withdrawal from the shareholding arrangements, however. They did so because they determined the Tibetan exiles, at that time, to be self-sufficient. They did so also because of a conflict that emerged between the norms and values they were trying to promote and the norms and values Tibetan exile leaders were trying to promote. Swiss officials were trying to use the businesses to compete in international markets. Tibetan exile leaders were trying to use them to promote their political cause. As a result of the conflict, Swiss officials withdrew first from day-to-day management, then from membership on the boards of directors, and finally from the shareholding arrangements themselves.

In 1966, five years after the Tibetan exiles constructed their first carpet factories, Swiss officials registered them under the Nepal Company Act as private limited companies.[27] Swiss officials also registered an export company, the Carpet Trading Company Private Limited (CTC), to enable the camp factories to export their products to a buyer they had located for them in Switzerland.[28] Swiss officials negotiated two separate shareholding arrangements for the businesses.[29] With the four camp factories, Swiss officials own all of the shares entirely. With CTC, Swiss officials initially owned 83 percent of the shares and the Dalai Lama owned 17 percent in the name of a Tibetan who already had Nepali citizenship.[30] Swiss officials served as the financial and political guarantors of all of the businesses. The CTC served as their only importer, exporter, and unofficial banker.

Swiss ownership of the shares entitled Swiss officials to serve on their boards of directors. Swiss representation on the boards enabled Swiss officials to appoint, promote, and dismiss the managers of all the camp businesses; to formulate their strategies for production, expansion, and sales; and to direct their day-to-day decisions. Swiss officials, in the early years of the Tibetan exile, were very active members of the board. Although they appointed Tibetans as general managers, they retained control over all day-to-day decisions. They used their positions to help the Tibetan exiles learn to compete in international markets. The Tibetan exiles themselves had other ideas, however. They resented Swiss involvement and resisted the norms and values they were trying to promote. A Nepali employee of the Jawalakhel Handicraft Center (JHC) at the time explains:

> The Tibetans had always in their minds why they should be so much under the control of the Swiss.... What the Tibetans wanted from the Swiss was just advice and not any interference in their activities.... Another reason was the somewhat harsh businesslike treatment shown by some Swiss personnel.... As refugees [the Tibetans] expected love, sympathy, and kindness, whereas some Swiss began to be much more business minded and wanted the Tibetans also to be the same, in order to survive in this competitive world. (Joshi 1983: 3)

Swiss officials believed the settlement camp businesses should be used to compete in international markets so as to enable the Tibetan exiles to become economically self-sufficient. Tibetan managers believed the businesses should be used to cultivate loyalty to the Dalai Lama's exile administration and the independence cause. The conflict between them led Swiss officials to withdraw first from day-to-day management and then from the boards of directors, as the transfer of the management of the JHC illustrates.

The transfer of the management of the JHC was precipitated by two related conflicts. The first involved a conflict over who should succeed to the general manager's position. Throughout the first decade of its existence, JHC's management structure comprised a Tibetan general manager, a Nepali assistant manager, and a Swiss official who supervised them both. All three reported to a JHC board of directors composed of two Swiss officials, two Tibetans, and one Nepali businessman. In 1971, the general manager resigned, and the board had to appoint a new one. Swiss officials, concerned that the JHC remain competitive, argued that skills and experience were the most important qualifications. They wanted the assistant manager to succeed to the position. The Tibetan members of the board, concerned that the JHC promote their political cause, argued that loyalty to the Dalai Lama's exile administration was a more important qualification. They wanted a representative the exile administration had sent to the factory to succeed to the position instead. Swiss officials considered the representative entirely unqualified for the position. A Swiss official explains: "Tibetan government managers [*sic*] were usually not up to the mark because they were chosen for political reasons and not for talent. Government officials usually appointed relatives when they could. Jawalakhel was especially bad for sectarianism."[31] Disagreement over the appointment continued until a Tibetan who was both well qualified and appropriately loyal could be found.

Soon after that issue was settled, another conflict emerged. The Tibetan members of the board complained that Swiss officials had signed agreements with the Nepal government but not with the Dalai Lama's exile administration (Joshi 1983: 13). Why was their relationship with the Nepalese formally recognized through intergovernmental agreements yet not their relationship with the Tibetans? Swiss officials explained that they had to sign an agreement with the Nepal government to be able to establish an office in Nepal at all and that they could not sign agreements with the Dalai Lama's exile administration. Their own government had never officially recognized the Dalai Lama's exile administration. It was also among the first to recognize the People's Republic of China. Signing an agreement with the exile administration would go against the spirit of early recognition.[32] As a concession to the Tibetans, one Swiss and the one Nepali board member withdrew. Tibetan board members, then in the majority, immediately arranged for the Dalai Lama's exile administration to appoint all future managers.

As a result of the change, Swiss officials initiated a withdrawal from their shareholding arrangements in the Swiss-Tibetan settlement camp businesses. The process has been slow. The shares that Swiss officials held in the Carpet Trading Company are the only shares that have thus far been transferred. They were transferred in May 1995 to five Tibetans with Nepali citizenship. They join the one other Tibetan who already held shares in CTC on behalf of the Dalai Lama.

The transfer of the shares of the four settlement camp factories has been more difficult. The Swiss and Tibetan exile officials I interviewed were in agreement about the many problems involved. First, successive general managers of all four factories have not kept copies of important business documents, such as license renewal certificates, so that Swiss officials fear problems may arise with the withdrawal of their influence.[33] Second, finding Tibetans with "good" Nepali citizenship, that is, acquired legally, and with the integrity not to abuse their positions, to take over the shares has not been easy. Third, Tibetan exile officials have asked that the Swiss and Nepal governments first sign an agreement to ensure there is a high degree of acceptance for the transfer of the shares. Since Nepal's democracy movement in 1990, however, the government has changed hands so frequently that Swiss officials have been unable to establish the level of cooperation necessary for such an agreement. Finally, Swiss officials want to make sure that they "cover all of the bases" before their withdrawal so that the Tibetans face no surprises.

Swiss ownership of the shares of the settlement camp businesses enabled the Tibetan exiles of the four Swiss-Tibetan settlement camps to incorporate into the Nepal state as business owners and achieve economic self-sufficiency. Swiss officials initiated their withdrawal from their ownership position in part because they determined the Tibetan exiles to be self-sufficient but also in part because the Tibetan exiles had started to use the Swiss-Tibetan businesses for their own purposes. Swiss officials remain committed to the assistance relationship, however, until the remaining shares of the businesses can be effectively transferred.

Incorporation into the International Carpet Market

Swiss officials helped the Tibetan exiles to incorporate not just into the Nepal state, but also, simultaneously, into the international carpet market. Management of the camp businesses was the most important issue to negotiate to enable them to compete in the market, as it required the Tibetan exiles to learn new values and skills. Swiss officials trained the Tibetan exiles in the values and skills they believed they needed to be able to compete. None of the Tibetans initially trained by Swiss intergovernmental officials now work in the Swiss-Tibetan settlement camp businesses, however. They used the values and skills they learned to start their own businesses and to achieve self-sufficiency separate from the settlement camp system instead. Those who did work for settlement camp businesses for any period of time left when the Dalai Lama's exile administration secured control over their management. They now compete with the settlement camp businesses for market share.

Swiss officials used three strategies to train the first generation of Tibetan carpet factory managers. The first involved the day-to-day management of the settlement camp businesses themselves, a practice they ended in the early 1970s. The second involved indirect supervision of the settlement camp businesses, a practice that continues to a certain degree today. The third involved a training program Swiss officials organized for the Tibetan exiles in Nepal. The program began in 1971 and lasted for three years. Twenty-two Tibetan children—fifteen boys and seven girls—aged 16 to 20 participated.[34] Swiss officials selected the program participants from the four Swiss-Tibetan settlement camps for their facility with numbers and their potential to become managers. The program involved daily classes at the CTC throughout the school year. Through the program, Swiss and American teachers taught the Tibetans values such as cleanliness, efficiency, and an international orientation as well as skills such as mathematics, bookkeeping, correspondence, geography, and foreign languages. The success of the program is demonstrated by the high percentage of program participants, nearly 80 percent, who went on to establish successful international carpet export businesses.[35]

Tsering Yangkyi, one of the program participants and now the owner of a successful carpet export business, recalls her life from that time:

> My parents were working in the Jawalakhel Handicraft Center. My sister and I were sent to Dharamsala for school. We were assigned to the Central School for Tibetans in Kalimpong. I entered into class seven. I was the girl's captain in one of the houses, so I could not come to Kathmandu for holidays, even when my parents called me to apply for the CTC program. My uncle came down to Kalimpong to tell me about it. I sent recommendation letters through him and my parents brought them to CTC. A man named Mr. Dit was in charge at the time. I was chosen for the program and so I came up to study for three years.... I remember learning accounting and Nepali and also how to sew and swim... I still use all of the skills even today... After the program ended, I wanted to work for the Tibetan community but there was an unfortunate event in my family... I finished the program but asked if I could help my family instead. (personal communication, August 1, 1995)

The Swiss program for Tibetan administrators was intended to train managers for the Swiss-Tibetan settlement camp businesses. It was intended, in the words of one program participant, to make the businesses "of the Tibetans, by the Tibetans, for the Tibetans."[36] None of the training program participants currently works for any of the settlement camp businesses, however. Of the program participants, only six worked for the camp businesses for any period of time. Most started private carpet businesses instead. Part of the reason involves the way in which the camp businesses were managed as they came under the control of the Dalai Lama's exile administration. Swiss-trained Tibetans found their values and skills to be in conflict with the exile administration's way of doing business. A Swiss official explains:

> Government-owned undertakings are always a problem. They are slow and indecisive. Corruption is rampant. Red tapism is always a problem. Even the Swiss had to wait for approval from the Tibetan government [*sic*] for certain things.... The trainees were better off using their skills in their own businesses rather than in the government factories where patience was more important.[37]

One of the program participants who did work for the settlement camp businesses supports his assessment with: "I didn't like the way decisions were made at CTC. Although I can see the benefits of CTC, I was frustrated by the length of time it took to get anything done. In general, communal undertakings do not agree with me. I am fine when I work one-on-one but I don't like to work with committees."[38] For the Swiss-trained Tibetans, managers from the Dalai Lama's exile administration were too slow in making decisions, did not feel any pressure to act when there was an opportunity, and were generally unresponsive to the market. The Swiss-trained Tibetans who did work for them found that their skills, experience, and ideas were increasingly underutilized. Like many other Tibetans in Nepal at the time, they chose to establish their own private carpet factories and to enter the international carpet market on their own instead.

The Normative Dynamics of Swiss Intergovernmental Assistance

The normative dynamics of the relationship between Swiss intergovernmental organizations and Swiss-assisted Tibetans involve a fundamental conflict between the goals of self-sufficiency and political loyalty. Swiss officials promote self-sufficiency by promoting certain values among the Tibetan exiles. Swiss-assisted Tibetans, for the most part, have accommodated those values. Doing so enabled them to establish many successful private carpet businesses in Nepal. Within the four Swiss-Tibetan settlement camps, however, the value of efficiency came into conflict with the value of political loyalty. Tibetan exile leaders managed the camp businesses in an inefficient manner, for the purpose of cultivating loyalty to themselves and their political cause. Their inefficient management caused them to become unable to compete in the market. They now rely on sympathy for the independence cause to remain in business.

Swiss officials, from the start of their relationship with the Tibetan exiles, have promoted among them the values of cleanliness, efficiency, and an international orientation. In the early years of the Tibetan exile, cleanliness was the focus for their efforts. The Tibetan exiles did not, at first, know how to live at lower altitudes. Continuing to live as they had in Tibet, they contracted diseases to which they were not immune. They were dying by the day. Swiss officials considered the first order of business to be to teach the Tibetan exiles how to keep clean. They:

> collected the men together by the water spigots and cut, washed, and combed their long hair to get rid of the bugs. Others instructed all of the [Tibetans] in the use of latrines... Nurses repeatedly explained that saving and eating raw meat in [Nepal's] hot climate would only exacerbate illness, often to no avail. The foreigners tried to teach the Tibetans to wash their bowls instead of simply licking them clean... most Tibetans rarely washed. Skin infections erupted from the rubbing of heavy clothing against dirty skin. (Forbes 1989: 30)

Cleanliness is a value that Swiss officials sought to promote not only for good health but also to help the Tibetans sell their goods, to interact with carpet buyers first on the local tourist market and then in international markets. Swiss-assisted Tibetans have largely accommodated the value of cleanliness. Tibetan exiles in the Jawalakhel camp wash daily at the public water pumps. They keep their clothes clean. Most men now keep their hair short. Many women keep their hair short as well, not just for fashion, as one Tibetan woman explained to me, but also because it is easier to keep clean. Every morning in Jawalakhel, Tibetan carpet shop owners can be seen sweeping out their shops and throwing water on the dusty street. They have even taken to washing their carpets thoroughly before they put them out for sale.

The extent to which Swiss-assisted Tibetans have accommodated the value of cleanliness became clear to me one day through a discussion I had with my Tibetan language teacher in Jawalakhel. He had asked to see photographs I had taken on a research trip to Tibet. When he saw one photograph of some children in Nyalam, he laughed at how dirty (*tsog-pa*) they are. Even though they have access to water, he said, the children do not wash (there is a river in the photograph). He then explained, however, that there is a saying in Tibetan that washing means risking your prosperity (*yang-shor*) so that people in Tibet do not wash very often. He also said that there is one special day every year in Tibet when Tibetan women wash their hair. On no other day do they wash it. What we see in his comments are his reflections on the relative value of cleanliness for Tibetans in exile, like himself, versus Tibetans in Tibet. That cleanliness had become one of his own values is evident in his initial response to the photograph (surprise and laughter); that cleanliness, as far as he knows, is not generally a value for Tibetans in Tibet is evident in his later reflections, on the way in which it is portrayed in Tibetan sayings.

Efficiency is another value Swiss officials sought to promote among the Tibetan exiles. In the early years of the Tibetan exile, getting the Tibetans to work more efficiently was a constant struggle for settlement camp managers. They experimented with a variety of incentive structures, yet none seemed able to convince the Tibetan exiles to work. A Tibetan manager recalls:

> The men especially did not like working in the factories. Spinning and carding wool was the women's work and in Tibet men would never touch women's work. Both the men and women were very lazy. In Tibet, this wasn't their job. There they would go and look after the cattle and yak all day and then come home, eat, and go to sleep. In the beginning, they felt very sorry for themselves. (quoted in Forbes 1989: 53)

In the early years, the Tibetans would work in the factories only a few hours a day. The carpets they made were so carelessly woven that they could not be sold. Their work improved only when, in 1965, Swiss officials switched to paying the Tibetans on a piecework, rather than hourly, basis. Only then did the Tibetans begin to find value in more efficient production (Forbes 1989: 53).

These days, the Swiss-Tibetan settlement camp factories, and indeed all Tibetan carpet factories with which I am familiar, produce carpets in accordance with a production schedule. Foreign buyers place orders for a certain number of carpets with particular patterns and colors. They supply color samples. They agree on a shipping date, often recorded in a written contract. Most factories maintain a production director who supervises the schedule for carding, dyeing, and spinning the wool; and weaving, trimming, and washing all of the carpets the factory produces. The production director at the Jawalakhel Handicraft Center keeps records of every stage of the process on preprinted "production schedule" cards that he uses also to determine how to pay the many producers involved. Efficient production ensures that the carpets meet the shipping date and that the production costs remain below the purchase price.

Another value that Swiss officials sought to promote among the Tibetan exiles is an international orientation. They did so, in a formal manner, by organizing classes for the Tibetan exiles to teach them geography and foreign languages. They did so in an informal manner in conversations with them about the world as they knew it. One result of this international orientation is that Tibetans are very flexible in their approach to the international carpet market. The Tibetan exiles produce carpets appropriate to many different markets. Tibetans explained to me that Americans like very busy looking carpets with red and black in them; they produce those kinds of carpets for the American market. Europeans, especially Germans, like carpets with softer pastel colors and abstract geometric designs; they produce those kinds of carpets, which they refer to as "modern design" carpets, for the European market. Tibetans also produce what they call traditional

Tibetan carpets that tend toward vibrant primary colors, with red borders and Tibetan and Chinese motifs, such as the dragon and the phoenix, the lotus flower, and the long-life symbol. Tibetan carpet shop owners I observed were adept at assessing what their customers from different countries might want. Their knowledge was based in part on experience yet also in part on what they could observe about fashion trends in different countries from foreign magazines and from their attendance at international carpet trade shows.[39]

Swiss-assisted Tibetans used the values and skills they learned through their interactions with Swiss officials to compete effectively in international markets. Germany soon became the principal market for Tibetan carpets, yet Britain, Switzerland, Belgium, the Netherlands, the U.S., Japan, and Taiwan remained important markets as well.[40] Bryan Huffner, former managing director of Oriental Carpet Manufacturers (OCM), a London-based carpet business that bought an estimated one-half to two-thirds of all carpets produced by private Tibetan factories in Nepal in the 1970s, explains why Tibetan carpets performed so well in these markets: "Many traditional carpet producing countries are entrenched in their traditional sizes, designs and colors. They will not, or cannot, make a carpet which is totally strange to them. In Nepal there was no problem of this sort.... The flexibility of the people throughout the industry [and the] exceptional fast and economic weaving on the rod led to a phenomenal growth in the industry" (Huffner 1992: 83).

The four Swiss-Tibetan settlement camp businesses were not alone in the development of the carpet industry in Nepal. Swiss-trained Tibetans who left the settlement camp businesses established many private factories and export companies on their own. U.S. international organizations helped another group of Tibetans, demilitarized guerrilla fighters, to establish their own network of carpet factories and export companies, based on the Swiss model. Tibetans also migrated into Nepal from India to participate in the carpet industry. Finally, many Nepali businessmen, initially engaged in other businesses, expanded into the carpet industry as well. By 1992, there were more than two thousand carpet businesses in Nepal, 80 percent of them in the Kathmandu Valley.[41] In 1992, they exported more than two million square meters of carpet, valued at more than $100 million (Shrestha 1992: 13).

All of the many carpet businesses in Nepal compete for market share largely on the basis of cost. Maintaining efficient low-cost production has thus become important to all of the businesses. For the Swiss-Tibetan settlement camp businesses, however, the value of efficiency comes into conflict with the value of political loyalty. Tibetan exile leaders, starting in 1975, have been managing the camp businesses in an inefficient manner, for the purpose of enticing Tibetans into their employment, and into camp residence, more permanently.[42] As one Tibetan explains:

FIGURE 1.1 Value of Carpet Exports from Nepal, 1984–1995

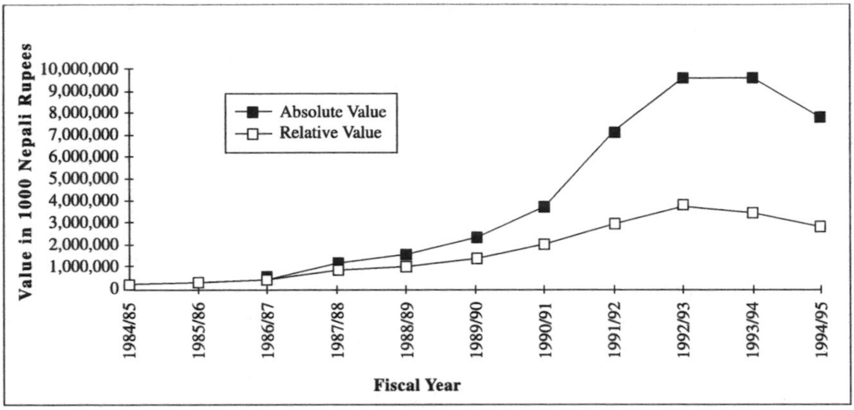

Source: Data were compiled from Nepal Trade Promotion Board statistics. Data for 1994/95 are based on 11 months.

It is the goal of His Holiness [the Dalai Lama] to use factory money for the benefit of the Tibetan people ... [to] keep Tibetans together so they can maintain the Tibetan culture ... then those people will think of themselves as Tibetan settlement people, just as someone who is employed by CTC thinks of himself as a CTC person and someone who is employed by the Snow Lion Foundation thinks of himself as a Snow Lion Foundation person.[43]

All of the settlement camp businesses have instituted incentive systems to entice Tibetan exiles into their employment and into camp residence more permanently. The JHC has the most generous of all incentives. It needs them to keep Tibetan exiles in the settlement camp and in the employment of the settlement camp businesses, as it has always been comparatively easy for Tibetans from Jawalakhel to leave the camp to establish carpet businesses of their own. Senon Dorje, one of the first Tibetans to leave the Jawalakhel camp in the 1970s, explains how he established his first carpet business:

> In 1973 or 1974, I decided to start off on my own. I rented some rooms in Pulchowk from some Nepali families and bought three or four looms ... my expenses were not so high. I did some weaving myself and hired some Tibetan friends from JHC to weave for me. Everyone worked from early in the morning until well into the night.... About 1979, it happened often that wholesale buyers came by. They were mostly from Germany, Britain, Switzerland, and Holland. They started to buy carpets.... When they realized I provide good quality carpets, I signed exclusive contracts them.[44]

"There were buyers even waiting at the airport to buy carpets," another Tibetan to leave the Jawalakhel camp explains, "At that time, the level of production throughout the industry was very low and the demand was very high."[45]

In 1975, the incentives the JHC used to entice Tibetan exiles into its employment and into camp residence included a free room in the camp, high wages, free day care, free medical treatment, and permission to sell privately made carpets on commission in the JHC salesroom. All of these measures, a Nepali employee of the JHC reports, "somewhat stopped the movements of trained workers" to other businesses (Joshi 1983: 11–12). Over the years, as the industry expanded, JHC's incentives had to expand as well. By 1995, the JHC was paying nearly double the wages paid in private factories. It provided free elementary education for children of all regular employees, and free secondary education at high schools affiliated with the Dalai Lama's exile administration. It subsidized room and board for old and infirm relatives at the settlement camp's old age home. It provided bonuses to all regular employees upon the birth of their children, and an annual bonus whether or not the JHC as a whole was profitable. By 1995, the JHC not only had no problems recruiting workers, it even had to start a waiting list.[46]

The incentives the settlement camp businesses offer to Tibetans are intended to keep the Tibetans in residence in the camps. The camps provide a place where representatives from the Dalai Lama's exile administration can cultivate loyalty to themselves and the independence cause more easily. Representatives from the Dalai Lama's exile administration regularly make speeches in the settlement camps about their activities, aimed to achieve Tibetan independence. They regularly organize political programs through the camp leadership. The Swiss-Tibetan settlement camps now serve as "technologies of power" for the cultivation of national consciousness (Malkki 1989, 1995b). They provide a place where the Tibetan independence cause can be maintained.

TABLE 1.1 Carpet Production Costs

	Private Factories		JHC (Tibetan weavers)	
	60 knot carpet	80 knot carpet	60 knot carpet	80 knot carpet
Dyed Yarn	1,367.50	1,545.00	1,465.00	1,642.50
Weaving Wage	350.00	600.00	582.00	845.00
Cotton Thread	120.00	150.00	120.00	150.00
Trimming Charge	25.00	25.00	25.00	25.00
Washing Charge	90.00	100.00	90.00	100.00
Washing Loss	75.00	109.16	75.00	109.16
Overhead Expenses	150.00	150.00	150.00	150.00
Total Per Square Meter	2,177.50	2,679.16	2,507.00	3,021.66
U.S. Dollar Equivalents	$43.55	$53.58	$50.14	$60.43

The incentives the settlement camp businesses offer may enable exile officials to cultivate loyalty, yet they prevent the businesses from being able to compete effectively in international markets. With JHC's incentives, labor costs average 50 percent more than those of other carpet businesses in Nepal. For the more remote settlement camp businesses, the high labor costs, combined with the cost of transporting carpets to Kathmandu for export, makes carpet production entirely unprofitable. The settlement camp businesses continue to produce carpets, however. They do so in order to keep Tibetans in residence in the settlement camps.

The Jawalakhel Handicraft Center and the Tibetan Independence Cause

The settlement camp businesses, unable to compete on cost, had to find other ways in which to remain in business. One solution was to establish other, subsidiary businesses that could compete on cost and use them to subsidize the settlement camp businesses. Another was to subcontract out export orders to other businesses with lower production costs.[47] A third involved cooperating with international organizations that oppose child labor. Through efforts such as USAID's Rugmark program, the settlement camp businesses agreed to continue not using child labor in their factories in exchange for assistance in marketing their carpets internationally.[48]

The primary means through which the settlement camp businesses have been able to remain in business, however, involves their efforts to market their reputation among supporters of the Tibetan independence cause. All of the Swiss-Tibetan settlement camps in Nepal serve simultaneously as tourist sites. They provide places in which tourists may both observe and participate in the maintenance of the Tibetan independence cause. The Jawalakhel settlement camp is the one most frequented by tourists, as it is the closest to the airport, is featured in tour books of many languages, and benefits from the many agreements the Jawalakhel Handicraft Center maintains with Kathmandu's major tour companies. In 1995, the JHC paid tour companies a 15 percent commission for the guide and a 2 percent commission for the driver on all carpets sold to the tourists they brought.[49] One Tibetan comments on the tour company business: "These people have been very good for business.... Unlike budget tourists who are always looking for a bargain, these people come through in two days ... stop in Bhaktapur, Patan, Kathmandu ... and buy carpets in the Jawalakhel showroom. The next day they are gone."[50]

Tours of the Jawalakhel Handicraft Center are led by clean, well-dressed English-speaking Tibetans. They show the tourists JHC's spacious, well-lighted, and well-ventilated weaving hall, filled with the cheerful, smiling faces of only adult Tibetan weavers. They tell the tourists about the atrocities the Chinese committed against the Tibetan people; about the poor Tibetan refugees who poured into Kathmandu in 1959, helpless and needy; about the camps the Tibetans established to help rebuild their lives; and about the school the JHC built to help preserve the Tibetan culture and the independence cause. The tour ends at the JHC showroom where tourists are encouraged to purchase a carpet. Tourists often choose to donate to the JHC whether or not they also buy a carpet. These donations help the JHC to remain in business despite its inability to compete in international markets on the basis of cost.

The visit of a French tour group to the JHC illustrates the type of interaction that often occurs. I witnessed the visit from the vantage point of the general manager's office where we had just been discussing JHC's cost structure. After the tour, a French man came into the office and said "I am really a friend of the Tibetan people and I'd like to make a donation." He was acting very humble and he remained in a slight bow the entire time. He refused any offer of tea or soda, and he gave the general manager two French bills that equaled about the price of a large carpet. The general manager gave him a receipt and said, very routinely: "In 1959, there were 450 people in the camp. Now, more than three decades later, there are more than one thousand.... Tibetans are still coming out of Tibet, but the situation is tricky politically. The Nepal government is sending many of them back."

"What can I do to help?" the French man asked.

"It is very difficult because your government cannot recognize Tibet without China getting mad," the general manager replied, "But as an individual, you can continue to help us."

The French man then smiled for the first time since he came into the office and said, while bowing very low, "Thank you very much." The general manager laughed and replied, "I should be thanking you for your donation."

By marketing its reputation among supporters of the Tibetan independence cause, the JHC and the other settlement camp businesses remain in business despite their inability to compete on cost in the international carpet market. This use of the settlement camp businesses is not what Swiss officials intended when they helped the Tibetan exiles to start them, however. Swiss officials intended the settlement camp businesses to enable the Tibetans to incorporate into Nepal, incorporate into the international carpet market, and become self-sufficient. One Swiss official, stationed in Nepal from 1973 to 1978 and 1990 to 1996, reflects upon the change in their use as follows:

> The biggest change I have seen in the Tibetan community between the 1970s and today is that today the Tibetans are no longer dependent upon outside help. They are more-or-less self-sufficient and they certainly have the capacity for self-sufficiency. They still do receive help but that is because they are very clever about exploiting the feelings of foreigners who support their political cause. Sometimes

I think that they don't need this help because they have enough themselves already, but then sometimes I think that if foreigners really want to give this help, then why shouldn't they accept it?[51]

Use of the camp businesses to cultivate loyalty to the Dalai Lama's exile administration and the independence cause prevents the Tibetans of the four Swiss-Tibetan settlement camps from becoming self-sufficient, as it prevents them from being able to compete on cost. The Tibetan independence cause also enables the settlement camp businesses to remain in business, however, as it attracts enough foreign assistance to subsidize them. Using the settlement camp businesses for such political purposes is not what Swiss officials intended when they initiated their international assistance program to Tibetans in Nepal. It is what Tibetan exile officials intend, however. The settlement camp businesses have thus become a principal site for the negotiation of the goals of international assistance. These negotiations involve a fundamental conflict between the goals of self-sufficiency and political loyalty.

Notes

1. Incorporation, rather than integration, is the analytical frame I prefer here, as it implies participation in legal and administrative structures without implying cultural or psychological adjustment to them (Soysal 1994: 30). Whether or not the Jawalakhel Tibetans feel integrated into Nepal, in other words, is not as important for my purposes here as whether or not they have been incorporated into the administrative structures of Nepal.
2. The U.S. State Department (1995) lists only water, timber, hydroelectric potential, scenic beauty, and limited but fertile agricultural land among Nepal's natural resources.
3. According to the 1991 census, Nepal's population numbers 18,491,097 people within 3,328,721 households, with 46.7 percent located in the plains; 45.5 percent in the hills; and 7.8 percent in the mountains (Central Bureau of Statistics 1995). Justice writes that only 12 percent of Nepal's land is arable (1986: 5). The U.S. State Department estimates 16 percent (1995).
4. Lévi (1909), Joshi and Rose (1966), Slusser (1982), Sever (1993), and Uprety and Acharya (1994) provide political and economic histories of Nepal. The Shahs are the royal family of Nepal. The Ranas are an elite family who controlled the government from 1846 to 1950.
5. Hagen (1994: 201) estimates that 30,000 Tibetans fled to Nepal between 1950 and 1959. The Information Office of the Dalai Lama (1981: 136) estimates 20,000.
6. The Information Office of the Dalai Lama (1981: 140) reports 8,000. Holborn (1975: 747) reports an initial 12,000, but a later 7,000 to 8,000, due to migration either back to Tibet or on to India. My own research, centered on the Kathmandu Valley, indicates that migration between Nepal, Tibet, and India continues. See Table A.1: Statistics on Kathmandu Tibetans from Refugee ID Applications for information about the arrival dates of Tibetan exiles in Kathmandu. Later arrivals (1980–1993) come from both Tibet and India.
7. Von Fürer-Haimendorf (1975, 1990) describes the relationships Tibetan exiles established with local populations in the northern hills to secure land and employment. Guest-host relations, long established through trade, assisted their efforts.
8. Tibetan exiles in Kathmandu say that the Tibetan god Po Thang Gonpo lives on the Tundikhel and, when appeased, protects the people who stay there.

9. Swiss intergovernmental organizations were initially reluctant to extend assistance to the Tibetan exiles. Their reports indicated that the Tibetan exiles did not need assistance. One report reads as follows: "It is difficult to understand why the Tibetans have fled; only the big landlords and lamas have been in danger. Indeed, the farmers and laborers have today under Chinese occupation a better living than before under the Dalai Lama. This explains the high percentage of monks who are predominantly Charlatans amongst the refugees" (Froesch, quoted in Forbes 1989: 27). Toni Hagen persevered in promoting a more sympathetic view of the Tibetan exiles, however, by emphasizing the needs of the poor among them (Forbes 1989: 27).

10. According to Hagen (1994: 206), the sole concern of the Nepal government "was to have the local Nepali population incorporated into the future programme in order to allow them also to share in ongoing developments and to prevent any jealousies ... from surfacing." Once he assured them that Nepali people would be included in the project, he was free to do as he pleased.

11. The humanitarian reputation of the Swiss, for years criticized by Jewish organizations, recently came under renewed attack for the role the Swiss banking industry is alleged to have played in Hitler's war effort (see, for example, William Safire, "Long-term Debt," *The New York Times*, February 3, 1997; Alan Cowell, "Swiss Begin to Question Image of Heroism in War," *The New York Times*, February 8, 1997; The Associated Press, "Switzerland Agrees to Set Up Fund for Holocaust Victims," *The New York Times*, February 12, 1997).

12. Hagen's plan, from the start, seemed destined to avoid what have been described by Harrell-Bond (1986: 3) as expensive, ineffective, and wasteful "anti-participatory aid programs," which "usurp the role of the host, suppress the creative energy of the refugee who could have helped himself, [and] provoke responses which are hostile and unproductive for all concerned."

13. Soysal (1994: 52) argues that Swiss immigration policy "emphasizes the individual migrant and labor market processes as the loci of incorporation" and "control[s] the size of the foreign population in accord with labor market demands." In contrast with other countries, which emphasize more civic-oriented models of incorporation, "Swiss officials pointed to market mechanisms as the principal framework for integration" (1994: 53).

14. The Swiss Popular Bank and the Swiss Association for Technical Assistance granted loans to the Tibetan exiles to fund the start-up of the Carpet Trading Company (CTC), the first carpet export company in Nepal (Joshi 1983: 10). Iten Maritz, a private multimillionaire, served as the first and only buyer for the Tibetans' carpets until 1977 when the manager of CTC himself traveled to Europe to find others (Joshi 1983: 11).

15. Walter Jutzi, Swiss official stationed in Nepal from 1973 to 1978 and 1990 to 1996, personal communication, May 3, 1995.

16. Walter Jutzi, personal communication, August 17, 1995.

17. Walter Jutzi, personal communication, May 3, 1995.

18. In Jawalakhel, the biggest landlord, a son of the last prime minister under Rana rule, sold the largest plot. Mudukar Rana, his son and my landlord throughout 1995, expressed regret over his father's generosity, as many of the Tibetans who resettled on the land have bigger and more elaborate houses than his own. According to Mudukar, his father was never sufficiently compensated for the land. At the same time that his father sold the land, however, the Birta Abolition Act of 1959 was being implemented. Given that his father's land was classified as birta land (land granted by the king to government families and their key supporters), and was therefore eligible for reclamation by the state, his father, in the end, may have lost the land without any compensation at all. For explanations of the different legal categories for land in Nepal, see Regmi (1965) and Sever (1993).

19. The 1964 Land Reform and Ukhada Land Tenure Acts restrict land ownership to citizens only.

20. Forbes (1989: 31) reports: "In November 1963... Father Moran received a call from the local magistrate saying that he had 24 hours to get all of the refugees out of the Kathmandu

valley. Stunned, Father Moran explained that this was impossible, that the refugees had nowhere else to go, that they had been given land and were slowly becoming settled. The official refused to discuss the issue. Since it was too late in the day to contact more sympathetic government officials, Father Moran decided he had no other choice than to obey the order."

21. T.R. Onta, executive director of the Nepal Red Cross Society and an employee of the Nepal Red Cross since its establishment, insists that the Nepal Red Cross started, informally, prior to the negotiations over the status of the Tibetan land. According to him, in about 1963, Nepali people started to take interest in humanitarian activities; one group formed an ad hoc committee for humanitarian affairs, but they were unable to form a Red Cross society, because at the time, the Nepal government had not yet signed the 1949 Geneva Convention. After Nepal signed the Convention in 1964, the committee applied for membership in the Federation of Red Cross Societies, which it received in the same year. It is not unreasonable to assume, however, that the Swiss Red Cross facilitated the committee's application for membership for the purpose of resolving the status of the Tibetan camp land. According to Hagen, the ICRC wanted a national Red Cross to administer the assistance program to the Tibetan exiles in Nepal and encouraged its establishment (1994: 209).

22. T.R. Onta, personal communication, May 26, 1995.

23. Former manager of the Carpet Trading Corporation (one of the Swiss-Tibetan businesses in Jawalakhel), personal communication, September 11, 1995. The Nepal Red Cross Society may have signed an agreement with the Jawalakhel Handicraft Center (JHC), another of the Swiss-Tibetan businesses, to protect the Jawalakhel settlement camp land independently of the 1964 Swiss-Nepal agreement. Walter Jutzi, a Swiss intergovernmental organization official stationed in Nepal from 1973 to 1978 and 1990 to 1996, reports that the JHC, rather than the Nepal Red Cross, has been paying taxes on the Jawalakhel land. He understands that to mean that JHC has come to some sort of ownership agreement with the Nepal Red Cross (personal communication, August 17, 1995, reiterated on September 14, 1995). Joshi (1983: 2) confirms there is an agreement, which he reports was signed in 1967. No one would explain to me, however, how the agreement protects the Jawalakhel land. Independently of even that agreement, JHC officials have taken one other precaution against the loss of their settlement land. The JHC has purchased other plots of land, which it is entitled to do as a private limited company in Nepal, and has built both residential and commercial properties on it (former manager of CTC, personal communication, September 11, 1995).

24. Karma Tashi, executive director of the Snow Lion Foundation, personal communication, September 7, 1995. Discussions I had with a number of Tibetan exile officials revealed their uncertainty about the citizenship issue today. They explained that certain Nepal government officials, in the early years of the Tibetan exile, proposed mass citizenship for all Tibetan exiles in Nepal, yet at that time, the Tibetans refused. Over the years, as the Nepal government has changed hands, different government officials have taken different positions on the issue. Reluctance on the part of Nepal's successive governments even to acknowledge the existence of the Tibetan exiles in Nepal, makes it difficult for the Tibetan exiles to determine what the status of the offer is today.

25. Walter Jutzi, personal communication, May 3, 1995.

26. Walter Jutzi, personal communication, May 3, 1995. The 1961 Industrial Enterprises Act restricts ownership of small-scale village and cottage industries to Nepali citizens only.

27. The carpet factories in the four Swiss-Tibetan settlement camps were registered as Jawalakhel Handicraft Center Private Limited, Chialsa Handicraft Center Private Limited, Tashi Palkhiel Handicraft Center Private Limited, and Dhorpatan Handicraft Center Private Limited (Joshi 1983).

28. The original name for the Carpet Trading Company was the Tibetan Carpet Trading Company Private Limited, yet within a year, the Nepal government requested that the word Tibetan be deleted from its name. Joshi (1983: 11) explains that: "As an independent

and sovereign state, Nepal had to preserve its position by giving shelter to the Tibetans. On the other hand, being a small country, very weak in all respects compared with China, she was afraid to displease the latter by giving open shelter to those who[m] the Chinese considered rebels. By chance, this occurred during the period when [Nepal] was under the direct rule of the late King Mahendra, who [had] abolished the pro-Indian Nepali Congress government. Naturally, His Majesty's Government could not displease the Chinese Government [at the same time]. As a small buffer state, its position was very delicate on both sides." The company was re-registered with its new name in 1969.

29. All information reported here about the shareholding arrangements derives from interviews I conducted with a former manager of the CTC; interviews I conducted with Walter Jutzi, a Swiss intergovernmental official; and a report prepared by H.D. Joshi (1983), one of the first Nepali managers of the Jawalakhel Handicraft Center.

30. CTC is now not just one company but two parallel companies managed by the same people. It is the Carpet Trading Company Private Limited as well as the Continental Trading Company Private Limited. CTC became two companies in 1973, in response to a law passed by the Nepal government that required all export businesses in Nepal to produce whatever they export. The law made the Carpet Trading Company ineligible to renew its business license the next year. In response to the law, Swiss officials, based on the advice of Nepal's home minister, started the Continental Trading Company Private Limited, which they registered as both a producer and an exporter of carpets. All assets from the Carpet Trading Company were transferred to the Continental Trading Company. The Carpet Trading Company was re-registered with responsibility only for transporting carpets from the remote settlements to Kathmandu. The ownership structure of the second CTC differs from the ownership structure of the first. The second CTC was registered in the names of two people with Nepali citizenship, a Tibetan-Newar who inherited citizenship from his father and a Newar who worked for CTC. They owned all of the shares for the new company, yet they allowed others to represent them on the board of directors. According to a former manager of CTC, there were never any problems with the new ownership structure. Both owners "have great integrity" as well as "good Nepali citizenship," acquired legally (personal communication, September 11, 1995). As insurance, it seems, both owners were also given loans through CTC as part of an agreement not to claim any profits from the company (Joshi 1983: G).

31. Walter Jutzi, personal communication, August 17, 1995. Ironically, the Tibetan whose appointment was blocked by the Swiss was re-appointed by the Dalai Lama's exile administration as the JHC general manager in 1994 and is now overseeing the withdrawal of the Swiss from factory ownership.

32. Walter Jutzi, personal communications, May 3, 1995 and August 17, 1995.

33. Walter Jutzi, personal communication, August 17, 1995. My own experience working in the Tibet Office to collect information on the Tibetan exiles using their identity card application forms supports Mr. Jutzi's evaluation of their documentation practices. Tibet Office documents were rarely complete. Documents were sometimes sent to subsidiary offices without recording either what was sent or where it was sent. Documents that were kept in the Tibet Office were merely bundled together with string and piled into various corners. High turnover among staff prevented anyone from knowing where certain documents were located.

34. Information on the training program derives from interviews I conducted with Karma Tashi, executive director of the Snow Lion Foundation and one of the program participants (personal communications, February 5, 1995 and August 23, 1995); Tsering Yangkyi, another of the program participants (personal communication, August 1, 1995); and Walter Jutzi, Swiss intergovernmental official and one of the program administrators (personal communication, May 3, 1995).

35. According to Karma Tashi, out of twenty-two program participants, seventeen own their own private carpet factories; one owns a restaurant; one emigrated to Switzerland; one

was one of the few women elected to the Tibetan Legislative Assembly in Dharamsala before she died in a tragic car accident; one was just lost somehow; and one was Karma Tashi himself (personal communication, August 23, 1995).

36. Karma Tashi, personal communication, February 15, 1995.
37. Walter Jutzi, personal communication, May 3, 1995.
38. Former manager of the CTC, personal communication, September 11, 1995.
39. Another way in which to analyze this difference between "traditional" Tibetan carpets and "modern" Tibetan carpets is in terms of the social history approach promoted by Appadurai (1986) in *The Social Life of Things*, and in particular, in his discussion of the relationship between knowledge and commodity valuation. Appadurai (1986: 41) proposes that the relationship involves, at minimum, two different kinds of knowledge—the knowledge that goes into the production of a commodity; and the knowledge that goes into the appropriate consumption of a commodity. These two types of knowledge interact in various ways throughout the social history of any given commodity. Changes in production knowledge may at times influence how the commodity is consumed. Changes in consumption may at times influence how the commodity is produced. In the case of Tibetan carpets, changes in consumption have, indeed, influenced how the carpets are produced. Tibetans now produce carpets of many different sizes, styles, and designs appropriate to many different markets. Given the flexibility in their designs, what makes all of these carpets distinctly Tibetan is an issue that has emerged. Why, in other words, would someone want to purchase a "Tibetan" carpet on the international market as opposed to a Chinese, Moroccan, or Turkish carpet? Tibetans have identified the weaving process as the essential element. A "Tibetan" carpet, they explain, involves the use of a rod in the weaving process so as to produce a thick double knot instead of the single knot process favored in China, Morocco, and the other carpet-producing countries worldwide. Tibetan carpets, they explain, are thicker and softer overall as a result.
40. Most estimates attribute 80 to 90 percent of the market to Germany (Shrestha 1992: 13); Kiran Man Singh, employee of USAID, personal communication, February 6, 1995.
41. Pradhan (1993). Bhawa (1994: 8) estimates as many as five thousand factories. What constitutes a factory is debatable.
42. Joshi (1983: 11). His observations are supported by comments made to me by the assistant manager of the JHC, personal communication, March 21, 1995.
43. Sonam Tsering, personal communication, August 7, 1995.
44. Senon Dorje, personal communication, July 30, 1995.
45. Kelsang Gyaltsen, personal communication, November 5, 1995.
46. Information on JHC's incentives derive from interviews I conducted with a number of people including JHC's liaison officer (personal communication, June 1, 1995); JHC's general manager (personal communication, February 9, 1995); JHC's assistant manager (personal communication, March 30, 1995); and JHC's accountant (personal communication, April 27, 1995).
47. The JHC, for example, owns shares in three other carpet businesses in Nepal and maintains regular subcontracting relationships with eleven other carpet production units (JHC assistant manager, personal communication, March 21, 1995).
48. Kiran Man Singh and Neal Cohen, USAID employees, personal communication, March 16, 1995. Factory owners who sign the Rugmark contract are entitled to use a Rugmark label on all carpets they make without child labor and another temporary label for other carpets made prior to the agreement.
49. JHC accountant, personal communication, April 29, 1995.
50. Karma Tashi, personal communication, February 15, 1995.
51. Walter Jutzi, personal communication, August 17, 1995.

2

Containing Communism

The U.S. and a Tibetan Democracy

U.S. intergovernmental organizations first became involved with the soon-to-be Tibetan exiles in July 1950.[1] U.S. soldiers were fighting in Korea when China's People's Liberation Army (PLA) attacked Tibet's eastern border town of Dengo and threatened to take the Tibetan government outpost at Chamdo. With only five hundred poorly trained and ill-equipped Tibetan soldiers in eastern Tibet (Knaus 1999: 71), with eighty thousand PLA soldiers waiting to fight them (Dalai Lama of Tibet 1990: 52), and with questionable support for the Tibetan government among the local population, the Tibetan government did not know, at first, how to respond.[2] China's new communist government was intent to incorporate Tibet into its territory. The Tibetans had no way in which to resist. Indian independence had removed British interests from the region, and all efforts on the part of the Tibetan government to secure an alternative source of support had failed.[3] The Dalai Lama fled from his capital at Lhasa to Yatung, on the border between Tibet and India, while his government appealed simultaneously to Beijing to withdraw its soldiers and to Britain, India, and the U.S. to help. Both Britain and India refused on the basis that Tibet's liberation was inevitable (Goldstein 1989: 661–791). The U.S., however, responded. U.S. State Department officials perceived the war in Korea and the Chinese attack on Tibet to be related. They perceived both to be part of the same international communist conspiracy determined to destroy the democracy of the West (Knaus 1999: 75). The U.S. government began its efforts to support Tibetan resistance against the Chinese. Its efforts include assistance to Tibetans in Tibet, Tibetan exiles in India, and the Tibetan exiles in Nepal. Its support has continued, in various forms, for more than fifty years.

This chapter analyzes U.S. intergovernmental assistance to the Tibetans from the perspective of its influence on the Tibetan exiles in Nepal. U.S. assistance to the Tibetan exiles in Nepal, it is important to keep in mind, is part of a much more extensive assistance relationship that involves, in some ways, all Tibetans in exile, if not Tibetans in Tibet as well. The Tibetan exiles in Nepal, in other words, are not the only Tibetans involved. U.S. officials assist the Tibetan exiles in Nepal through the Dalai Lama's exile administration, an organization represented in Nepal by the Tibet Office yet with its headquarters in Dharamsala, India. The Dalai Lama's exile administration, through the Tibet Office, oversees twelve out of the fifteen formal Tibetan settlement camps in Nepal, including the four camps initially established by the Swiss (see Map 0.1).

U.S. assistance has helped the Tibetan exiles in Nepal in many ways. It helped one group of approximately four thousand Tibetan exiles for more than a decade to fight a guerrilla war against China from bases in Nepal. It helped that same group to resettle in Nepal at the end of the guerrilla war, in settlement camps with carpet factories, based on the Swiss model. It helped another group to establish and maintain the Dalai Lama's exile administration. More recently, it helped a group of one thousand Tibetans exiles, 10 percent of them from Nepal, to migrate to the United States.

U.S. intergovernmental organizations maintain two related narratives about the Tibetan exiles in Nepal that legitimate assistance to them. The first portrays the Tibetan exiles as fellow anti-communists. This narrative dominated the discussions of the Tibetan exiles among U.S. officials for the first thirty years of the U.S.-Tibet relationship and still serves to legitimate assistance to the Tibetans among Cold War veterans within the U.S. government. The other narrative portrays the Tibetan exiles as advocates for global democracy. This narrative now dominates discussions about the Tibetan exiles, particularly within the U.S. Congress and among younger officials. U.S. support is intended to promote the development of a democratic system of governance, one that could serve as a model for a future Tibet. Toward that end, U.S. officials promote such values among the Tibetan exiles as equal opportunity and representative government.

The Tibetan exiles have done much to accommodate these democratic norms and values. In 1963, soon after the Dalai Lama arrived in exile, they adopted a constitution for the future of Tibet, not only based on the U.S. model, but in fact, written by an American, Ernest Gross (Knaus 1999: 252). Also in the 1960s, they founded the Assembly of Tibetan People's Deputies, popularly elected from among the settlement camp inhabitants, and mandated to advise the Dalai Lama's Cabinet of Ministers. In 1990, they adopted the Charter for the Tibetan Exiles, a plan for governing the Tibetan exile settlements in even more democratic manner, through elected representation and a system of checks and balances among three branches of government. The Charter provides for the Cabinet of Ministers, previously appointed by the Dalai Lama, to be elected by the popularly elected assembly. It provides for the development of an independent judiciary, based in Dharamsala, and for popularly elected local assemblies within each Tibetan exile settlement.

Tibetan exile elite, at the same time that they have accommodated democratic norms and values, however, have resisted them as well. The norms of equal opportunity and representative government incite the most resistance. The norm of equal opportunity conflicts with a norm widely held among Tibetans of allegiance to family and kinsmen. Tibetan elite are accustomed to using their political positions to assist their families. They resist the idea of using them to create equal opportunities for all Tibetans in exile. The norm of representative government conflicts with a norm of enlightened government. Tibetan Buddhism maintains the idea that the Dalai Lama and other religious leaders are more enlightened than ordinary people.[4] Tibetans legitimate governance by the Dalai Lama, and those who rule in his name, based on his superior insight.

This chapter analyzes the normative dynamics of the relationship between U.S. intergovernmental organizations and the Tibetan exiles in Nepal. It argues that the relationship is characterized by a fundamental conflict between the normative framework of government the Tibetans maintained in Tibet, under the Dalai Lamas, and the normative framework of democracy. It proceeds in five parts. The first discusses the history of the relationship. It analyzes the role U.S. intergovernmental organizations played in support of Tibetan resistance, in support of Tibetan resettlement, and in support of the development of a Tibetan democracy. The second analyzes the normative dynamics of the relationship. It focuses on the various ways in which Tibetan exiles in Nepal discuss democratic norms and values and in particular on the ways in which they struggle to reconcile the norms of representative government versus enlightened government, equality versus hierarchy, and equal opportunity versus allegiance to family and kin. The third focuses on the conflict between the norms of equal opportunity and allegiance to family and kin. It analyzes the U.S.-Tibet Resettlement Project, and specifically the ways in which the Dalai Lama's exile administration allocated the one thousand U.S. visas through the project. The fourth analyzes the way in which democratic norms and values conflict more generally with the normative framework of government under the Dalai Lamas. It focuses on a struggle between the Jawalakhel local assembly and the Tibet Office to define the parameters of democracy for the Tibetan exiles in Nepal. The final section analyzes how the Tibetan exiles, despite their continuing struggles with the idea of democracy, promote the idea that the Dalai Lama's exile administration is now fully democratic. It argues that they do so to ensure that U.S. intergovernmental assistance to them continues.

History of the U.S.-Tibet Relationship: Cold War Anti-Communism

We may analyze the history of the relationship between U.S. intergovernmental organizations and the Tibetan exiles in terms of three distinct phases, on the basis of the goal U.S. officials sought to achieve within each. Throughout the first phase, from 1951 to 1971, U.S. officials sought to assist the Tibetan guerrilla movement to resist Tibet's incorporation into the People's Republic of China (PRC). Throughout the second phase, from 1971 to 1989, U.S. officials sought to resettle the Tibetan exiles into Nepal in settlement camps with carpet factories, based on the Swiss model. Throughout the third phase, from 1989 to the present, U.S. officials have sought to help the Tibetan exiles to establish a democratic government, with the potential one day to return to Tibet. Throughout all three phases, U.S. officials have legitimated their assistance in terms of democratic norms and values. The Tibetan exiles have struggled to accommodate these norms to ensure that the assistance relationship continues.

Tibetan Resistance (1951–1971)

U.S. assistance to the Tibetans began as far back as 1951, even before the Tibetan exile. U.S. officials took interest in the Tibetans, as they perceived the incorporation of Tibet into the PRC to be part of a communist conspiracy directed, in part, against themselves. A U.S. official involved with the Tibetan project explains the mind-set within the U.S. government at the time that lent itself to such a view: "President Truman was intent upon stopping the spread of communism. The State Department too was fiercely anti-communist.... This was all during the Korean War. Everyone was expecting World War Three to start. People were panicked.... The U.S. was even going to invade Cuba to get the communists out."[5]

U.S. efforts to assist the Tibetans were entirely covert at the start; they involved two initially distinct groups. The first consisted of members of the Dalai Lama's family and other Tibetan political elite. U.S. officials, as far back as 1951, began to work with them to try to convince the Dalai Lama to flee into exile. U.S. officials wanted the Dalai Lama to flee so as to be able to use him to recruit support for their own anti-communist efforts in Tibet. With the Dalai Lama in exile, they thought, he could denounce the Chinese and make a public request for U.S. assistance; then British, Indian, and U.N. support for U.S. efforts in Tibet would be easier to secure.[6] U.S. officials helped one of the Dalai Lama's brothers, Thubden Jigme Norbu, to emigrate to the United States (Goldstein 1989: 794; Norbu 1960: 244). They helped another of his brothers, Gyalo Thondup, to establish an office in Darjeeling, India to gather information on communist atrocities in Tibet (Avedon 1984: 47). Their offers to the Dalai Lama himself proceeded from support for Tibetan autonomy, to support for Tibetan self-determination, to asylum for himself and one hundred of his followers in the United States (Goldstein 1989: 776–808). In 1959, the Dalai Lama finally decided to flee, in a context of great uncertainty and apprehension about China's intentions in Tibet and about how much assistance to expect from U.S. officials once in exile.[7] An estimated 80,000 Tibetans fled in his wake; 20,000 of them to Nepal (Information Office of the Dalai Lama 1981: 136). Even with the Dalai Lama in exile, however, British, Indian, and U.N. support for U.S. efforts failed to materialize. U.S. assistance had to proceed on a covert basis. The Dalai Lama ended up claiming asylum in India.

The second group consisted of eastern Tibetans (Khampas) who had organized to resist the incorporation of their lands into the PRC. These Tibetans inhabited the eastern borderlands between Tibet and China, areas that had been ruled by Chinese warlords and semi-autonomous Tibetan kings off and on for centuries. China's efforts to incorporate Tibet into the PRC began in 1950 in these borderlands with communist propaganda meetings and with the reallocation of lands. Tibetans whose lands had been confiscated and whose leadership positions had been usurped began to organize in the hills as militant bands intent to resist the Chinese (Avedon 1984; Andrugtsang 1973). The U.S. CIA collected information about their efforts through the intelligence office Gyalo Thondup had established in Darjeeling. In 1957, the U.S. CIA, through Gyalo Thondup and his colleague, Amdo Lhamo Tsering, began to assist them as well.

U.S. assistance to the eastern Tibetans was also entirely covert; it included a number of distinct efforts. In 1956, U.S. CIA officials recruited six eastern Tibetans, trained them on the Pacific island of Saipan, and airdropped them, along with weapons and radio equipment, into eastern Tibet secretly at night (Avedon 1984: 47; McCarthy 1997: 240; Knaus 1999: 138). The goal was for them to gather information on resistance efforts and to identify leaders to whom more extensive assistance could be extended (Knaus 1999: 138). Starting in 1957, U.S. officials recruited an additional 200 to 250 Tibetans (Avedon 1984: 119) to participate in an even more extensive training program at a military base in Camp Hale, Colorado (Knaus 1999: 216–233). The program lasted for seventeen years, seven of them at Camp Hale itself (Knaus 1999: 217–219). Its goal was to train Tibetans in guerrilla warfare. It included instruction in weaponry, map reading, radio operations, encryption, propaganda techniques, and the history of communism (Knaus 1999: 219). At the end of that program, forty-nine of the trainees were also airdropped into Tibet (Knaus 1999: 233). The remainder joined guerrilla operations that had been organized in India and Nepal. Starting in July 1958, the U.S. CIA also started to airdrop military equipment into Tibet. From 1958 to 1965, the U.S. CIA completed thirty airdrops consisting of an estimated 550,000 to 800,000 pounds of military equipment (McCarthy 1997: 242; Knaus 1999: 279). That equipment included rifles, machine guns, bazookas, grenades, ammunition, wireless radios, cameras, and medical supplies (McCarthy 1997: 242). It was dropped from American planes secretly at night into drop zones identified by CIA trainees.

The assistance the U.S. provided to both groups of Tibetans did little to prevent China from incorporating Tibet into the PRC. The military assistance was, in the words of one CIA official, "too little too late" (McCarthy 1997: 242). The public relations effort through the Dalai Lama failed to recruit international support for further U.S. efforts. What the assistance relationship did accomplish, however, was to provide the U.S. with critical information on China's People's Liberation Army (PLA) and its operations (Knaus 1999: 249). U.S. officials, with the approval of President Eisenhower himself, decided to continue in their efforts, and to extend their assistance to the Tibetans in exile as well (Knaus 1999: 237).

U.S. officials intended assistance to the Tibetans in exile to accomplish two goals. The first was to continue their public relations effort to recruit support for U.S. involvement in Tibet. U.S. officials continued to work with the Dalai Lama and other Tibetan political elite to accomplish this goal. In 1959, upon the Dalai Lama's arrival in exile, they started an annual subsidy of $15,000 to him (Knaus 1999: 275). They hired a public relations firm to teach him and his officials how to publicize their case (Knaus 1999: 204). They also sponsored three groups of six to eight young English-speaking Tibetans to attend Cornell University in the U.S. to prepare them to establish the Dalai Lama's exile administration. Twenty-three Tibetans attended (Knaus 1999: 285). Those who returned to India were employed in the CIA offices in Darjeeling and Delhi and in the offices of the Dalai Lama's exile administration in Dharamsala.

The second goal was to continue gathering information on PLA activities in Tibet. U.S. officials continued to work with the eastern Tibetan guerrilla fighters to accomplish this goal. The guerrilla fighters, after escorting the Dalai Lama into exile, had regrouped in Darjeeling in 1959. There, they decided to move their basis for operations to northern Nepal, in the ethnic Tibetan semi-autonomous kingdom of Mustang (Avedon 1984: 122; Knaus 1999: 242). An estimated four thousand Tibetans were then involved. The U.S. CIA continued to airdrop military equipment to them and to advise them in their efforts. Leadership under the Camp Hale graduates, in particular, provided them with more order and coordination than they otherwise would have had:

> With the airdrops came almost forty graduates from Camp Hale. They brought M-1's and Springfields, heavy 80-millimeter recoilless guns and 2-inch mortars as well as solar batteries to run hidden radio hookups, scramblers for coding messages, machine-gun silencers, "death pills" and miniature cameras for espionage. Under their instruction, khaki uniforms were adopted and daily life became more regimented with a 5:00 a.m. rising followed by calisthenics, singing of the Tibetan

national anthem, farming, survival training and maneuvers in the hills. (Avedon 1984: 123)

From Nepal, the Tibetan guerrillas conducted raids and intelligence missions into Tibet. They cut radio lines and blocked supply routes. They blew up bridges and arsenals. Most importantly for U.S. officials, they collected information on PLA activities in Tibet, which U.S. officials in turn used to recruit support for the continuation of their activities from other branches of the U.S. government (McCarthy 1997: 235).

For the Tibetans themselves, U.S. assistance throughout this period provided a certain amount of hope. They were struggling to resist the Chinese for their own reasons. U.S. officials were one of the few groups willing to help them. U.S. assistance provided the Tibetans with training in practical skills that they would later use to help rebuild their lives in exile. Tibetan exiles in Nepal who were involved with U.S. efforts at the time discuss the role U.S. assistance played in their lives. One Tibetan exile, for example, now the owner of a large carpet export business in Nepal, recalls the work he did for the CIA at the time:

> My father served in the Tibetan government and I would have [too] if I stayed in Lhasa, but I went to Kalimpong in 1956.... In Kalimpong, I attended school and learned English from a British ex-army officer.... There were a lot of movements going on in my life then. For the next five years, I was involved in the Khampa [eastern Tibetan] movement and I did a lot of traveling. I even went to Tibet.... I did translation work for the CIA because I was one of the few people who knew both Tibetan and English.... Any Tibetan would have done what I did.... We were all united.... It was not like it is now. (personal communication, July 18, 1995)

Another Tibetan exile, one of the Cornell graduates and also the owner of a large carpet export business in Nepal, recalls his involvement as well:

> When the trouble started in Tibet, I had not yet finished school [in Kalimpong, India] and I was worried because I could not contact my parents.... Lhamo Tsering asked me to come to Darjeeling for a top-secret meeting that was very important for the Tibetan cause. I met Gyalo Thondup who told me that I was going to a far away place and that it was an important mission.... I was sent to the United States, to Colorado [where] I served as the interpreter for a special training group.... In 1963, I was assigned to the secret Delhi office coordinating all of the guerrilla activities.... In 1965, I was sent to study in the United States. For two years I studied political science, economics, and business at Cornell University.... I was part of the second group. All of the trainees became part of the Tibetan exile government when they returned [except for] at least three people [who] stayed in the U.S. I worked in the Delhi office until 1969 when I started to work in the Boudha factory. (personal communication, September 17, 1995)

Not all of the Tibetan exiles who were involved with U.S. efforts at the time are entirely happy about U.S. involvement, however. Some criticize the U.S. for not helping them enough. Baba Yeshe, the initial leader of the Tibetan guerrilla camps in northern Nepal, now living out his days in retirement in Kathmandu, recalls with some bitterness the short-comings of U.S. assistance:

> I am from Baba [Batang] in Kham.... I was the leader from Kham Dzong and I brought seventy-five people to fight.... In 1959, when His Holiness [the Dalai Lama] escaped, we helped him. We arrived with him in India.... We decided then to continue to fight from Mustang.... The Americans promised to send weapons, food, and clothing.... We discussed who would go.... I was chosen because I do not have a family [he is a monk].... For the first eight months ... the Americans did not send any food or weapons, not anything. We had to eat our shoe soles to stay alive. It was winter and very cold. After many months, the Americans sent food and weapons and good clothing by airplane. It was at night and the packages dropped from the sky. (personal communication, August 18, 1995)[8]

For another Tibetan exile, the owner of several Tibetan restaurants in Kathmandu, U.S. assistance not only did not help the resistance movement enough; it also did not help him enough. He wanted to emigrate to the U.S. He explains his efforts to do so:

> I worked for Gyalo Thondup for nine years [and] was sent to America to learn guerrilla warfare.... When I returned to India, I worked to collect people for the Tibetan military.... [After a number of years] I made my way to Dharamsala because I heard the Americans were sending fifteen to twenty boys every two to three years to go to school in the U.S. I got a job working in the Dalai Lama's mother's house.... What I really wanted to do was go to the U.S. to study but the three groups closed before I could go and they never sent a fourth group.... They did not select people the right way to go. People's fathers and brothers influenced the selection and I had no father and no brothers with me for support. I was sent to Delhi for vocational training.... I went only because I could not go to America. (personal communication, November 17, 1995)

U.S. assistance to the Tibetan guerrilla movement ended through a combination of internal and external factors. In 1969, the CIA had decided that the guerrilla movement was no longer serving its goals (Avedon 1984: 125; Knaus 1999: 296). A succession struggle within the guerrilla movement led to its ultimate defeat. The succession struggle started when Gyalo Thondup, in 1968, recalled Baba Yeshe from Mustang and replaced him with the younger CIA-trained Wangdu Gyatsotsang (Knaus 1999: 294).[9] Baba Yeshe was reassigned to be chief of security in Dharamsala, but instead of accepting the position, he returned to Mustang, rallied 250 of his troops, and seceded (Avedon 1984: 125). As the two groups fought each other, chaos ensued. The Nepal government was in a process of transition at the time—King Birendra was enthroned in 1972—and could not tolerate disorder. Mustang was sealed off and ten thousand Nepali troops were deployed to disarm the guerrillas (Avedon 1984: 126).

Baba Yeshe and his group surrendered to the Nepal army in exchange for honorary Nepali citizenship, medals for loyalty, and resettlement assistance from the Nepal government. Other Tibetan exiles consider him a traitor for doing so. One Tibetan explains: "In Tibetan society, surrendering is the worst thing anyone can do. No matter what, even if their leader dies, Tibetans are supposed to fight to the death... [Even] if [Tibetans] see someone else surrender, they have no respect for that person and they kill him right away.... When Baba Yeshe surrendered... he and all of his followers were immediately expelled from Tibetan society" (personal communication, August 25, 1995).

Baba Yeshe himself explains why he surrendered:

> I was the leader of the Mustang group for many years and then all of a sudden, Gyalo Thondup sent [Wangdu] up to Mustang to be in charge. Why did I have to give everything over to him? I was called down to Delhi to meet with Wangdu Dorje [an official in the Dalai Lama's exile administration] and I was kicked out of the Tibetan community. What could I do? I returned to Nepal and approached the king to ask how he could help.... We surrendered our weapons and were given land and citizenship. What could I do? The Tibetan government kicked me out. What choice did I have? (personal communication, August 18, 1995)

The Nepal government made the same offer of assistance, in exchange for surrender, to Wangdu and his group in 1974, but they refused (Avedon 1984: 126). Only after the Dalai Lama made a personal plea, conveyed via audiotape carried by his brother-in-law Phuntsok Tashi, did most surrender. Even then, Wangdu and at least 150 others tried to flee (Avedon 1984: 128). For several months, the Nepal army chased the renegade group from one village to the next throughout northern Nepal until Wangdu finally was shot, and the rest were captured. Those who did not either die during the chase, or commit suicide when captured, were brought down to Kathmandu under heavy guard.[10] The first phase of the relationship between U.S. intergovernmental organizations and the Tibetan exiles came to an end.

Tibetan Resettlement (1971–1989)

The second phase of the relationship began with the end of the guerrilla war and involved the incorporation of the demilitarized guerrilla fighters into Nepal in settlement camps with carpet factories, based on the Swiss model. U.S. officials helped the demilitarized guerrillas to locate land on which to resettle, to start carpet factories and a carpet export company, and to learn the skills they needed to be able to live constructive civilian lives in Nepal. CIA-trained Tibetans and other guerrilla leaders, led by Gyalo Thondup, managed the U.S.-Tibet settlement camps and carpet businesses until 1978. In 1978, the Dalai Lama's exile administration took over their management. The exile administration's Finance Department now uses the U.S.-Tibet businesses as a source of income for the exile administration.

Without CIA documents, still considered classified for this period of U.S. assistance, it is difficult to demonstrate the extent of U.S. involvement. Knaus's (1999: 299) account of U.S. CIA assistance to the Tibetan exiles mentions U.S. support for the carpet businesses Gyalo Thondup started in Pokhara and Kathmandu, Nepal. He does not discuss the details of the relationship, however. For a number of reasons, it is reasonable to assume that U.S. officials were as involved in the establishment of the U.S.-Tibet settlement camps and carpet businesses as the Swiss were in the Swiss-Tibetan camps. First, given the amount of government-level negotiation required to start the Swiss-Tibetan businesses, it is unlikely that Gyalo Thondup started his without similar support. Second, most of the managers of the Gyalo Thondup businesses have been CIA-trained Tibetans, whose personal relationships with CIA officials could have been used to recruit more extensive support. Third, when the carpet industry as a whole faced severe wool shortages in the early 1980s, only the Gyalo Thondup businesses were able to secure an alternative source of wool, from New Zealand, which they kept, according to managers of the Swiss-Tibetan businesses, totally secret. The Swiss-Tibetan businesses had to use their Swiss diplomatic connections to find a comparable source of wool.[11] I am assuming that the Gyalo Thondup businesses used their CIA connections to acquire New Zealand wool. Finally, a U.S. CIA official involved with the Tibetan project at the time confirms the establishment of CIA-funded carpet factories in Darjeeling.[12] If the CIA established carpet factories in India, it is not unreasonable to assume they established them in Nepal too.[13]

At the end of the guerrilla war, U.S. intergovernmental organizations helped to resettle approximately three thousand guerrilla fighters in thirteen settlement camps in India and Nepal. In Nepal, these included Boudha, Swayambhu, Balaju, Pokhara, and Helitar (for Wangdu's group) and Jorpati, Lumbini, and Trisuli (for Baba Yeshe's group). The camp lands were acquired through a variety of means. Gyalo Thondup purchased lands in Boudha and Pokhara in 1969 in the name of a Newar-Tibetan with Nepali citizenship. UNHCR purchased lands in Swayambhu and Balaju in 1967 in the name of the Nepal Home Ministry (Holborn 1975: 752). The Nepal Home Ministry gave the land in Helitar, also called the Jampa Ling settlement, to the Tibetan community, as one inalienable plot, in 1975.[14] King Birendra gave the Jorpati, Lumbini, and Trisuli settlements to Baba Yeshe and his group, as inalienable plots, in 1975. Many different organizations, UNHCR and the Nepal Red Cross among them, provided initial, temporary assistance to the settlements. The U.S. Agency for International

Development monitored the establishment of the settlements and the provision of assistance.

In the U.S.-Tibet resettlement camps (Boudha, Pokhara, and Helitar), former guerrilla leaders established a number of camp businesses (carpet factories, an export company, and two hotels) to provide more long-term economic support to the camp inhabitants. Tibetans, in their everyday discussions, refer to these businesses only as the Yabshi businesses, a title that refers to the Dalai Lama's family and that recognizes the role Gyalo Thondup, the Dalai Lama's elder brother, played in their establishment.[15] Tibetans also claim that the businesses were all "self-help" organizations (Forbes 1989: 61), yet their claims are difficult to maintain, as they cannot explain how the businesses were sustained. All of the businesses had management problems, as could be expected from any effort to transform guerrilla fighters into carpet weavers. UNHCR funded counseling services for them (Holborn 1975: 753).[16] Even then, the businesses initially produced very poor quality carpets, as the first manager of HIMCAR, the export company U.S. officials helped the Tibetans to establish, reports:

> The carpets being made by the ex-guerrillas were horrible.... When they were spinning wool, sometimes they would spin a piece as thick as a person's finger. And then they would have to make carpets out of that! (personal communication, July 18, 1995)

A Tibetan involved in the establishment of the Boudha factory explains further:

> Business then was not like business today. At the time, the foreign market was just opening up and the number of carpets produced in Nepal was minimal.... The Boudha factory made less in one year than my factory makes in one month.... Workers were paid a fixed salary every month whether or not they produced, and so there was not so much production then. (personal communication, September 17, 1995)

The businesses required an outside source of funding to sustain them until they could recruit and train other carpet weavers to work for them. The CIA, it is likely, served as that source.

By 1989, all of the Gyalo Thondup businesses were officially registered with the Nepal government in the names of Tibetans, and Tibetan-Newars, with Nepali citizenship. Their management is now divided between the Dalai Lama's exile administration and the Mustang Organization, an organization established by former guerrilla fighters to help manage the U.S.-Tibet settlement camps in Nepal. The businesses have since expanded to include five carpet factories, an export company, shares in a wool trade company, two hotels, a restaurant, two bookstores, and two handicraft shops. They provide employment to the former guerrilla fighters and they help fund the Dalai Lama's exile administration.

Tibetan Democracy (1989–present)

The third phase of the relationship between U.S. intergovernmental organizations and the Tibetan exiles began with renewed congressional interest in them, following the exile administration's International Campaign for Tibet and the Dalai Lama's 1989 Nobel Peace Prize. During this phase, from 1989 to the present, U.S. officials have provided both material and symbolic support to the Tibetan exiles to encourage them to develop a democracy. Legislation passed in the 101st to 104th Congresses included provisions to:

1. Condition China's most-favored-nation trade status[17]
2. Establish Voice of America broadcasts in the Tibetan language[18]
3. Provide scholarship funds for thirty Tibetan exiles to study in the U.S. every year[19]
4. Provide $2 million in direct assistance to Tibetans in India and Nepal[20]
5. Allocate one thousand special resident visas to Tibetans in India and Nepal to immigrate to the U.S.[21]

Initiatives through Congress have become increasingly supportive.[22] Their goals and intentions are multiple.

On one level, congressional initiatives are intended to appease an increasingly mobilized Tibet support constituency within the U.S. itself. Increasing numbers of U.S. citizens have taken interest in Tibet and the Tibetan independence cause, a result, in part, of the International Campaign for Tibet that the exile administration initiated in 1987. Congressional hearings on Tibet are now replete with questions about the number of Tibet support groups, Tibet research programs, and Tibetan Buddhist retreat centers that have been established in various congressional districts. Congressional representatives are concerned, on one level, to represent the interests of their own constituencies.

On another level, congressional initiatives appeal to the human rights principles of the representatives themselves. Congressional representatives support assistance to the Tibetan exiles as a means to compensate for their inability to assist Tibetans in Tibet. A report that accompanies a September 1995 Tibet support bill illustrates the way in which congressional officials relate support for the exiles with relief for Tibetans in Tibet: "The people of Tibet continue to live under a repressive and brutal occupation by China. The Chinese government is engaging in a regimen of population transfer ... [to] dilute Tibet's unique traditional culture. The situation in Tibet has resulted in tens of thousands of refugees fleeing into India, a country that has little ability to assist them. The Committee recommends that best efforts be undertaken to provide $2,000,000 in refugee assistance for Tibetan refugees" (www.tibet.com).

On a third level, congressional initiatives are intended to promote the values of democracy among the Tibetan exiles. A U.S. consular officer in Kathmandu explains: "The main problem preventing the U.S. from fully supporting the Tibetan exiles is their lack of democracy. The U.S. is not fond of theocratic governments and especially of people who unquestioningly support any leader, even if he is the Dalai Lama" (personal communication, September 8, 1995). A Tibetan in Kathmandu explains further: "The U.S. government is very direct about what it wants. The U.S. says it wants all countries in the world to become democratic.... It gives aid when countries take steps toward that goal and it withdraws aid when countries take steps away from that goal" (personal communication, August 28, 1995).

In response to congressional initiatives, the Dalai Lama's exile administration, in 1990, ratified a new Charter for the Tibetan Exiles, a document that outlines how democracy should be implemented within the exile communities. Exile officials portray the Charter as only the most recent of their ongoing efforts to develop a democracy. They cite the development of the popularly elected Assembly of Tibetan People's Deputies in 1960, and a 1963 constitution for the future of Tibet, as evidence of earlier efforts. The Charter is the first of their efforts to democratize the Tibetan exile communities themselves, however. Jamyang Norbu, a Tibetan scholar from Dharamsala, explains:

> Though popularly elected, the Assembly had no real legislative function, and since it was not influential in the appointment or removal of ministers of the Dalai Lama's Cabinet, its role was essentially symbolic.... The constitution too had its limits. Executive power rested solely with the Dalai Lama and the Cabinet that he chose.... The constitution itself was considered to be a draft and only to be implemented when Tibet was independent ... no clear democratic principles were propounded ... for the actual running of the government-in-exile. (Norbu 1990: 14)[23]

The 1990 Charter provides for the democratization of the Tibetan exile communities in three ways. It provides for the Cabinet of Ministers, previously appointed by the Dalai Lama, to be elected by the popularly elected assembly; for the development of an independent judiciary; and for the development of popularly elected local assemblies within each Tibetan exile settlement. Whether or not the Charter eventually leads to the democratization of the Tibetan exile communities, its most immediate effect has been to prompt a debate about democracy among the Tibetan exiles. Fundamental questions about the role of government in society have emerged and have led the Tibetan exiles to ask what, exactly, democracy means. Tibetan exiles now struggle to reconcile the norms and values that maintained the system of government they knew in Tibet, under the Dalai Lamas, with democratic norms and values.

The Normative Dynamics of U.S. Intergovernmental Assistance

The normative dynamics of the relationship between U.S. intergovernmental organizations and the Tibetan exiles involves a fundamental conflict between the normative framework of government Tibetans maintained in Tibet, under the Dalai Lamas, and the normative framework of democracy. U.S. intergovernmental organizations promote democratic norms and values among the Tibetan exiles. These norms and values at times conflict with the normative framework of the system of government Tibetans maintained in Tibet under the Dalai Lamas and have, in part, re-created in exile under the leadership of the Fourteenth Dalai Lama. We may discuss the conflict of values in terms of such contrasts as representative government versus enlightened government, equality versus hierarchy, and equal opportunity versus allegiance to family and kin.

The system of government Tibetans maintained in Tibet before the exile was based fundamentally on a principle of enlightened government. It was based on the idea that enlightened beings, the Dalai Lamas in particular, should serve as the head of government. The Dalai Lamas are a line of religious leaders who served as the head of the Tibetan government from at least the seventeenth century (Shakabpa 1967: 123). Tibetans believe the Dalai Lamas to be manifestations of the Bodhisattva Chenresig; a bodhisattva is a supreme enlightened being, a near-Buddha, who takes rebirth in the human realm to help all humankind advance on the path toward enlightenment (Ray 1986). Tibetans believe the Dalai Lamas also to be reincarnations of each other. They consider the Fifth Dalai Lama, for example, to be the reincarnation of the Fourth, and so on down the line of succession. The present Dalai Lama, the fourteenth in his lineage, explains:

> I am held to be the reincarnation of each of the previous thirteen Dalai Lamas of Tibet (the first having been born in 1351 A.D.), who are in turn considered to be manifestations of Avalokiteshvara, or Chenrezig, Bodhisattva of Compassion… As for my own religious practice, I try to live my life pursuing what I call the Bodhisattva ideal. According to Buddhist thought, a Bodhisattva is someone on the path to Buddhahood who dedicates themselves entirely to helping all other sentient beings towards release from suffering. The word Bodhisattva can best be understood by translating the *Bodhi* and *Sattva* separately: *Bodhi* means the understanding or wisdom of the ultimate nature of reality, and a *Sattva* is someone who is motivated by universal compassion. The Bodhisattva ideal is thus the aspiration to practice infinite compassion with infinite wisdom. (Dalai Lama of Tibet 1990: 11, 204–205)

Within the Tibetan government, the Dalai Lamas, thus, not only held absolute authority (Richardson 1984: 18; Goldstein 1989: 11), they also served as religious teachers and models for spiritual accomplishment.[24]

Beneath the Dalai Lamas, the Tibetan government was organized on a principle of hierarchy. It was a bureaucratic system composed of officials who represented aristocratic landholding families and landholding monastic organizations (Goldstein 1971: 170–182). It was a highly stratified system of ranked positions that determined not only what each official did for a job but also how much land he could hold, what he could wear, where he could sit, how other officials were expected to address him, and what he was expected to contribute to government celebrations (Goldstein 1973: 452; Goldstein 1989: 12–13; Taring 1970: 16, 46; Yuthok 1990: 30–31). Tibetan officials negotiated the performance of their rank in their daily interactions. Relative rank was an important part of the identity of the Tibetan political elite (Taring 1970: 21–33, 66–68, 105–106; Goldstein 1989: 146–171).

The Tibetan government operated on a principle of allegiance to family and kin. Government officials, including members of the Dalai Lama's family, if not also the Dalai Lama himself, used their positions to help their family and kin. They did so to ensure that they maintained access to estates, and to the government positions that guaranteed estate-holder status, across generations (Goldstein 1973: 452). Estates (land and people to work the land) were a primary source of wealth in Tibet. They were a limited source of wealth, however, as there is comparatively little fertile land in Tibet, and Tibetans did little to open up new lands for agricultural purposes (Goldstein 1973: 449). The number of estates was fixed. The number of officials claiming access to estates was not fixed, however. With each new Dalai Lama, a new family (his natal family) entered the political elite and needed estates appropriate to their status. These estates were confiscated from other government officials (Goldstein 1973: 449). Government officials confiscated estates to enrich their families and favorites as well. Estates were the basis of the system of patronage Tibetan officials used to build political loyalty (Goldstein 1973: 453).

Tibetan exiles now struggle to reconcile the norms and values that maintained the system of government they knew in Tibet, under the Dalai Lamas, with democratic norms and values. As they struggle to reconcile the two normative frameworks, they interpret and reinterpret what they mean by democracy in very interesting ways. When Tibetan exiles in Nepal discuss democracy, they interpret it variously to mean the end of Tibet's hierarchical system of governance, equal access to government resources, equal rights to command respect, and equal opportunity. Some even discuss democracy as a ritual they should adopt because the Dalai Lama has asked it of them. We see in these various interpretations a conflict between the norms of representative government versus enlightened government, equality versus hierarchy, and equal opportunity versus allegiance to family and kin. We see a struggle, for example, over the issue of equality versus hierarchy in the comments one Tibetan woman, a member of the former government elite in Tibet, made to me. She explained, with some bitterness, that democracy means the aristocracy should no longer control the government: "My husband's family was a government service family and I hope that my son can continue the tradition.... In the past it was expected that the sons of government families would go into government service.... These days, anybody can go into government service. Every child has to earn his way himself. This is what they call 'democracy'" (personal communication, July 12, 1995).

In a similar manner, other Tibetans reasoned that if democracy means equal access to the government, it should also mean equal access to government resources. One story follows that in Chialsa, a Tibetan settlement in northern Nepal, the Cooperative Society once received a large donation and then met to decide what to do with the money. During the meeting, some of the camp leaders suggested dividing the money up and giving it to all people equally. "We Tibetans have 'democracy,' now and so all should get an equal amount of the money." Other leaders said that it would be better to show that the donation had some results for the settlement. "If everyone in the camp just ate the money, there would be no results."

Still other Tibetans interpret democracy to mean that no one should have to work for anyone else, that everyone is entitled to equal social position. Tibetans in Nepal tell a story about the visit of two officials from the new Tibetan assembly in Lhasa (*si-chu dro-tsog*) to a monastery in Kathmandu. With the two officials was an attendant who, in his youth, had studied at the Potala palace's Tse school, and was intended for an important government position. When the Tibetan government was dissolved, however, he was arrested. Only after his release did he begin to work in the lowest government position, as a caretaker. While in Kathmandu, he had to wash the clothes of the two officials he attended and to clean up after them. When his relatives saw him, they scolded him by saying, "You should not be doing the work of a servant. We have a democracy. You should not have to work like that."

Related to the idea that no one should have to work for anyone else is the idea that everyone is entitled to the same degree of respect (*gu-shab*). In Boudha, a neighborhood northeast of Kathmandu, another story follows, there used to be a house in which eight Tibetan families lived. Three lived on the first floor; three on the second; and two on third. One of the women on the first floor was of very low class, from a family of butchers or blacksmiths, professions considered particularly polluting among Tibetans. Her husband had died; she had many, many children; and she was very poor. People were always a little afraid of her, as the story goes, because she was very talkative (*kha mangpo*) and would say anything, but everyone always listened when she spoke. There was also a woman on the first floor who had married a high lama (a Tibetan religious teacher). She was considered very high class and dignified. One day when this woman walked out of the house, she was dressed in her finest clothes and was walking in a very dignified manner. The poor but very talkative woman saw her and was very jealous, and so she screamed out at her, "You think that you are so high and dignified!

Wife of a lama! You in your nice clothes! You expect me to pay respect to you?! I will do nothing! The Dalai Lama has given us democracy! You are no better than me!"[25]

The various ways in which Tibetan exiles interpret the idea of democracy reveal a struggle not only between the values of equality and hierarchy but also between the values of representative government versus enlightened government. We see this struggle even in the issue of how to translate democracy into the Tibetan language. Some Tibetans translate democracy as *mangtso* (dmangs-gtso), spelled with a silent "d" and silent "s" on the first syllable. Others translate it as *mangtso* (mang-gtso), without the silent characters. Both translations are pronounced essentially the same, yet their derivation and meanings differ. The former (dmangs-gtso) derives from Tibetan religious texts and is used to discuss the lowest caste in the Indian caste system. The word, thus, connotes that the lowest caste should rule. The eleventh Assembly of Tibetan People's Deputies considered this idea too close to communism, so they changed the spelling to mean that everyone together, the masses (*mang*), should rule.[26] Some Tibetan exile newspapers continue to use the former spelling, however, as the debate continues: If democracy means rule by the people, who are the people who should rule?

One Tibetan, a former monk, argued with me that it is enlightened people who should rule. He interpreted democracy to refer to how regular people (*mi kyuma*) as opposed to enlightened people (*p'agpa*) conduct their lives. Regular people do whatever the masses (*mang*) do. Enlightened people do what they think is right. It is dangerous to let regular people run the government, he then reasoned as follows:

> If you have fifty stupid people (*kugpa*) in the Assembly all talking and the one person who is intelligent has no chance to speak, that is dangerous. Even if you have fifty intelligent people but one hundred stupid people, then it is the stupid people who make decisions.... In Tibetan exile society, people who work for Taiwan, if they have more people in the Assembly, they can make decisions that benefit Taiwan.... What would happen to the Tibetan exile government and the Tibetan cause? (personal communication, September 11, 1995)

Based on such an argument, that democracy could threaten the Tibetan cause, and that decisions are best left to enlightened people, such as the Dalai Lama, the exile administration has maintained control over most decisions at the same time that it has declared itself a democracy. As Samdhong Rinpoche, chairman of the Assembly of Tibetan People's Deputies, has argued, democracy among the Tibetans is a gift given by the Dalai Lama from above; it did not result from a struggle from below. Lobsang Gyatso, a cartoonist with the *Tibetan Review*, illustrates his comments in Figure 2.1.

Tibetan exile officials, rather than rejecting democracy as unsuitable, however, reinterpret it in ways to make it useful. In 1995, for example, the

FIGURE 2.1 Tibetan Democracy

assistant chairman of the Assembly of Tibetan People's Deputies, during a
meeting convened to explain new election procedures, argued that democracy does not mean freedom of speech. It means that certain people are
allowed to talk about certain things, and other people are allowed to talk
about other things, but not everyone is allowed to talk about everything.[27]
His explanation served to dismiss a question raised by a young Khampa
(eastern Tibetan) who had asked, very respectfully, why the Assembly had
not filled two seats left empty by resignations of Khampa representatives the
previous term. The question was controversial, as it evoked concerns among
Khampas about not being represented fairly in the Dalai Lama's exile
administration, yet it was a question that had been discussed for months,
and the Tibetans wanted answers. In a similar manner, Tibetan Youth Congress representatives in Kathmandu complain they never have the chance
to discuss issues that emerge within Kathmandu itself, such as housing
allowances and salaries of exile administration officials. Tibet Office meetings are convened to discuss events that occur in Delhi, Dharamsala, or
America, places in which they have no influence, yet not in Kathmandu.

Tibetan exile officials regularly cite Assembly elections as evidence of the
development of a democracy in exile.[28] The development of political parties to advance candidates for the elections further supports their claims.
Tibetan exile officials regularly come into conflict with the people they are
supposed to represent, however, over how to interpret the concept of
democracy within a Tibetan worldview and within the Tibetan exile context. How much power should remain with the Dalai Lama as opposed to
the common people? How much privilege should remain with government
positions? Does the exile context justify the postponement of democratic

reforms in the name of national unity? These questions pervade the Tibetans' debates.

The U.S.-Tibet Resettlement Project: Equal Opportunity as an Emergent Norm?

The U.S.-Tibet Resettlement Project illustrates how some of these debates play out in practice. It illustrates, specifically, the debate about government privilege. The project began with the U.S. Immigration Act of 1990 (section 134), which allocated one thousand special resident visas for Tibetans from India and Nepal to immigrate to one of a number of "cluster sites" in the U.S. At these sites, volunteers from the Tibetan-U.S. Resettlement Committee were to help the Tibetans find housing, work, and other necessities. For the Tibetans, the project represented an unprecedented economic opportunity. Many Tibetans even migrated from Tibet into India and Nepal to attempt to secure a visa. One young Tibetan shopkeeper, a newcomer to Kathmandu, explains: "I too want to go to the U.S. When I came to Nepal, I applied to go as one of the thousand but I had no luck.... All of the people I know, when you ask where they want to go, they say that they want to go to the U.S. Many newcomers even go straight from Kathmandu to the U.S. They do not have to stay in Nepal at all."[29]

Another Tibetan exile in Nepal reflects on the value of a U.S. visa as follows: "Monthly salaries in the U.S. are equal to yearly salaries here. That is why Tibetans who live in the U.S. can come to Nepal and do nothing.... Tibetans I know in the U.S. make seven dollars an hour, and when they live all together in one place, they make a lot of money. A friend of mine in St. Paul works in a vegetable market and never has to buy vegetables. She does not have any problems with anything.... I want to go to the U.S. too. If my luck increases, I will go. If my luck decreases, I will stay" (personal communication, April 25, 1995).

Tibetan exile officials, aware of the value of the U.S. visas, positioned themselves as intermediaries in their allocation. Although it is standard U.S. policy for U.S. officials to allocate special visas through a lottery system, a series of agreements between the U.S. State Department and the Tibetan-U.S. Resettlement Committee allowed the exile administration's Home Department to allocate the visas instead.[30] What the Home Department did was to devise a number of categories for the visas and to conduct lotteries within them.[31] The net effect of the allocation system was to provide Tibetan exile officials, and their families, a better chance to receive one of the visas. The wife of one Tibetan exile official explains: "We had a good chance to go to America because government workers and their families had a special advantage.... My husband has no brothers and sisters and so I had an even better chance. I wanted to go, but my husband did not allow me to apply because we have a young child. I later heard that if I was chosen, my sister could go in my place ... but we did not know then" (personal communication, April 12, 1995). Tibetan exiles in Nepal criticized the Dharamsala officials for using their positions to secure a better chance. They argued against government privilege in favor of equal opportunity. One Tibetan exile explains: "It is the same with all opportunities.... The people in Dharamsala always make special chances for themselves. Most of the time, announcements do not even arrive in Nepal until after the deadline.... Even if people in Nepal are qualified, they have no chance.... With the thousand chances to go to America ... most went to people in Dharamsala because the people there reserved some for themselves" (personal communication, April 20, 1995).

Tibetan exiles in Nepal drew parallels between the way in which the visas were allocated and the way in which the thirty U.S. scholarships per year are allocated. They complained that, in both cases, the Dharamsala officials reserve special opportunities for themselves. Exile officials explicitly reserve one-third of all U.S. scholarships for themselves and their families. The requirements for the others (which include payment of all taxes to the exile administration, adequate performance on Tibetan language and history exams administered in Delhi, and attendance at schools affiliated with the exile administration up to class twelve), effectively exclude the Tibetans in Nepal. Few Tibetans in Nepal have had the chance to attend Tibetan exile schools up to class twelve (the only Tibetan exile high school in Nepal was constructed in 1992) and out of those who studied in India, many are not willing travel to Delhi for the exams. As one Tibetan in Nepal explained: "The fellowships through Dharamsala are somewhat of a joke. They always go to children of exile officials. No one in Kathmandu would ever get one" (personal communication, April 20, 1995).

Exile officials reserved one hundred U.S. visas for Tibetan exiles from Nepal. The Tibetans who were chosen emigrated to the U.S. in 1992. In 1995, those Tibetans became eligible to apply for visas for their relatives under the U.S. government's family reunification policies. Tibetan exile officials viewed those policies as another opportunity for themselves. The way the process was supposed to work is that the Tibetans in the U.S. were supposed to contact their relatives in Nepal to tell them to apply directly to the U.S. embassy for their visas. What happened instead is that the Tibet Office called a meeting of all Tibetans in Nepal to discuss the process and the Tibet Office's role in it. Although only sixty to seventy Tibetan exiles were eligible to emigrate, hundreds attended the meeting. As one Tibetan who attended the meeting explains: "It is certain there were people there who did not have any relatives in the U.S., who went to see if they could get a chance.... For example, there is an unmarried girl from Jawalakhel who went to the U.S ... and now many boys are trying to find a way to say they are her husband.... Someone here could fax a marriage certificate to her to sign and she could fax it back ... it could be brought to a Nepali office for a signature and then some boy will be lucky" (personal communication, September 6, 1995).

Tibetan exile officials in Nepal attempted to use their positions to influence who would become eligible to emigrate. Tibetans who are disloyal to the exile administration, they argued, should not be allowed to emigrate. In one of several attempts to prevent a Tibetan from emigrating, a Tibet Office representative argued with U.S. officials that a Tibetan who was suspected of working for the Chinese government should be considered ineligible. A U.S. Consular Officer explains: "I had to explain to him that the U.S. has no interest in whether or not he works for the Chinese government and that the U.S. sometimes even grants visas to Chinese people who work for the Chinese government.... The procedures now involve only the regular process of reunifying family members. They are not part of a special political program" (personal communication, September 8, 1995). That particular Tibet Office representative wanted his daughter to have a chance to emigrate in place of the suspected spy. He mistakenly thought that if the suspected spy could not emigrate, that would make the visa available for reallocation.

Tibetan exile officials regularly position themselves as intermediaries in the provision of U.S. intergovernmental assistance. That position enables them to exercise a certain amount of authority over fellow Tibetan exiles. It also enables them to use their positions to assist their families and kin. In examples like the U.S.-Tibet Resettlement Project, we can see how allegiance to family and kin conflicts with the norm of equal opportunity. Fundamental questions about the role of government privilege arise.

The Jawalakhel Local Assembly: Representative Government as a Tibetan Norm?

We see another conflict of norms in a struggle that proceeded throughout 1995 between the Jawalakhel local assembly and the Tibet Office to define the parameters of democracy for Tibetan exiles in Nepal. The local assembly struggle reveals conflicts among multiple norms. They include equal opportunity versus allegiance to family and kin, representative government versus enlightened government, the necessity to develop a democracy for the exile communities versus the postponement of democracy to the future, in an independent Tibet. Throughout the struggle, Jawalakhel's local representatives legitimated their arguments in terms of equal opportunity and representative government. Tibetan exile officials legitimated their arguments in terms of enlightened government as well as in terms of their role of defenders of the Tibetan independence cause. Both sides used the rhetoric of democracy, yet both interpreted the term to serve their own interests.

The struggle began in 1992 when, in accordance with the provisions of the 1990 Charter for the Tibetan Exiles, Tibetan exile officials created local assemblies in each of the Tibetan exile communities in Nepal. In the Kathmandu Valley, they created four local assemblies in each of four districts–Boudha, Swayambhu, Jawalakhel, and Kathmandu. Eleven to fifteen representatives were elected into each. Because the local assemblies were new, and because the Charter itself is not very explicit on what they are supposed to do, the representatives disagreed over how to proceed once the assemblies had been established.[32] Although there was general agreement that the assemblies were supposed to make law for the administration of the community, how laws were supposed to be made was initially unclear. The director of the Tibet Office explained to me that, "The local assemblies function in the same way as state governments in the United States." When pressed to explain what he meant by that, however, he confided: "The Boudha, Swayambhu, and Kathmandu local assemblies are doing absolutely no work at all, and the people in Jawalakhel are over-ambitious and try to do everything. This is the problem. How do you make the others work and at the same time stop the Jawalakhel people from working?" (personal communication, July 28, 1995).

The Jawalakhel local assembly, in 1995, was led by an ambitious young Tibetan, educated in Tibetan exile schools in India. Described by other Tibetans as pushy, he is critical of the way in which exile officials work, despite his own position as an exile administrator for one of the settlement camp businesses. He sought election to the Jawalakhel local assembly, he explained, to change the exile administration. He argued: "The government does not need people who work on behalf of their own people [family and regional group] only. It needs people who are going in the right direction and are very straight. It needs people who are working for all Tibetans and for the Tibetan cause and are working for the Dalai Lama. The government does not need tricky people or smart people but ... very good people with steady minds" (personal communication, October 30, 1995). The local assembly, he explained, can help limit the effects of exile officials who work for their own people only, who are not going in the right direction: "The local assembly ... is responsible, generally, for looking after the Tibetan community in a particular area.... There is an office that looks after the camp people that is run by the exile government, and they have every right to look after the people in the camp, but, are they administrating in the right way or not, that is for the assembly to decide.... The assembly is like an opposition party that looks after the administration" (personal communication, October 30, 1995).

Jawalakhel local assembly members developed two strategies to enable them to limit the decision-making powers of exile administrators. Both efforts started to transform the Jawalakhel local assembly into a labor advocacy organization until exile officials sought, effectively, to limit their influence. The first strategy involved convening monthly meetings to discuss any problems in the community that came to the attention of local assembly members. Not surprisingly, as the assemblies were new and their influence undemonstrated, few exile officials attended the meetings. In order to compel them to attend, local assembly members started to listen for rumors in the Tibetan community about problems that had occurred with particular officials so as to convene meetings specifically about them. During its first year in office, the Jawalakhel local assembly called the Jawalakhel factory manager into meetings twice, and both times he felt compelled to attend, he explained, simply to defend his own name.[33]

The second strategy involved placing local assembly members on the boards of the settlement camp businesses and schools to enable them to influence decisions as they were being made. This strategy, unlike the first, invited opposition immediately from exile officials. As soon as the administrative boards received letters from the Jawalakhel local assembly explaining that one of their members would attend board meetings as a representative of the people, they searched for ways to stop them. As the director of the Tibet Office argued: "Could you imagine how the businesses would operate if there were local representatives on their boards? The representatives would be worried only about their own re-election, so they would do whatever it takes to please the people.... They would give out gifts and bonuses and allocate money to all sorts of events ... and then how could you possibly run the businesses? The businesses would not last" (personal communication, July 28, 1995).

Aware of his opposition, the chairman of the local assembly explained he needed to move slowly to introduce the representatives to the boards. He proposed, at first, that the representatives should attend board meetings only as observers, so that they could report to the people what was decided. His intent was to transform them into regular board members, however, as he explained:

> We are moving very slowly in order not to create any problems. We must move slowly or there will be opposition. We are trying ... always to see both sides of everything. We have not yet used our full power and have not made too many clauses and conditions. If we were to do that, particularly with the businesses, then if there is a problem, for example if the factory does not make so much money this year, then the administration will blame the problems on us.... We have to move very slowly and not insist on our full power. We are being very careful. (personal communication, October 30, 1995)

The exile administration met to discuss what to do about the assemblies and decided that the Jawalakhel local assembly did not have the right to representation on the boards of the settlement camp businesses. Because they are only a local assembly, the logic followed, their right of representation was limited to the local area. All organizations that operate outside the Jawalakhel area were exempt. Only the Atisha School was left, as it serves only the Jawalakhel community. As the vice-chairman of the local assembly already served on Atisha's board in another capacity, the easiest solution was to make him a dual representative.

Soon after that decision, however, the Jawalakhel local assembly tried to use the Atisha School as a precedent to argue for dual representation on the other boards. Unable to resolve the issue locally, the Jawalakhel local assembly chairman discussed the issue with the vice-chairman of the Assembly of Tibetan People's Deputies while he was in Nepal to explain election procedures. The vice-chairman decided in favor of the administration (personal communication, October 30, 1995). Critics of the decision argued it was contrary to democracy: "For a long time, the Tibetan government has been run by the administration only. Now it should be run as a democracy. Who should the factories and schools, medical clinics and government organizations benefit? The Tibetan people, not just the people on the administrative boards.... The Tibetan people also need to be on the boards ... so they can benefit too" (personal communication, August 7, 1995).

In the wake of the decision, the director of the Tibet Office, in his capacity as district election commissioner, sought to restructure the local assemblies. "These days, there are local assemblies in Boudha, Kathmandu, Swayambhu, and Jawalakhel," he explained, "But with the next elections, there will be only one local assembly for the Kathmandu Valley" (personal communication, July 28, 1995). With only one local assembly, it becomes less likely that the Jawalakhel representatives will be re-elected into office. Aware of what the director of the Tibet Office was trying to do, however, the chairman of the Jawalakhel local assembly used the language of democracy to object. As he argued: "It would not be good for the Tibetans ... if there is only one assembly.... Each district needs its own assembly so its members can go among the people and know their problems.... Only if all the people in Kathmandu want only one assembly, then should there be only one.... If it is only the director of the Tibet Office who wants one assembly, then he should not be allowed to make one. Why? Other people had to fight for democracy, but His Holiness the Dalai Lama gave the Tibetans democracy" (personal communication, October 30, 1995).

"Sometimes the idea of democracy is inappropriate," the director of the Tibet Office argued in response:

> First, a democracy is never really a democracy because only some people can speak very well and it is the ideas of those people that are followed.... And then you have the people who shout all the time, and their ideas are the ones that are heard. And then you have people who are uneducated, and most of our people are uneducated.... How can you have a democracy like that? In a future Tibet, we need to have a democracy, but as for right now in exile, maybe we should have a limited democracy.... Maybe until we get our country back ... we should let the administration run the government. (personal communication, July 28, 1995)

Based on the argument that democracy is inappropriate for the exile community, as it may cause disunity or may result in the end of the independence cause, exile officials have maintained control over the Dalai Lama's exile administration at the same time they have declared it to be a democracy. As one Tibetan exile argued: "Just as it was in Tibet, people think that the government is the government.... They never think that they themselves are responsible for the government.... Government people, too, think that the government is not the business of the people.... If you ask has democracy been implemented throughout Tibetan society, you would have to answer no" (personal communication, November 22, 1995).

Tibetan exiles continue to struggle to implement democracy within the Tibetan exile communities. The Jawalakhel local assembly issue is only one example of their efforts. As they proceed in the struggle, Tibetan exiles regularly come into conflict over how to interpret and implement the concept of democracy. Within the exile communities, pressure is mounting on the exile administration to resolve these conflicts now. As younger Tibetans continue to be educated in Tibetan exile schools about the ideals of democracy and continue to expect a democracy to be implemented within their own communities, we can expect exile officials to have to start to accommodate them. How Tibetan exile officials respond will determine the viability of the exile administration, and the independence cause, in the future.

The Maintenance of the U.S.-Tibet Relationship

Despite the ongoing debates about whether or not democracy is appropriate for the Tibetan exile communities, in June 1992, after only some of the provisions of the 1990 Charter had been implemented, Lodi Gyari, former exile official and current president of the International Campaign for Tibet, argued before the U.S. Senate Foreign Relations Committee that a "fully-functioning democratic government now exists among Tibetan exiles" and now "wants to take democracy back to the Tibetan people in Tibet." His argument led to a request for further U.S. assistance, which Gyari implied the Tibetans are entitled to receive based both on the history of the U.S.-Tibetan relationship and on the democratic transformations the Tibetans had already effected. As he argued:

> In the 1950s until the early 1960s, certain agencies of the U.S. government were actively involved in helping the Tibetan resistance movement, and that resistance movement was to overthrow the illegal occupation of Tibet by the Chinese government. So, obviously, if U.S. government agencies were directly physically assisting such a movement, was it not a clear implication that they thought that the Tibetan people had the right to fight for their independence? That was done by successive administrations of the U.S. government. Or were they just using us as pawns? (U.S. Senate Foreign Relations Committee 1993)

Gyari's request was supported by Hollywood actor Richard Gere, founder of the Tibet House and member of the board of the International Campaign. Gere's statement emphasized the fundamental goodness of the Tibetan people and their intolerable suffering under Chinese rule. Asked what it is the Tibetans want, Gere replied "freedom," a comment that aroused general congressional laughter. Asked more seriously, he replied, "Money. Money to run the exile government" (U.S. Senate Foreign Relations Committee 1993).

Through exchanges such as these, Tibetan exile officials maintain their relationship with U.S. intergovernmental organizations despite their unwillingness to implement democracy now, within the exile communities, and not just to wait for a future Tibet. Given that a debate, at least, exists among Tibetan exiles about what democracy means and whether or not it is appropriate, there is the possibility that, in the future, the exile administration will, indeed, become more democratic. Should it do so, however, it is uncertain what will become of the exile administration and the independence cause. It is this context of uncertainty that maintains the exile administration as debates about the meaning of democracy continue.

Notes

1. U.S. officials had contacted certain members of the Dalai Lama's government in Tibet years before an assistance relationship began. In 1943, during World War II, the U.S. Office of Strategic Services sent two army officers, Captain Ilia Tolstoy and Lieutenant Brooke Dolan, to Lhasa to search for a supply route to Western China (Goldstein 1989: 391–397). Captain Tolstoy, to facilitate his request for permission to travel through Tibet, offered the Tibetan government wireless equipment, assistance in manufacturing a Tibetan typewriter, and support for Tibetan representation at a peace conference at the end of the war. He assured the Tibetans that "the U.S. government was in full sympathy with weak and small countries that wished to retain their independence" (Goldstein 1989: 393). Tibetan officials, always looking for ways to resist Chinese hegemony, responded enthusiastically to his offers. Foreign Secretary Surkhang stated that, "What the Tibetan government wished to see was America backing up Great Britain in her effort to maintain Tibetan independence. The Tibetan government trusted that this help would be forthcoming" (Goldstein 1989: 395, citing India Office records). The two Americans completed their journey, surveyed the Tibetan terrain, and returned to the U.S. with the first official maps of the area, along with other information of strategic military potential. The Tibetan government remained uninvited to any post-war peace conference. The U.S. Department of State retained its official position that Tibet was a protectorate of China.
2. Eastern Tibetans (Khampas) had many grievances with the Tibetan government, most of which involved taxation and ill-treatment (Goldstein 1989: 178, 640). When the PLA first attacked in 1950, many Khampas sided against the Tibetan government (Goldstein 1989: 681).
3. Goldstein (1989) provides a detailed account of Tibetan efforts to secure support. The Tibetan government sent delegates to an Asian relations conference in Delhi in 1947; a Tibetan trade mission to the U.S., Britain, and China in 1948; and numerous appeals to the

U.S., Britain, India, Canada, and the United Nations to argue for U.N. membership. Based on U.S. State Department documents, Goldstein (1989: 607–610), argues that the U.S. did reconsider its policy toward Tibet after the 1948 trade delegation visit. State Department officials decided to wait to see whether or not the communists would secure control over China and if so, how the Soviet Union would respond.

4. Tibetans refer to people whom they consider to be supreme enlightened beings, like the Dalai Lama, as *p'agpa*; they refer to ordinary people as *mi kyuma*.

5. U.S. CIA official, personal communication, April 18, 1996. U.S. State Department communications from the time also convey the idea of an international communist conspiracy. U.S. officials in Kabul, for example, ask: "What might be the cause of [China's] attacks in Tibet when the Korean problem has not yet been finished? Some of the Commentators affirm that the Chinese aggression in Tibet and the aggravated activities of Ho Chi Minh against Viet Nam are both designed to counter recent events in Korea" (Enclosure 2 of U.S. State Department Despatch 161 from the American Embassy in Kabul to the U.S. Secretary of State in Washington, DC, dated November 15, 1950, from *Confidential U.S. State Department Central Files. China: Foreign Affairs, 1950–1954*. Frederick, MD: University Publications of America).

6. U.S. State Department memoranda from the time demonstrate U.S. unwillingness to provide overt assistance without British, Indian, or U.N. support. The "Announcement Regarding Support for Self-determination for the People of Tibet," for example, discusses a commitment to the Dalai Lama "both to support self-determination ... and to make a public declaration, when a suitable opportunity presents itself...." The announcement anticipates that "debates in the United Nations General Assembly regarding the problem of Tibet" would be successful. The debates the U.S. anticipated never occurred. The announcement was never published. U.S. assistance continued instead on a covert basis. (Memorandum from John A. Calhoun, Director, Executive Secretariat, Department of State, to Brigadier General A.J. Goodpaster at the White House, dated January 28, 1960. *Confidential U.S. State Department Central Files. China: Foreign Affairs, 1950–1954*. Frederick, MD: University Publications of America.)

7. There are many accounts of the events that led up to the Dalai Lama's decision to flee into exile. They include Dalai Lama (1962: 164–216; 1990: 123–143), Avedon (1984: 50–73), Goldstein (1989: 776–808), and McCarthy (1997: 197–199). The group that escorted the Dalai Lama into exile included some Tibetans working for the U.S. CIA (Dalai Lama 1990: 140). McCarthy (1997: 201) denies the allegation that the U.S. CIA kidnapped the Dalai Lama, however. By all accounts, it appears that the decision to leave Tibet was his own.

8. Knaus (1999: 242) confirms the details of his account. He estimates that two thousand Tibetans were left starving in northern Nepal.

9. There were many differences between the two leaders, and the groups that supported them. Baba Yeshe is from Batang (a semi-autonomous polity in eastern Tibet), is older, and as a monk, represented traditional Tibetan leadership and authority. Wangdu Gyatsotsang is from Lithang (another semi-autonomous polity in eastern Tibet that used to fight occasionally with Batang), is younger, and as a CIA-trainee, represented the modernity that many young Tibetan guerrillas aspired to achieve.

10. Details on the end of the Tibetan guerrilla movement derive from Avedon (1984: 126–128); *The Rising Nepal*, September 13, 1974, p. 1; and *The Rising Nepal*, October 13, 1974.

11. Former manager of the CTC, personal communication, September 11, 1995.

12. U.S. CIA official, personal communication, March 23, 1996.

13. A highly secretive atmosphere surrounds the Gyalo Thondup businesses. Whereas other carpet business owners and managers were very happy to speak with me and to show me their factories, managers of the Boudha factory, on my first and only visit, stopped me from talking with people. They insisted that I needed official permission to ask any questions of anyone. Incessant delays over many months prevented such permission from materializing. Forbes (1989: 62) writes that it is in order to protect OCM's carpet designs that outsiders

cannot enter the Boudha factory without permission (OCM is one of their buyers). I had no problem with other business owners who also export to OCM, however.

14. Karma Tashi, executive director of the Snow Lion Foundation, personal communication, July 27, 1995. According to Karma Tashi, at the time the Nepal government gave the land in Helitar to the Tibetan exiles, they had no land documents for that area of Nepal. Recently, the Nepal government surveyed the land and gave the relevant documents to the settlement leader in 1990.

15. All families of successive Dalai Lamas in Tibet were granted the title Yabshi, a highly honorific term that, in Tibet, referred to the Dalai Lama's father and his estates.

16. Holborn (1975: 753) reports that UNHCR allocated $55,000 in 1971 and $46,000 in 1972 for several projects involving the resettlement of Tibetans from northern Nepal. Counseling services are included among the itemized project expenses.

17. The 103rd Congress, through Foreign Relations Authorization Act, Fiscal Years 1994 and 1995 (section 513), authorized conditions on China's most-favored-nation trade status to protest human rights abuses in Tibet and China. The United States-China Acts of 1991 and 1992, passed by the 102nd Congress, also authorized conditions.

18. Foreign Relations Authorization Act, Fiscal Years 1990 and 1991 (section 218) established Voice of America Broadcasts in Tibetan. Foreign Relations Authorization Act, Fiscal Years 1994 and 1995 (section 309) established Radio Free Asia, of which Tibetan-language broadcasts are only one part.

19. Foreign Relations Authorization Act, Fiscal Years 1988 and 1989, allocated scholarship funds for fifteen Tibetan students and professionals to study in the U.S. Foreign Relations Authorization Act, Fiscal Years 1990 and 1991 (section 216) allocated funds for thirty Tibetans.

20. Foreign Operations, Export Financing and Related Programs Appropriations Act, 1991, provided $500,000 for 1990 and $500,000 for 1991 to the Department of State to allocate on behalf of Tibetans in India and Nepal; and Foreign Operations, Export Financing and Related Programs Appropriations Act, 1993, provided $1,500,000 as a one-time only grant for the Department of State to allocate. The Department of State allocated the 1993 grant to the Dalai Lama's exile administration for the stated purpose of resettling newcomer Tibetans in India and Nepal. It is believed to be the single largest grant to the Dalai Lama's exile administration; it represents 22 percent of the exile administration's annual budget (Samdup 1992: 7).

21. The Immigration Act of 1990 (section 134) allocated one thousand special resident visas for Tibetans from India and Nepal.

22. Foreign Relations Authorization Act, Fiscal Years 1992 and 1993 (section 355) declared Tibet to be an occupied country and the Dalai Lama and his exile administration to be Tibet's true representatives as recognized by the Tibetan people. Foreign Relations Authorization Act, Fiscal Years 1994 and 1995 provided funds to establish a USIA office in Lhasa (section 221), and to finance educational and cultural exchange with Tibet (section 236). Foreign Relations Authorization Act, Fiscal Years 1996 and 1997, vetoed by President Clinton, would have been the strongest statement of support for Tibet to date in that it provided for the post of special envoy to Tibet and the Tibetan exiles; recognized the Dalai Lama and his exile administration as the true representatives of the Tibetan people; and expanded Tibetan-language radio broadcasts.

23. According to Norbu (1990: 16), the Assembly was popularly elected from 1960 to 1981, yet in 1981, elections were suspended and it was decided that the Dalai Lama should appoint all Assembly members himself instead. Elections did not resume until after the 1990 Charter had been adopted.

24. The Dalai Lamas in theory were absolute rulers, yet in practice, few Dalai Lamas lived long enough, or acquired enough power within the government, to play such an influential role (Goldstein 1973: 447; Petech 1988: 126–133). The Fifth and the Thirteenth Dalai

Lamas are notable in Tibetan history for the strong roles they are believed to have played (Shakabpa 1967: 123, 246–273).

25. The Tibetan, represented more-or-less as pronounced, follows: "Oh, mi-tsang chen-po ray shad! Mi tho-bo ray! La-ma acha ray shad! Tug-lo dzig-po kön-ah! Nga ku-shabs che-kyi-yö! che-kyi-med! Gyalwa Rinpoche mang-tso nang a! Keh-rang yag-ga ma-ray!

26. Minutes of the eleventh Assembly of the Tibetan People's Deputies.

27. Observations at Jawalakhel, September 10, 1995. The right to free speech is very controversial among Tibetan exiles, for there are numerous examples of exile government censorship of its opposition. One Tibetan exile publication, called *Democracy* (dmangs-gtso), dedicated an entire issue to examples of exile government censorship (volume 6, number 16, July 31, 1995). Ironically, within a year, the publication was forced to close.

28. See, for example, "Democracy is an Integral Part of the Tibetan Freedom Struggle," *Tibetan Bulletin*, May–June 1996, and "Twelfth Exile Tibetan Parliament Constituted, Elects New Kashag," *Tibetan Bulletin*, July–August 1996.

29. News of the project spread quickly through Tibetan-language Voice of America broadcasts and personal networks. Many Tibetans I met in Nepal, Tibet, and India discussed how they fled into exile for the sole purpose of securing one of the thousand U.S. visas. When they did not receive one, some returned to Tibet while others waited in India for another chance. Rumors spread that more U.S. visas would soon be allocated.

30. U.S. consular officer in Nepal, personal communication, September 8, 1995.

31. The first division was into three categories: 75 for Tibetans with relatives in the U.S.; 100 for Tibetans in Nepal; and 825 for Tibetans in India. The second was into "Tibetans Not Firmly Resettled"–those who had never received assistance (200 visas), who were impoverished (150 visas), or who had only recently come from Tibet (100 visas)–and "Tibetans Most Likely To Be Resettled Successfully"–those with English-language or professional skills (200 visas), with a record of service to the exile administration (100 visas), or with a record of service to the community (150 visas). Although explicitly the categories reserved only 100 visas for exile administration officials, implicitly they reserved 525, given that exile administration officials are the most likely to have relatives in the U.S., to have English-language and professional skills, and to have served the exile administration and community (associate secretary of the Home Department, personal communication, July 27, 1994).

32. The Charter states only that the Assembly of Tibetan Peoples Deputies "shall have the power to exercise all authority in respect to the formation and ratification of all business matters of the respective Tibetan settlements as specified by law provided that the Tibetan administrator and assistant Tibetan administrator shall be consulted before making the final decision."

33. The first time, weavers in the Jawalakhel factory had complained that they were not getting new carpet graphs on time. As they are paid on a contract basis, they believed they were losing money from the delay. The second time, there were some other workers in the factory whose manner of payment had been changed from a salary to a contract basis. They, too, complained they were losing money. The local assembly brought their interests to the attention of the factory manager, and at least the first of the issues was resolved (chairman of the Jawalakhel Local Assembly, personal communication, October 30, 1995).

3

Friends of Tibet

Variations on a Theme of Liberal Humanism

In July 1996, in Golden Gate Park in San Francisco, nearly 100,000 people gathered for the Tibetan Freedom Concert. Organized by Adam Yauch, co-founder of the Milarepa Fund and member of the rock group the Beastie Boys, the concert attracted such renowned performers as Yoko Ono, Sonic Youth, Smashing Pumpkins, and Bjork. Although not all of the performers considered themselves Tibet-support activists per se, they all performed under "Free Tibet!" banners nevertheless, as they helped to raise money to finance the education of Tibetan students at Namgyal High School in Kath-mandu, Nepal.[1]

The Milarepa Fund is only one of several hundred voluntary organiza-tions that assist the Tibetan exiles.[2] Some, like the Milarepa Fund, the Inter-national Campaign for Tibet, and Association Tibet Libre, are single-interest Tibet-support organizations. Others, such as the Scientific Buddhist Associa-tion, the Vajradhatu Foundation, and the Foundation for the Preservation of the Mahayana Tradition are international Buddhist organizations. Still oth-ers, such as Asia Watch, Amnesty International, and the International Com-mittee of Jurists are international human rights organizations. There are many differences among these many organizations. Some have significant financial resources, many offices in many countries, and professional salaried staff members. Others have only one small office or operate out of the home of a volunteer. They all have two related aspects in common, however. The first is that, as voluntary organizations, they all involve some level of personal identification. In contrast with intergovernmental organizations, whose offi-cials support Tibetans, irrespective of personal identification, when it is part of their job, friends of Tibet support Tibetans because Tibet is important to their own personal lives, goals, and visions for the future of humanity. The second is that they all promote the values of liberal humanism. I define liberal humanism here as a set of beliefs that emphasizes the individual as the most basic social unit, with the right to live a life of his or her own choosing. Friends of Tibet promote the values of liberal humanism, whether defined in terms of human rights, Western Buddhism, or multiculturalism. They do so by discussing the Tibetan culture and way of life as an option not only for Tibetans, but for anyone who wants to participate. Friends of Tibet themselves act to participate in the Tibetan way of life. They do so through the relationships they maintain with the Tibetans they assist.

This chapter analyzes the relationship between these many friends of Tibet organizations and the Tibetans they assist in Nepal. The Tibetans they assist consist primarily of school children, monks, and nuns. For friends of Tibet, monks and nuns symbolize, more than anyone else, the sacred wisdom of the Tibetan past. Children symbolize, more than anyone else, hope for a better future. Tibetan exile monasteries, established for the monks, and Tibetan exile schools, established for the children, are the principal recipients of friends of Tibet assistance. The ongoing relationships they maintain with friends of Tibet organizations provide them with the funding they need to remain in operation.

This chapter argues that friends of Tibet, although they discuss their relationship with the Tibetan exiles as intended to preserve and protect a traditional Tibetan culture in exile, actually promote the transformation of what it means to be Tibetan toward the accommodation of their own norms and values. The normative dynamics of the relationship involve the promotion and accommodation of the values of liberal humanism. Friends of Tibet promote the values of liberal humanism; the Tibetans they assist act to accommodate their values. What it means to be Tibetan transforms as a result.

The chapter proceeds in four parts. The first asks "Why Tibet?" as it analyzes the factors that contributed to the emergence and development of the hundreds of friends of Tibet organizations currently in existence. It argues that one of the reasons that Tibet has become so popular is that it has come to represent the preservation and maintenance of a liberal humanist tradition. The second analyzes the normative dynamics of the relationship between friends of Tibet and the Tibetan schools in Nepal. Within the schools, I argue, Tibetan exiles accommodate the values of liberal humanism relatively easily. Schools are a primary setting within which the Tibetan exiles invent new Tibetan traditions.[3] The third analyzes the normative dynamics of the relationship between friends of Tibet and Tibetan monasteries in Nepal. Within the monasteries, I argue, Tibetan exiles are less willing to accommodate the values of liberal humanism. As friends of Tibet become increasingly involved in the interpretation of what Tibetan Buddhism is and how it should be practiced, what it means to be Tibetan and who has the right to decide has become the focus for intense, highly personalized transnational debate. The final section expands the context of the debate to include the interpretation of the Tibetan political cause. Relationships the Tibetan exiles maintain with the many organizations that assist them have shaped the way in which the Tibetan exiles themselves discuss and promote the Tibetan political cause. As Tibetan exiles promote their cause, whether they interpret it to be independence or the preservation of their culture in exile, I argue, they promote the values of liberal humanism as well.

Why Tibet? The Origins and Development of Friends of Tibet Organizations

The face of the Dalai Lama appears juxtaposed with Ray Charles and Karl Marx in a Harvard Square storefront window collage. Tibetan monks walking through a barren landscape inform television audiences that Lotus Notes is better than telepathy. Jetsun Pema, the Dalai Lama's sister, shares the screen with Brad Pitt in *Seven Years in Tibet,* one of two 1997 Hollywood Tibet films. Since 1989, when the Dalai Lama was awarded the Nobel Peace Prize, symbols of Tibet have become incorporated into American pop culture's repertoire of images, as Tibetan independence has become a cause célèbre among people as influential as Senators Pat Moynihan, Ted Kennedy, and Jesse Helms; Hollywood actors Richard Gere, Steven Seagal, and Harrison Ford; business executive Peter Hires; composer Phillip Glass; and billionaire heiresses Andrea Soros and Gigi Pritzker.

What is it about Tibet that attracts such popular attention? How does the Tibetan cause become important to people who have never been to Tibet and never lived among Tibetans? Why do people pledge, as one Tibet-support activist pledged on-line, that they "will never rest until the fate of Tibet is once again back in the hands of the Tibetans"?[4] Why Tibetans instead of so many others?

Three factors together help to explain the emergence and development of these many friends of Tibet organizations. The first is the fantasy factor, the imagination of Tibet as Shangri-La, and of the Tibetan way of life as without suffering. The second is the leadership factor, the work of particular individuals to organize around a shared interest in Tibet-as-Shangri-La. The third is the impression management factor, the accommodation of the language of liberal humanism by the Tibetan exiles themselves to maintain friends of Tibet support.[5] All of these factors together contributed to the emergence and development of friends of Tibet organizations.

The Fantasy Factor

Long before the Tibetan exiles ever even left Tibet, Tibet became an important setting for Western fantasies and imagination.[6] An account by Herodotus of giant ants mining gold in Tibet may be the oldest source for these fantasies, yet it was through Europe's travel writers and imperial officials that they developed into a narrative tradition. Heinrich Harrer, Alexandra David-Neel, Sven Hedin, William Rockhill, and many others described Tibet as a wild and inaccessible land filled with strange and wonderful events. Like Xanadu and Timbuktu, Tibet became a metaphor for a land far, far away. It became Shangri-La.

What is Shangri-La? Why do we imagine Tibet as Shangri-La? How does the Tibet-as-Shangri-La narrative promote the development of friends of Tibet organizations? Bishop's (1989) analysis of travel writing on Tibet from the eighteenth century until the Tibetan exile provides the basis for an answer. It examines the successive themes that emerged within the story we tell ourselves about Tibet. In the eighteenth century, Bishop argues, as Tibet was unmapped, unexplored, and inaccessible, we imagined it to be full of mystery and magical events (1989: 27). In the nineteenth century, as Tibet became a frontier of British India, we imagined that great wealth, possibly large deposits of gold, lay hidden and untouched in its treacherous landscape (1989: 96). Later in the century, we imagined Tibet, as the highest place on earth, to be a refuge, similar to Mount Ararat. After a global catastrophe, we imagined, Tibet would remain the only place left untouched to re-seed the humanity of the future (1989: 101). In the twentieth century, we imagined Tibet to be a timeless remnant of a medieval past whose wisdom Europe had lost. The impulse to try to save Tibet from the evils of the West emerged (1989: 173). Finally, just prior to the Tibetan exile, we imagined Tibet as a utopia, a land of hope and aspiration, of wisdom and meaning, where great spiritual masters, who "could help the West find its way again," reside in peace (1989: 210).

In 1933, British author James Hilton combined these many themes into a best-selling novel, *Lost Horizon*, in which four main characters, British and American expatriates, are kidnapped and brought to Tibet to live in its timeless and peaceful paradise forever. The book gave the sacredness of Tibet a name, Shangri-La; defined its purpose, to preserve all that is beautiful and good; and provided a set of characters with whom readers could identify. In 1949, when Lowell Thomas, Jr. traveled to Tibet, for example, he imagined himself as part of the wise and great civilization described in James Hilton's book: "Once we crossed the Himalayas into Tibet we were indeed travellers in the land of the Lost Horizon. And it seemed as though we were dreaming–acting the parts of characters in James Hilton's novel, on our way to Shangri-La" (Thomas 1950: 17).

Three years later, Frank Capra produced a movie, also called *Lost Horizon*, which brought new life to the story of the stranded expatriates. Transformed through Hollywood's conventions of the time, the movie opens with a question that asks its viewers enticingly: "In these days of wars and rumors of wars–haven't you ever dreamed of a place where there was peace and security, where living was not a struggle but a lasting delight?"[7] What would such a place be like? What is Shangri-La? In the movie, it has waterfalls and tranquil pools, beautiful women and attentive natives, banquet tables and music rooms, vast deposits of gold and the secrets of eternal youth, all governed, with an authority exercised only in moderation, by a wise and ancient (and Christian) sage, the two-hundred-year-old Father Perrault. Shangri-La promised to be an escape from all suffering, even death, a haven where wisdom could outlive passion, and the meek could inherit the earth.

That a Shangri-La could exist, for real, somewhere on this earth, is a very tempting idea, particularly for people who see problems with their own society that they feel powerless to resolve. If only there were a place where one could go where people are good. Bishop (1989: 211) argues that Tibet became such as place: "By the close of the Second World War, the searching had become desperate. The disillusionment was all-embracing. Tibet seemed to offer hope, not just for a personal despair but for the malaise of an entire civilization, and perhaps for the whole world." Tibet, Bishop argues, became "intimate and *essential*" to our imagination. It became Shangri-La.[8]

The imagination of Tibet as Shangri-La provided the basis on which friends of Tibet organizations first developed. Friends of Tibet imagined the Tibetans as exiles not from Tibet as a real place but from Tibet-as-Shangri-La, the wise and ancient civilization we discuss within our own narrative tradition. The imagination of Tibet-as-Shangri-La differentiates the Tibetan exiles from other claimants to international assistance. It portrays them as more worthy of recognition and support. We see the influence of this Shangri-La image of Tibet in such early statements of support as the following letter, written by a founding member of the U.S.-based Tibetan Friendship Group, in celebration of the arrival of a number of Tibetan exiles in the United States. After describing the exiles and their various occupations (most were monks and students), the author writes:

> All of this pursuit of meditation brought to us by our brothers of the East is needed in the America of today, along with the expansion of liberal Christian groups. And when I read of the prophecies of the Buddha and Padma Sambhava of the coming of Buddhism to the land of the Red Man, I am reminded that nearly 100 years ago the Ancient Wisdom was brought out into the world, as the Theosophical Society formed in New York City in 1875, with its motto: THERE IS NO RELIGION HIGHER THAN TRUTH. (Lewis 1975: 22–23, emphasis in the original)

The author compares the Tibetan exiles with a number of other religious groups, mostly Christian, and argues that their wisdom is needed in the "America of today."

The role that the Tibet-as-Shangri-La narrative has played in the development of friends of Tibet organizations can also be seen by comparing the way in which exiles from Tibet versus exiles from Xinjiang, a Chinese province just north of Tibet, have been discussed in the U.S. and Europe. Xinjiang and Tibet are similar in many ways. Xinjiang, like Tibet, enjoyed considerable autonomy, if not independence, prior to its incorporation into the People's Republic of China (Benson 1990; Lipman 1998). Xinjiang, also like Tibet, counts among its inhabitants a number of groups who seek independence from China.[9] Xinjiang, unlike Tibet, however, lacks a narrative tradition that portrays it as a place where one can go where people are good. In part, as a result, Xinjiang lacks the popular attention in the West that Tibet has for so long enjoyed. There are few to no "friends of Xinjiang" organizations in the West.

Since the Tibetan exile, the Tibet-as-Shangri-La narrative has continued to expand to encompass a variety of additional themes. In the 1960s and 1970s, as a result, in part, of the migration of Tibetan Buddhist leaders from the exile communities in Nepal and India to the West, Tibet-as-Shangri-La took on a Buddhist theme. In contrast with the decidedly Christian nature of Shangri-La in both the book and the movie *Lost Horizon*, Tibet-as-Shangri-La, after the Tibetan exile, becomes Buddhist. In the 1980s and 1990s, in the wake of the Tibetan exile administration's International Campaign for Tibet, Tibet-as-Shangri-La took on themes such as the right to self-determination, the preservation of indigenous knowledge, the protection of the environment, and support for multiculturalism. Through novels, speeches, articles, and websites, a narrative about Tibet as a Buddhist, human rights, and environmental rights Shangri-La continues today.

The continuation of the Tibet-as-Shangri-La narrative is most evident in a 1996 novel composed by two authors from the U.S., Eleanor Cooney and Daniel Altieri, self-identified human rights activists and supporters of the Tibetan cause. Entitled *Shangri-La*, the novel is intended as a sequel to James Hilton's *Lost Horizon*, yet the novel also reinterprets *Lost Horizon* to accommodate these new themes. In the novel, the authors describe Tibet as a human rights and environmental rights issue. The novel portrays the Chinese Communists as enemies not only of the Tibetans but of anyone who believes in freedom, human rights, and the protection of the environment. Comments a reviewer solicited from both authors about the novel and what it means to them demonstrate the way in which they imagine Tibet as, in essence, a good place. "Something used to be right in Tibet," Cooney explains, "People were happy. And I don't think it's right anymore." Altieri adds: "To write this, I had to believe it was possible, even in this late time, to have a land still hidden in this trodden Earth of ours.... You want to believe that such an experiment would be possible on this planet—a place where you can reseed humanity. You want to believe something like that could really last."[10]

Hollywood actor Richard Gere promotes a similar interpretation of Tibet-as-Shangri-La in his speeches in support of the Tibetan exiles. In one of his speeches, for example, Gere argues:

The social system which evolved in Tibet was based on the high Buddhist tenets of truth, love, compassion and enlightened altruism. Although their system wasn't perfect, the people were happy. This 1,200 year old heritage has much to offer our increasingly impersonal world. The Tibetan world-view of compassion and non-violence is not just rhetoric ... but exists in the heart of each and every Tibetan.... This wisdom of love, if embraced by all the leaders of the world, could bring only peace and harmony to our strife-torn planet. There is no other way to proceed.[11]

The Internet has become a primary site for Buddhist, human rights, and environmental rights narratives of Tibet-as-Shangri-La as well. One website, constructed by followers of the Engaged Buddhism movement, imagines Tibet as an integral part of a variety of political causes. The creators of the site, it is clear, have a vision for Tibet that goes beyond anything Tibet as an actual place could possibly offer. Quotations from the Dalai Lama, Noam Chomsky, Martin Luther King, Jr. and Mahatma Gandhi are juxtaposed to argue for causes as various as Guatemalan street children to a boycott of Pepsi, to Hawaiian independence to opposition struggles in Burma and East Timor. Links to other sites include those to Amnesty International, UNICEF, and the League of Women Voters as well as to World Tibet Network News, Tibet Information Network, and the Free Tibet Home Page. The site portrays Tibet not as a real place but as a metaphor for a liberal humanist tradition endangered by evil state and corporate interests.[12]

Many other friends of Tibet sites share similar narratives. Another focuses on the life of Palden Gyatso, a Tibetan monk who was imprisoned in Tibet for thirty years. As the narrative alternates between a rhetoric of Tibet-as-a-real-place and Tibet-as-Shangri-La, it confuses Palden Gyatso's real life with a lurid storybook fantasy. Palden Gyatso becomes a "diminutive and elfin faced" monk who, despite "the forces of evil," manages to "live happily ever after":

> Once upon a time there was a mystical kingdom called Shambala, fringed with the bewitching Everest and magical Kailas, home of the Hindu gods. Wise people also knew this land by the name Tibet. This land was then ravaged, captured by the forces of evil and turned into a nightmare world of genocide, electric shock torture and starvation. Palden Gyatso, a diminutive and elfin faced Tibetan monk only just escaped with his life.... Palden Gyatso has suffered enough. As he says, "Individuals are very powerful." You can do something to insure that he lives happily ever after.[13]

Other friends of Tibet focus on the environmental rights aspect of the Tibet-as-Shangri-La narrative. They project onto the Tibetan past an environmental ethic popular in Western societies today. One, for example, argues: "For centuries, Tibetans lived in their vast, sparsely populated country in perfect harmony with their environment.... [Their] views ... are very similar to those of most animal and wildlife protection agencies. The difference with the

Tibetans ... is that the same criteria [were] extended beyond the animal world, taking into account all beings of the six realms" (Yeshi 1991: 264). The other makes a similar argument with: "There is no other country or people on this planet [who] have succeeded in living in total harmony with their environment ... for centuries, the Tibetans lived in isolation, unexposed to the influences of the modern world [and] due to the belief in the inter-relationship between the flora and fauna and other natural elements, there was a general taboo against exploiting the environment" (Fink 1991: 257). Both authors characterize the Tibetans as fellow environmentalists who, by their very nature, support environmental rights causes.

Through all of these forms–novels, speeches, articles, and websites–the Tibet-as-Shangri-La narrative has continued to expand to accommodate additional themes. Many people have begun to take an interest in Tibet not because of anything they may know about the Tibetans themselves, but because the Tibet-as-Shangri-La narrative has become associated in their minds with their own norms and values. Friends of Tibet conflate saving Tibet with saving all that they think of as good and worthy, as Richard Gere so poignantly explains: "Saving Tibet as a spiritual and cultural entity ... is saving ourselves. We need it around."[14]

The Leadership Factor

The Tibet-as-Shangri-La narrative is not wholly responsible for the development of the many friends of Tibet organizations that exist today. Leadership, funding, and organizational skills were also necessary to transform individual personal engagement into effective organizations. Friends of Tibet organizations developed over three phases, with different groups of leaders coming to the forefront within each. As these organizations promote the Tibetan cause, they also promote an activist political culture mobilized in terms of their own norms and values. That political culture has transformed the way in which the Tibetan exiles themselves define and discuss their cause.

During the first phase, in the 1950s and 1960s, at the start of the Tibetan exile, the first people to start friends of Tibet organizations were the many travelers, explorers, and imperial officials who had, at various times in their lives, lived either in Tibet or among Tibetans. They were the first to develop an assistance relationship with the Tibetan exiles and to promote the Tibetan cause in the West. They include Lowell Thomas, Jr., author of *Out of this World*, and a traveler in Tibet throughout the 1950s. He helped to form the American Emergency Relief Committee for Tibet, an organization that provided initial support to Tibetan exiles in Nepal and India. They also include Peter Aufschnaiter, an Austrian explorer in Tibet, and companion to Heinrich Harrer, author of *Seven Years in Tibet* (Hagen 1994: 208; Forbes 1989: 28). Prince Peter of Greece and Denmark, an anthropologist who conducted research in Tibet in the 1950s, began a program to help Tibetan children in

Nepal and India (Knaus 1999: 171). The Tibet Society and Relief Fund, the Transhimalayan Aid Society, and Swiss Aid to Tibetans were also established by these initial Tibet friends.

In the late 1960s, and throughout the 1970s, a different group of leaders emerged. They are people who took interest in Tibet through their involvement with Western Buddhism. They are members of the hippie, free love, and new age countercultures who helped support Tibetan Buddhism, along with Zen Buddhism, Transcendental Meditation, the International Society for Krishna Consciousness, and many other new religious organizations (Bharati 1979: 3–11).[15] Their interest in Tibet derived from the access they thought it would provide them to sacred knowledge and eastern wisdom. As one observer writes of the followers of Chögyam Trungpa, founder of the Vajradhatu, Naropa, and Karme Chöling institutes, and one of the first Tibetan religious leaders to emigrate to the West: "A section of what used to be called the counterculture desired a guru, and here he was in the flesh.... The confused came to be made sound.... His devotees ran to the upper middle class, white, with impressive academic credentials.... If they did not turn their pockets inside out for their teacher–and some did–they made good fund raisers."[16] The Tibetan Nyingma Relief Foundation, the Foundation for the Preservation of the Mahayana Tradition, Rokpa International, and the Ganden Foundation derive directly from the Tibetan Buddhist organizations established during this phase.

In the 1980s and 1990s, human rights and environmental activists also began to develop friends of Tibet organizations, just as the Dalai Lama's exile administration began its International Campaign for Tibet, a systematic effort to associate Tibet with a variety of Western political causes.[17] The International Campaign for Tibet, the International Committee of Lawyers for Tibet, Students for a Free Tibet, and Eco-Tibet were all founded during this phase. Amnesty International, Asia Watch, and Cultural Survival began to take greater interest in Tibet as well.

Although organized at different times and in different contexts, these many friends of Tibet organizations, as they promote the Tibetan cause, also promote an activist political culture based fundamentally on a liberal humanist worldview. That worldview emphasizes the rights of individuals to live as they choose. It holds government responsible to protect those rights. Friends of Tibet engage in activities intended to hold various governments responsible for protecting individual Tibetan rights and liberties. Their activities include letter-writing campaigns, political demonstrations, and fundraising events. The Tibet Society, for example, promotes six ways to help Tibet:

1. Join the Tibet Society (by donating £15 per year)
2. Write to Members of Parliament about Tibet
3. Write to national or local papers about Tibet

4. Organize a talk on Tibet
5. Organize a local branch of the Tibet Society
6. Donate to the Tibet Relief Fund

The International Campaign for Tibet, similarly, promotes "Seven Things You Can Do For Tibet"; the Tibet Foundation outlines eleven ways to help. What all of these efforts have in common is their roots in an activist political culture, committed to the rights of individuals to pursue their own way of life.

The Impression Management Factor

The third factor in the development of the many friends of Tibet organizations that exist today is the impression management factor, the use of the language of liberal humanism by the Tibetan exiles themselves to maintain friends of Tibet support. The Tibetan exiles now promote their cause through the language of liberal humanism. They promote it in terms of human rights, women's rights, environmental rights, and global multiculturalism.

The Dalai Lama's exile administration, its Department of Information and International Relations (DIIR) in particular, is most instrumental in promoting the Tibetan political cause in this manner. Its many publications tend to accord with whatever cause is most fashionable among Western political activists at the time. In 1988, just as deforestation and global warming were becoming fashionable, the DIIR published "Where did Tibet's Forests Go?" a pamphlet that opens with the following: "Conservation of forests is a major contemporary global concern. From the mighty Amazon to the foothills of Nepal ... destruction of the world's forests is endangering nature's delicate ecological balance" (DIIR 1988: 1).

In 1991, when the preservation of indigenous knowledge became more fashionable, the DIIR promoted the Tibetan political cause more often as a variant of cultural survival. As Sakya Trizin, one of Tibet's foremost religious leaders, argued in an interview in *Chö-Yang*. "The Tibetan situation is difficult and it is important that the world is continuously made aware of Tibet's plight. [Tibet] has many old cultural and religious traditions which are important and which can contribute to the whole world.... When such an ancient tradition is on the verge of extinction, it is important not to let it die" (DIIR 1991: 73).

In 1995, when women's rights became more fashionable, the DIIR published its first-ever National Report on Tibetan Women, a document remarkable for its attempt to incorporate women, for the first time, in the exile administration's official version of Tibetan history. The document opens with: "Traditionally, Tibetan women enjoyed a higher social status than their counterparts in many other societies. They also played an active part in the affairs of family and society. Since the occupation of Tibet by

Chinese military forces, Tibetan women have suffered oppression, exploitation, subjugation and discrimination" (DIIR 1995).

The document proceeds to contrast all of the problems Tibetan women face under Chinese rule (such as forced abortions, denial of equal opportunities, denial of civil and political rights, and denial of adequate health care facilities) with all of the benefits they enjoy under Tibetan rule. Most remarkable is the report's attempt to portray Tibet before the exile as a matriarchy. It argues:

> In [Chinese] annals ... there is a reference to the existence of a "women's kingdom" in southeastern Tibet. In this kingdom, the society is described as being matriarchal and matrilineal where political power appeared to have been in the hands of women.... In Tibetan history one also finds that there were times when certain individual women played prominent roles.... The mothers of the Tibetan emperors ... are believed to have played active roles in the polity of the state.... The Chinese authorities have time and again tried to portray traditional Tibetan society in a negative light ... [yet] at no point of history were the Tibetan women subjected to foot-binding, veiling, dowry or concubinage. It is not fair to compare the status of Tibetan women in the past to that of [the] present under Chinese occupation. It is more justified to compare Tibetan women in Tibet with their counterparts in exile. The women in Tibet enjoy none of the human rights and freedom that are taken for granted in exile. (DIIR 1995)

The DIIR emphasizes that Tibetan women in exile enjoy human rights and freedom. Women's rights were very fashionable among friends of Tibet at the time, just prior to the United Nations Fourth World Conference on Women in Beijing.

The Dalai Lama also uses the language of liberal humanism to promote the Tibetan political cause. He focuses repeatedly on two themes. The first is the environmental theme, the idea that Tibet was an environmental haven in the past and could again become one in the future. A speech he delivered in Dharamsala, India, entitled "Message on the Protection of the Environment," illustrates how he uses the environmental theme not only to promote the Tibetan cause but also to teach Tibetans themselves how to accommodate an environmental ethic in their own lives:

> In Tibet previously there was a good tradition of instituting laws to safeguard hills and valleys for unprotected and unsupported wild animals and birds and for the protection of various defenseless creatures. We should maintain the continuity of this tradition .... [but] to discard fruit-peels, paper, plastic, bottles, old clothes, food leftovers and other kinds of garbage ... [to] urinate and defecate everywhere ... [to] tie worn clothes and fallen hair to branches of trees ... looks extremely unattractive, so from now on this habit should be abandoned.

The second theme the Dalai Lama uses to promote the Tibetan political cause is the zone of peace theme. He introduced this theme in a speech he delivered before the European Parliament, controversial among Tibetans for its implication that less than independence would be acceptable. He argued that if Tibetans regained political control of Tibet, "the whole of Tibet" would be transformed into a zone of peace, "a sanctuary in which humanity and nature can live together in harmony." He argued: "In the future, Tibet need no longer be an occupied land, oppressed by force, unproductive and scarred by suffering. It can become a free haven where humanity and nature live in harmonious balance; a creative model for the resolution of tensions afflicting many areas throughout the world."[18]

In accordance with the Dalai Lama's speeches, Tibetan exiles themselves promote the Tibetan cause through the language of liberal humanism. A Tibetan from Dharamsala, for example, described his homeland in Tsang in a way that resembles closely the Dalai Lama's words: "In Tibet, it was Tibetan nature [*gomshi*] to protect the environment [*khoryug*]. Tibetans never mined the earth ... the precious things in the earth [*terkha*] belong to the gods.... Also, in Tibet, there were thick forests and many animals. In Tsang, the trees grew so big it took six people holding hands together to extend around each one.... The Dalai Lama says everyone should protect the environment as we did in Tibet."

Tibetan exiles use the zone of peace theme to define their own concerns as well. A discussion I had with my Tibetan language teacher illustrates. After we debated the many reasons other countries should support Tibet, he argued: "If Tibet became independent, then it could be a zone of peace that would protect all of Asia." Asked why countries outside of Asia should support Tibet, he argued that, as a zone of peace, Tibet is a model for all humanity: "If China continues what it has done to Tibet, that leaves a black mark [*tsen-nag*] on world history. If the world does not fix the problem now, then the whole world will degenerate to the law of the jungle [*shing-nag gi tim*]. Just as dogs and buffalo and other animals fight until the most powerful wins, so that will happen to the world" (personal communication, November 13, 1995).

Tibetan exiles now use the language of liberal humanism to promote their own concerns. They promote their concerns as human rights, women's rights, and environmental rights issues. In doing so, they reinterpret their own culture, values, and traditions through a liberal humanist worldview. Ironically, therefore, friends of Tibet, although they discuss their efforts to assist Tibetan exiles as intended to preserve and protect a traditional Tibetan culture, also serve as a means to transform what it means to be Tibetan toward the accommodation of liberal humanism.

The Relationship between Friends of Tibet and Tibetan Exile Schools in Nepal

Friends of Tibet assist the Tibetan exiles primarily in the form of donations to Tibetan exile monasteries and schools. Tibetan exiles have made it a priority to re-establish their monasteries and to establish a network of schools throughout the exile communities. The monasteries are meant, in part, to replace those destroyed by the Chinese communist regime in Tibet (Dalai Lama of Tibet 1962: 117–118; Shakya 1999: 267).[19] Tibetan exile elite considered the schools important as well. The Dalai Lama writes of their importance as follows: "The children have been a special anxiety to me–there are over five thousand of them under sixteen. It is even harder for children than for adults to be uprooted and taken suddenly to an entirely different environment.... We had to do something to improve their health–and their education was a matter of great importance" (Dalai Lama of Tibet 1962: 226).

In Nepal, friends of Tibet helped to finance the construction and maintenance of two separate networks of schools. The first consists of a network of twelve schools now administered jointly by the Snow Lion Foundation (SLF) and the Tibetan exile administration. These schools now educate an estimated 1,200 Tibetan students. Swiss intergovernmental organizations provided the initial funds for these schools. They then founded the SLF to solicit funds from within the Tibetan exile community itself for their maintenance. The SLF was far more effective in raising funds from foreign organizations instead. By 1995, foreign donations to these schools had eclipsed donations from within the Tibetan exile community, as data I compiled from the SLF archives illustrates (see Figure 3.1).

The second network of Tibetan exile schools in Nepal consists of private schools founded by Tibetan exile elite outside of the framework of the Dalai Lama's exile administration. By 1995, fifteen of them had joined together to form the United Schools Association. Together, they educate nearly two thousand Tibetan and ethnic Tibetan students in Nepal. A number of Taiwanese organizations, including the Mongolian and Tibetan Affairs Commission, provide funding to them.

FIGURE 3.1 Snow Lion Foundation Sources of Income, 1975–1995

Source: Data compiled from Snow Lion Foundation annual reports, 1974–1995.

Friends of Tibet play a role not only in financing these two networks of schools but also in promoting their own values within them. Within the schools, Tibetan exiles accommodate the values of their sponsors relatively easily. Schools are a primary setting within which the Tibetan exiles invent new Tibetan traditions. Hobsbawm (1981: 1) defines an invented tradition as a set of practices that develops in the present political context yet that implies continuity with the ancient and historic past due to its ritual repetition. Examples include the Scottish Highland tradition (Trevor-Roper 1981), the British-Indian form of the durbar, or Imperial Assembly (Cohn 1981), and the use of national flags, national anthems, and national emblems by new nation-states (Hobsbawm 1981: 11). What all of these examples have in common—what constitutes invented traditions—is their development during times of rapid social and political transformation (Hobsbawm 1981: 4), their use in inculcating certain values and behaviors in those who participate in them (Hobsbawm 1981: 1), and their perceived continuity with the ancient and historic past (Hobsbawm 1981: 1). Political elite use invented traditions to inculcate such values as patriotism, loyalty, duty, or school spirit (Hobsbawm 1981: 10) with the larger goal of legitimating particular actions or cultivating group cohesion (Hobsbawm 1981: 12).

The incorporation of Tibet into the People's Republic of China, and the consequent exile of an estimated 80,000 Tibetans into Nepal, India, and other countries, brought on a period of rapid social and political transformation for Tibetans both inside Tibet and within the exile communities.[20] Within the exile communities, Tibetan political elite needed institutions through which to cultivate social cohesion and help the Tibetan exiles to adapt to their changing political circumstances. Secular schools were one institution they used, yet because secular schools were a relatively new institutional form for the Tibetans, the Tibetan exiles had no established norms to guide how they should function. In contrast with Tibet's monastic system, with its long-established canon of Buddhist texts, ritual practices, and rules for advancement, the Tibetan exile school system was essentially a blank slate.[21]

Tibetan political elite used the secular school system they developed in exile to promote new traditions among the Tibetans. Some of these traditions are intended primarily for the students and their families, with the goal of cultivating social cohesion among them. They include annual talent shows; an annual sports day competition; and an annual graduation ceremony. Others are intended specifically for the schools' sponsors, such as the traditional Tibetan culture show that schools perform for sponsor visits. Through these performances, the Tibetan exiles portray their culture as a unique way of life not only for Tibetans, but for anyone who wants to participate. Tibetan exile students learn this value as part of what it means to be Tibetan. They learn to think about their own culture as one of many life choices others may adopt.

The Atisha Primary School in Jawalakhel, Nepal, is an ideal site for discussing these traditional Tibetan culture shows. As the Atisha School is situated next to the JHC, it is a very convenient stop for tourists and potential sponsors; it frequently plays this showcasing role. Throughout 1995, many tourists and sponsors passed through the hallways of the Atisha School and observed the children through the classroom windows. Some, like the Danish couple who sponsor Tibetan children in another school, wanted only to take photographs. Others, such as the British man who wanted to study refugee education, sat in on classroom discussions. Still others, such as the representative from the U.N. Working Committee on the Rights of Children, wanted to speak to the children, in this case, to ask them if they know what their rights are.

In April 1995, four representatives from Association Tibet Libre, the Atisha School's principal sponsor, visited the Atisha School as well. Their visit illustrates some of the dilemmas the Tibetan exiles face in defining what they mean by the traditional Tibetan culture. On one hand, the Tibetan exiles wanted to invoke and use symbols that represent to them some form of continuity with the way of life they knew in Tibet. On the other, they wanted to use symbols recognizable to their sponsors as well. At the Atisha School, what the students performed as the traditional Tibetan culture is a curious mix of behaviors and practices. Their performance included fife and drum music (instruments introduced into Tibet by British army officers only after the turn of the twentieth century), the Tibetan national anthem (invented, again, only after the turn of the century), yoga exercises (adopted from India and Nepal only after the exile), British school uniforms (again, adopted only after the exile), and a tremendous showing of gratitude for the foreign assistance they receive. The Atisha students enacted this behavior not only to express gratitude but also to facilitate a request for further assistance, to fund the construction of an Atisha high school. The Tibet Libre representatives stayed in Kathmandu for a week and, as they were also making a film for French television, brought their video camera with them wherever they went. At the end of the week, Atisha School representatives initiated their request.

Association Tibet Libre's Visit to Shangri-La

It was a typical morning in late April. The sun was shining, vegetable sellers were setting up their stands, shopkeepers were tossing water onto the dusty paths, and buses, taxis, and *vikram* scooters, belching black smoke behind, were speeding down the narrow road in front of the Atisha School in Jawalakhel, Nepal. Inside the gates of the Atisha School, nothing typical was happening, however. First, there was music–fifes and drums and cymbals– and it was only Tuesday. The students play music during their morning exercises only on Fridays. That it was a special day was evident, therefore, even to the many Tibetans in the factory next door, as they crowded, pushing each other, against the iron bars of the factory windows to watch.

What they saw, in the courtyard of the school, were the children, in their British-style school uniforms, lined up in morning-assembly formation. The older children, playing their musical instruments, were grouped off to one side. Above the students, perched on the bridge between the two school buildings, stood a group of French people. Their leaders were a young woman in a tank top, hiking shorts, and boots, and a bearded man in dirty jeans who pointed his video camera down at the children. As they filmed the scene, the children performed a most elaborate version of their morning exercises. They sang a poem composed by the Sixth Dalai Lama, the Tibetan national anthem, and the Nepali national anthem, and they marched around the courtyard, with a pause at the position of honor, the group of French people on the bridge. They then performed yoga exercises, first standing and then sitting, before they settled in line again. All faced the front of the school.

The guests descended the stairs from the bridge. Behind them, they lugged a very large white cloth bag. The children at the back of the assembly started to guess what the bag might contain, what the guests might have brought them all the way from France. The guests positioned themselves, the big bag between them, at the front of the school. As they proceeded to draw out the presents, one by one, the headmaster announced the names of the students from slips of paper pulled out of a hat: "Karma Dawa ... Thinlay Dolma ... Tashi Gyaltsen...." As the students stepped forward to accept the presents, they bowed their heads and outstretched their hands, and the bearded man with the camera leaned in and focused on the bright, young eyes that looked up to see what each would receive.

What each child received was hardly worth the pageantry. Used clothes donated by volunteers from France was all that the bag contained, and as the clothes were distributed through a lottery system, most were inappropriate for the students who received them. A young girl received a pair of men's trousers far too big for anyone in Nepal, yet she smiled genuinely into the camera anyway, as it was considered lucky for her name to be called. She was followed by a young boy, who received a frilly turquoise-color summer halter top, which he called a "baby's dress," as he slid it on over his school clothes to model for his friends. Only one present was appropriate for the recipient, a pair of men's trousers for a tall boy, and the teachers at the back of the courtyard murmured in approval. The procedure went on for more than an hour, the French sponsors filming the grateful refugees accepting presents from the charitable Westerners the whole time, when finally, at the suggestion of the headmaster, who could see the students getting restless, they stopped calling out names and gave the remaining clothes to the staff assistant to distribute. The students marched together into the school, then, and the teachers started classes for the day.

The Tibet Libre representatives then made two additional requests. The first was to film the students in their classes. Although Atisha is an English-medium school, they requested to film only the Tibetan and Nepali classes. As they did, the Tibetan teachers started to talk among themselves in Tibetan. Neither of the Nepali teachers had shown up for school, and they were joking about who would teach Nepali for the purpose of the film. As all of the Tibetan teachers had been educated in India, they all knew Hindi much better than Nepali. Who would teach Nepali? The Tibetan science teacher finally agreed to do it, and the French sponsors filmed her, the children laughing at her pronunciation the whole time.

The second request was to film the parents. Although Tibet Libre gives all of its sponsor money in one lump sum to the SLF, they insisted on filming the parents gratefully accepting fake checks from them. The headmaster graciously agreed, yet as a result, the staff assistant had to spend the rest of the day running around the camp looking for parents willing to appear in the film. It was difficult to convince them, as all of them had carpet factory work to do. At the same time, however, no one wanted to offend the sponsors. Finally, a few agreed.

After filming the parents, the Tibet Libre representatives proceeded to the JHC factory to film the workers and to the SLF building where Tibetan exile officials thanked them for their support and asked if they needed a ride to the airport or anything else during their stay. At another meeting, the headmaster arranged before they left, he presented them with the plans for the construction of Atisha high school and requested further assistance.

The Invention of Tradition

The performance the Atisha students enacted for the Tibet Libre visit is only one of many examples of a tradition Tibetan exile elite have invented specifically for Western sponsors. Tibetan exile elite also regularly send reports, letters, and brochures to their sponsors. In their communications, they take care to represent the school in terms that their sponsors expect. A Christmas card Atisha's headmaster designed soon after the Tibet Libre visit illustrates their concerns. While designing the card, he repeatedly asked me, in particular, whether the card should fold in the middle or lie flat; whether the photograph should be in black-and-white or color; whether the border should be a Tibetan long-life design or straight line; whether "Tashi Delek" in Tibetan or "Season's Greetings" in English should be printed on the inside. What is it that the sponsors want to see? A report he prepared received similar attention, as did a twenty-fifth anniversary booklet prepared by the SLF. As Christmas cards, reports, and twenty-fifth anniversaries were all new, the Tibetan exiles sought a balance between symbols comprehensible to sponsors and symbols representative of the preservation of the Tibetan culture in exile.

Ironically, the traditions the Tibetan exiles invent as part of the preservation of the Tibetan culture in exile teach Tibetan students that what it means to be Tibetan is to accommodate the values of their sponsors. What it means to be Tibetan, as a result, is changing just as much outside Tibet–within the exile communities–as within Tibet. Speaking English, exchanging Christmas cards, and celebrating twenty-fifth anniversaries are neither more nor less Tibetan than speaking Chinese, exchanging mooncakes, and celebrating the harvest festival. None of these practices preserve any aspect of traditional Tibetan culture, yet all become some aspect of what it means to be Tibetan.

The phrase "Tashi Delek" provides another example of this process. Tibetan exiles use "Tashi Delek" as an approximation of the English "good day" or "hello." Tibetans in Tibet use the phrase only as part of a much longer New Year's greeting. Tibetan exile students insist the phrase was used also in pre-1959 Tibet to mean "good day" or "hello" and is a traditional part of their culture. It is the Tibetans in Tibet, they insist, who have changed. Both Tibetans in Tibet and Tibetans in exile, it is clear, have changed, however. Both invent new traditions to accommodate their present political circumstances. Both interpret what they invent as part of what it means to be Tibetan.

Tradition, Culture, and a Contest of Authenticity

This difference between the way in which Tibetans in Tibet and Tibetans in exile understand what it means to be Tibetan has led to a contest for authenticity. Who, indeed, are the "real" Tibetans, the "true" representatives of traditional Tibetan culture? Tibetans in Tibet contest the claims that Tibetan exiles make to greater authenticity, less tainted by Chinese culture and tradition. Tibetans in Tibet perceive the exiles as equally tainted by Western culture and tradition. We see this contest of authenticity in a confrontation between Tibetan women from Tibet and Tibetan women from the exile communities at the 1995 U.N. World Conference on Women in Beijing. The confrontation demonstrates how both groups interpret the accommodations they make in their present political circumstances to be part of what it means to be Tibetan.

Delegates from Tibet as well as from the Tibetan exile communities attended the 1995 U.N. World Conference on Women. At the conference, the delegates from Tibet argued that Tibetan women are happy under Chinese rule, far happier than they were under Tibetan rule (Tibetan Women's Delegation 1996). The delegation from the exile communities argued that Tibetan women are tortured and oppressed under Chinese rule and that only under Tibetan (exile) rule are they able to enjoy human rights and freedom. Fifteen separate friends of Tibet organizations, eight from the United States, assisted the Tibetan exiles in their efforts to promote their view.[22]

The divergence in their views clashed most dramatically during a workshop the exiles organized on women and development in Tibet. During the workshop, delegates from the exile communities argued that women are systematically oppressed under Chinese rule. Immediately after they finished speaking, two women from Tibet tried to show transparencies that, it was expected, would contradict what the exile delegates had said. The exile delegates refused to let them speak, and a conflict between the two groups ensued. One of the exile delegates reports that a delegate from Tibet

> started yelling at us in Tibetan and saying why are you guys doing this, why are you all lying and spreading these lies, and how could you know anything of Tibet, especially you, and she was pointing at me and the two younger ones. You're so young, how could you know anything. You've never been to Tibet and you don't even speak proper Tibetan. She threw a lot of insults at us that were very demeaning and hurtful. (Jinpa 1995: 14)

Each side accused the other of lying. Tibetan exiles claimed that Tibetans from Tibet cannot speak for themselves and say only what the Chinese government tells them to say: "We know they cannot speak freely. We know that they are under instruction to denounce us, and insist only they are genuine Tibetans" (Wangmo 1995: 15). Tibetans from Tibet claimed that the exiles say only what Westerners tell them to say: "Why are you begging for help from white people? You are all liars. You don't know anything" (Jinpa 1995: 15). As if only to illustrate what the delegates from Tibet were saying, a man from Amnesty International stood up in the midst of the argument and defended the exiles by saying that Amnesty has been working on the Tibetan situation for a long time and knows that what the exiles say is true (Jinpa 1995: 14).

Tibetan exiles maintain that they represent the truth about Tibet and are the true representatives of its culture and tradition. Tibetans in Tibet maintain that they are the true Tibetans. Both are influenced by their present political circumstances. Both interpret the new traditions they invent to be an essential part of what it means to be Tibetan.

Accommodation within the Tibetan Exile School System

Within the Tibetan exile communities, the school system promotes the idea that part of what it means to be Tibetan is to accommodate the norms and values of the people who support Tibetans. Within the schools, Tibetan exiles accommodate these values relatively easily. Pragmatically, some Tibetans argue that some accommodation of the values of their sponsors is necessary. As one Tibetan exile leader argues: "This is a competition. We know that they have to give it [the money] somewhere. The question is who can impress them first with the best project" (Devoe 1983: 146). Other

Tibetan exiles argue that accommodating the norms and values of their sponsors may even be beneficial. They explain that although Tibetans, as Buddhists, are supposed to have great compassion, it is Westerners, and particularly Christians, who really help people. One Tibetan schoolteacher, for example, explained that she was very surprised to see how much love (*champa*) Western teachers give to students. "Tibetans are always talking about compassion (*nyingje*)," she explained, "But at most, they give poor children a rupee or two, always from a distance. They never touch strange children and certainly never pick them up and hug them and clean the snot off their faces. It is only Christians who do." "The Christian religion has some good points," the headmaster of the Atisha School, likewise, once said, "It makes people generous.... Christian people are always giving things away, whereas Buddhists do not." Within the schools, Tibetan exiles have embraced the values of their sponsors and used them to reinterpret their own traditions.

The Relationship between Friends of Tibet and Tibetan Monasteries in Nepal

Within the monasteries, however, Tibetan exiles have responded with much greater anxiety as they witness the effects that friends of Tibet organizations have had. Tibetan exiles resist the introduction of liberal humanism into their monastic tradition. They interpret the changes foreign sponsorship has introduced as a threat to their culture and traditions.

Tibetan exiles in Nepal, by 1995, had established forty-five Tibetan monasteries and nunneries, most of them in Boudha, to house nearly one thousand Tibetan monks and nuns.[23] Although these monasteries and nunneries resemble those in Tibet in terms of their organizational structure and curriculum, in many other respects, they differ significantly. The primary way in which they differ involves how they finance their operations. In Tibet, monasteries were largely self-sufficient in terms of operational income; they supported their ongoing activities primarily through taxes on the vast estate lands they held (Goldstein 1973; Schüh 1988). In exile, in contrast, monasteries are not self-sufficient; they have become dependent on foreign donations. Tibetan lamas (religious leaders) solicit foreign donations in a number of ways. The primary way is through speaking engagements to Buddhists in Western countries. Tibetan lamas, according to one estimate, can earn as much as $40,000 to $60,000 through just one tour of the U.S. or Europe. When they establish dharma centers (teaching centers) in the U.S. or Europe, they create a more continuous source of foreign funds. According to one source, 77 percent of all Tibetan lamas in exile have traveled to the U.S. or Europe, and 51 percent have emigrated to Europe, the U.S., Canada, Australia, or New Zealand to resettle in dharma centers. They use

TABLE 3.1 Travel and Resettlement of Tibetan Lamas

Tibetan Buddhist School (Number of Lamas in Survey)	Lamas Who Have Toured Europe or North America	Lamas Who Have Resettled in Europe or North America
Gelug (74)	56 (76%)	37 (50%)
Sakya (15)	13 (87%)	9 (60%)
Kagyu (37)	30 (81%)	22 (59%)
Nyingma (17)	11 (65%)	7 (41%)
Bon (3)	3 (100%)	0 (0%)
Total (146)	**113 (77%)**	**75 (51%)**

Source: Data derive from Coleman (1993).

the foreign donations they solicit through their tours and dharma centers to finance their monasteries in Nepal and India.

Recognizing Westerners as Tibetan Buddhist reincarnates is a comparatively new way in which Tibetan lamas solicit foreign funds. In Nepal, Tibetan lamas have recognized at least two Western children as important reincarnates. One of them, from Seattle, has been enthroned at Tharlam monastery. The other, from Spain, is at Kopan monastery. Tibetan lamas have recognized prominent adults as reincarnates as well. One Tibetan lama has even recognized Hollywood actor Steven Seagal as an important reincarnate.[24] Recognizing Westerners as reincarnate lamas helps to establish an even more durable set of foreign connections than what speaking tours and dharma centers can offer. It creates a life-long connection between the Tibetan lama and his new student.

The way in which Tibetan monasteries and nunneries finance their operations in exile has introduced a number of other changes as well. Tibetan exile monasteries employ English and other foreign language translators, for example, so that they are more accessible to the Western Buddhists who want to study within them. Another change involves the sense of connection between Tibetan Buddhist leaders and their monasteries. Whereas in Tibet, Tibetan lamas usually had only one monastery, in exile, they maintain many monasteries and dharma centers in many countries.[25] Whereas in Tibet, lamas and their monasteries were so close that they usually also shared the same name, in exile, lamas choose whatever name is fashionable among Westerners.

All of these changes cause considerable anxiety among the Tibetan exiles who perceive them, and the values they represent, to be a threat to their culture and traditions. Tibetan exiles express considerable concern over the amount of time their lamas spend in Western countries, for example. They worry about the loss of their lamas, and the knowledge they embody, to wealthy Westerners. As one Tibetan, in reference particularly to lamas with a *geshe* degree, the highest degree in the Gelugpa school of Buddhism, comments:

Tibetan *geshes* spend more time in dharma centers in Western countries than they do teaching Tibetans. Why? Westerners pay high salaries for *geshes*.... Monasteries provide only room and board. The *geshes* go where the money is, and now Tibetan monks in the monastery, when they disagree about a particular point of the teachings, have no one to ask what is the right answer. In the future, maybe Westerners will have to teach Tibetans what Tibetan Buddhism is. (personal communication, July 9, 1995)

Tibetan exiles also express concern over the participation of Western students in Tibetan exile monasteries. Some Tibetans argue that Western students never really help Tibetans at all but are just hippies (*khyampo*) and drug addicts in need of help. I heard one such comment the day after the Oklahoma City bombing. Tibetan teachers at the Atisha School were discussing what might have been the cause. Unlike the American press, which immediately suspected Muslims, they immediately suspected drug addicts. Their speculations led to a discussion about all of the unstable (*mi-tempo*) and emotional (*sempa chung*) Westerners they had met. "Now they are all coming to our monasteries!"

Tibetan exiles express concern also about the participation of Western women in their monasteries. Discussions I had with a number of Tibetans in Nepal in 1995 around a particular event that had occurred illustrate their concerns. The event is all the more interesting, as it did not, in actuality, involve a monastery, yet it was reinterpreted among Tibetans as if it did. The event involved the death, most probably of a drug overdose, of the youngest son of a very rich Tibetan family in Boudha. The Tibetan had a Western girlfriend who was with him before he died. She had been arrested but the Tibetan family involved argued that she should be sent back to her country instead of being held in Nepal.

The story was not so simple as it circulated throughout the Tibetan community, however. As it spread, it accumulated more and more commentary, so that after a few months, the event was said to have occurred in a monastery, and the man who died was said to have been a monk, although still the youngest son of a very rich Tibetan family. Two Western women who were studying in the monastery, the story follows, were fighting over the monk because they were in love with him. Out of jealousy, one killed the monk. I asked the people telling the story if the Tibetan might have died of a drug overdose, but the storytellers insisted their version of the story is more likely, as they know about monasteries in Boudha that allow Western women to stay in them: "These women take showers outside naked where everyone can see.... There are a lot of Western women like this who want to have sex only with monks. They have a real thing for monks."

This story is only one of many that depicts Western students as unstable, unable to control themselves, and a threat to Tibetan monks and monasteries.[26] What it conveys most clearly is the anxiety with which Tibetans respond to the increasing involvement of Westerners, particularly Western women, in their religious organizations. Western participation introduces norms and values that Tibetans find quite strange, and at times threatening. Tibetan exiles resist accommodating these norms and values. They argue that they, as Tibetans, should decide what Tibetan Buddhism is and how it should be practiced. What it means to be Tibetan and who has the right to decide has, as a result, become the focus for considerable debate. We may interpret the debate in terms of issues of cultural authenticity and the ownership of tradition.

What Is Tibetan Buddhism?

Buddhism has undergone significant changes every time it has spread to a new region of the world and accommodated the belief systems already there (Robinson and Johnson 1996). That Tibetans and Westerners should understand Buddhism differently should be expected. That Western Buddhists should interpret Tibetan Buddhism through their own liberal humanist worldview, focused on the enrichment of the individual self, should be expected as well. Tibetan exiles resist the way in which Western practitioners reinterpret Tibetan Buddhism to involve a focus on the individual self. Dagyab Rinpoche, a Tibetan lama living in Germany, explains:

> Tibetan teachers and Western followers of Tibetan Buddhism may agree that the gradual spread of Buddhism in the Western society is to be welcomed ... [yet] if we go into detail, things are not so clear, smooth, and simple. I think one of the main problems is that most of the teachers and the disciples only believe that by using the phrase "Tibetan Buddhism" they are talking about the same thing. In fact they are not, and this misunderstanding is maintained persistently, because there is not enough genuine communication between teachers and their Western disciples, only a lot of illusions and projections–on both sides. (1992: 15)

We may characterize the difference between the way in which Tibetans and Westerners define and practice Tibetan Buddhism in terms of the framework of veneration versus imitation (Bond 1988: 162–167; Fields 1981: 371). Veneration involves the worship and support of the Buddha, the teachings, and the community of religious practitioners (monks and nuns). It is a merit-making activity that Tibetan exiles consider a worthy and entirely appropriate form of religious practice, particularly for lay practitioners (non monks and nuns). As one Tibetan exile explains, not everyone has the time, circumstances, or mental capacity to live the life of the Buddha (as a monk or nun). For most Tibetans, veneration is the more important part of their religious practice: "Many people in Tibetan society, especially women, do not have time to study and meditate properly because they work so hard. It takes free time and money and facilities to study Buddhism–all these things together.... Very few people have this" (personal communication, April 27, 1995).

For Western practitioners, imitation tends to be more important than veneration. Buddhist practice, for them, tends to involve studying the behaviors and opinions of different lamas and adopting what is useful as their own. Western practitioners, in other words, tend to view Buddhist practice in terms of how it enriches themselves as individuals much more so than how it creates and supports a religious community. Fields (1981: 371) explains: "Most Western Buddhists… have little interest in supporting monks and nuns. Indeed the idea of the 'transference of merit,' whereby the support that lay people give monks and nuns is transformed into merit leading to future benefit seems to run counter to the spirit of most North American Buddhists, who tend to see Buddhism as a do-it-yourself religion. Americans want to practice Buddhism themselves."

Tibetan exiles criticize Western practitioners for the degree to which they interpret Tibetan Buddhist practice to be an individually oriented activity, aimed at the enrichment of the individual self. They criticize Westerners for trying to enrich themselves through association with their lamas. One Tibetan exile in Nepal, reflecting upon her experience in a dharma center in France, explains:

> When Westerners say "my religion" and "my main lama," that is strange. Tibetan people do not talk that way…. For example, when a woman from Paris came to stay, she said that her main lama was one lama in Paris. I know this lama and he is very handsome (*zigpo*) and has a lot, lot (*mangpo, mangpo*) of girlfriends who are his students. Other Westerners at the dharma center said he is not a real lama…. There were a lot of arguments and the woman left…. Tibetans do not identify with their lama like that. There is one saying that if people stay with their lama for more than three days, they will quickly learn all of his faults (*kyön*). Maybe if they learn his faults, they will turn against him and the teachings. (personal communication, August 16, 1995)

Many Tibetan exiles, as a result of these differences, view with skepticism the Western practitioners who arrive in Nepal to practice Buddhism, especially when they cannot speak or read Tibetan. They do not understand Westerners' attempts to associate so closely with their lamas to be Buddhist practice. A Tibetan lama explains: "Western students seem to want to study only the most difficult of all Buddhist practices, and soon they focus on how they can learn to develop the power to avoid ejaculation during sex. It would be better for them to investigate how you know who has this power and who does not… It is impossible to know just by looking at someone and there are many lamas who pretend."[27]

Tibetan exiles resist the way in which Western practitioners associate Tibetan Buddhism with the enrichment of the self, particularly the sexual self. They criticize Tibetan lamas for accommodating this intense individuality in their teachings. They argue that only they, as Tibetans, should define what Tibetan Buddhism is, that Westerners should not be allowed to reinterpret Tibetan Buddhism to accommodate their own norms and values. Western students have responded to their criticisms. The debate has proceeded, in part, through interactions between Tibetans and Western Buddhists in monasteries in Nepal and also in part through English-language Tibetan Buddhist publications.

Who Has the Right to Decide?

We see on one side in the debate Western practitioners who argue that Tibetan Buddhism is a form of knowledge that, once acquired, entitles one to the right to decide how it should be practiced. On the other side are Tibetans who argue that Tibetan Buddhism is an essential part of their culture and identity, inherited by birth, and that only Tibetans have the right to decide. Whereas one Western practitioner in Kathmandu, for example, claimed that: "Tibetans are no longer interested in the true meaning of the dharma. They just touch their heads to the texts (*pechas*) instead of studying what is in them… It is only in the West now that you can find teachers who are masters and who are empowered to give certain initiations. The United States is the new home of the dharma." A Tibetan woman responded with: "If Westerners think that they are the experts, that is very strange. We are born Buddhist."

The debate, thus, is essentially about authenticity and cultural ownership. Tibetan exiles resist the way in which Western Buddhist practitioners and other friends of Tibet claim ownership over Tibetan Buddhism. They interpret those claims to be a threat to their values, culture, and tradition. Their perception of a threat is exacerbated by the financial control Western Buddhists and other friends of Tibet exercise over Tibetan lamas and their monasteries. Tibetans fear what might happen to their own communities, and even to their own identities, in a context of such control. Tsering Wangyal, a Tibetan from Dharamsala, for example, argues: "If the Western Buddhist centers continue to grow, and if Tibetans continue to be financially dependent on them…. Western influence could easily intrude upon the Tibetan culture as a whole, thereby endangering the unique Tibetan identity. If adequate precautions are not taken now, the future generation of Tibetans wishing to study Buddhism may only find the Western variation at their disposal, with books and teachers especially designed for Western minds" (Wangyal 1979: 4).

Western Buddhist practitioners, and other friends of Tibet, continue to assert their claims to participate in the Tibetan culture, however. They claim it as a right and a lifestyle choice. Keith Dowman, a Western scholar of Tibetan Buddhism, for example, argues: "In general, it should be evident … that now that the dharma has been transmitted to the West it is no longer an exclusive Tibetan domain… it is unrealistic to expect Western initiates to remain mute observers–however limited their understanding may be; and that Tibetan culture may sometimes benefit from outside input (1993: 84).

Tibetan exiles resist their assertions and claim Tibetan Buddhism as their own. Tenzin Thinlay, a Tibetan from Los Angeles, argues in response to Dowman: "Tibet and its people, religion, and culture have been ravaged over the last forty years by Chinese Communists. As we and our tradition have sought refuge and hope of a new life in the West, we face another, far more subtle threat. When 'experts' with limited understanding take it upon themselves to define our culture and experience for us, to intrude their beliefs and agendas where ours should be, then they have ravaged us as surely as those with guns" (1993: 8).

We see in these exchanges the limits to the degree to which Tibetan exiles are willing to accommodate the values of the people who support them. Tibetan exiles resist the introduction of Western norms and values into their religious organizations. They criticize the way in which their lamas, in particular, accommodate liberal humanism in their teachings and religious practices. They worry about the effects that their accommodation has on the Tibetan culture. They argue that Tibetan Buddhism is a domain for Tibetans alone to define.

Tibetan Independence versus the Preservation of the Tibetan Culture in Exile

The relationship between the Tibetan exiles and the friends of Tibet who assist them has influenced the interpretation not only of Tibetan Buddhism but also of the Tibetan political cause. Tibetan exiles, the political elite in particular, now promote the Tibetan political cause in terms of Western norms and values. Two interrelated but sometimes conflicting interpretations of the Tibetan political cause have developed as a result. One, shaped by the language of self-determination, interprets the Tibetan political cause to be independence. The other, shaped by the language of global multiculturalism, interprets it to be the preservation of the Tibetan culture in exile. Although the two goals can be seen as complementary, some Tibetans, increasingly frustrated by the perpetuation of their exile, advocate independence as the "real nature of the Tibetan political struggle" and fault friends of Tibet for its lack of achievement. Whether the Tibetan exiles interpret their political struggle as independence or the preservation of the Tibetan culture in exile, they frame their struggle in terms of a liberal humanist worldview. As they promote their political struggle, the Tibetan exiles also promote the values of liberal humanism.

Tsering Shakya, in "Tibet and the Occident: The Myth of Shangri-La," argues most effectively that the "real nature of the Tibetan political struggle," is Tibetan independence. For him, the ideas and activities of friends of Tibet serve only to distort the Tibetan struggle and distract Tibetans from their goal. "The myth of Shangri-La has influenced the Western perception of the Tibetan political struggle," he writes, "and has obscured and confused [its] real nature...." (1992: 15). "The danger is that Tibetans are also beginning to be seduced by the myth.... The tendency is to promote the Tibetan political struggle in terms of the populism of the West rather than in the daily concerns of [the Tibetan] people."

For Shakya, friends of Tibet do nothing to help Tibetans to achieve independence, for what they want, instead, is only the perpetuation of their own Shangri-La. "After all," he writes, "now there was a good chance of encountering the all-knowing lamas in the towering streets of Manhattan, the bustling crowds of Oxford Street and the fashionable boulevards of Paris" (1992: 14). Even Tibet, Shakya argues, has become only a part of the Shangri-La fantasy, a "Disney World for the Western bourgeois," where even "the ruined monasteries and tortured faces of the people" have become "part of the tourist attraction" (1992: 15). Tibetans and their interests, Shakya argues, have no room in such fantasies, as they reduce Tibetans "to an endangered species" for friends of Tibet to imagine they help to save. "Just as today it is fashionable to speak of saving the world from ecological destruction," he writes (1992: 16), so have "a flood of coffee table books on Tibet" been published "each preaching the need to save Tibet from ecological disaster."

Shangri-La-inspired interpretations of Tibet, Shakya argues, have not only distracted and confused Tibet's Western friends, but have also distracted other potential sources of support for Tibetan independence. "The majority of Third World countries see Tibet as merely an instrument of Western political interests," he argues, so that "whereas issues like South Africa and the Palestinian problem are seen as real political concerns, Tibet is seen is a lost cause." He writes: "If the Tibetan issue is to be taken seriously, Tibet must be liberated from both the Western imagination and the myth of Shangri-La" (1992: 16).[28]

Not all Tibetans agree that the "real nature of the Tibetan political struggle" is Tibetan independence, however. For some Tibetans, independence no longer seems feasible so that the preservation of the Tibetan culture in exile has become their goal. As one Tibetan argued:

> There are many things about Tibetan culture that should be saved. For example, Tibetans used to wear felt boots in Tibet. Now, no one in the exile community wears them. There may not be anyone who knows how to make them. Even if young people want to learn how to make them, it is too late to ask anyone.... It is the same with *chubas* [Tibetan robes]. If you look around, many people are wearing Western clothes instead of *chubas*.... With the next generation, no one will know how to make *chubas* and then that too will be lost. There is also a special way of mixing *pak* [barley flour in tea] that allows you to mix it without even a single grain of *tsampa* spilling over the edge of the cup.... All of these skills are lost and soon we will have nothing that is unique. (personal communication, October 31, 1995)

Samdhong Rinpoche, a professor at the Central Institute for Higher Tibetan Studies and the chairman of the Assembly of Tibetan People's Deputies, also makes a strong argument for a preservation interpretation of the Tibetan cause. For him, independence, if achieved through violent means, is unacceptable. He argues that the principal responsibility of all Tibetans, their birth-duty, is instead: "the preservation and dissemination of the unique inner sciences and cultural tradition that were preserved and enhanced over thousands of years by the Tibetans of early generations, who considered these to be more precious than their own lives. In modern times, these traditions have a close bearing on the well-being of all humanity. Therefore the ultimate goal is not just political freedom for Tibet ... our ultimate goal is the preservation, maintenance and dissemination of the sublime cultural traditions of the unique inner sciences for the sake of all sentient beings."[29]

Whether their goal is the preservation of the Tibetan culture in exile or independence for Tibet, Tibetan exiles promote their goals in terms that accommodate the liberal humanist values of the friends of Tibet organizations that assist them. They promote Tibetan independence through the language of self-determination. They promote the preservation of the Tibetan culture in exile through the language of global multiculturalism. Tibetan exiles learn this language as part of their own norms and values; it becomes a part of what it means to be Tibetan. The relationship between friends of Tibet and the Tibetan exiles they assist, although discussed as intended to preserve and protect traditional Tibetan culture, actually serves as a means to transform the Tibetan culture. It is one way in which the Tibetan culture has changed.

Notes

1. Yoko Ono, for example, explained that "Freedom and peace are important for not just Tibet but for our homeland, our planet, and that's what we're working on...." Yuka, of the Japanese band Cibo Matto, likewise, commented "To witness people standing up for an Asian country is particularly exciting to me."
2. Coleman (1993: 37–204) lists nearly four hundred single-interest Tibet-support organizations, located worldwide, with the largest concentrations in Europe (159) and North America (126). One Free Tibet web site (www.tibet.org), likewise, lists 255 active single-interest Tibet-support organizations.
3. Hobsbawm (1981: 1) defines an invented tradition as a set of practices that develops in the present political context yet that implies continuity with the ancient and historic past due to its ritual repetition. Invented traditions, he argues, inculcate certain values and behaviors in those who participate in them.
4. Tibetan On-Line Resource Gathering Site, September 1996.

5. I use the concept of impression management, as defined by Goffman (1959), here to emphasize the instrumentalist approach the Tibetan exile elite take when recruiting and maintaining friends of Tibet support. The impression management framework, as I discuss in the introduction, overstates the ability of the Tibetan exile elite to control the effects of their impression management strategies, however. These strategies encourage the Tibetan exiles to accommodate the values of the friends of Tibet organizations that assist them. They promote a process of transformation that is far more than skin deep.

6. Although it is common in anthropology today, in a context of a renewed focus on the study of Europe, to deconstruct the categories "West" and "Western," the categories are useful here. Both Nepalese and Tibetans use the categories extensively as a point of contrast to themselves. The people whom Nepalese call *videshis* and Tibetans call *injees* are light-skinned, light-haired foreigners from the United States, Britain, Australia, New Zealand, Switzerland, Germany, and other northern European countries. They are presumed to share similar characteristics despite whatever differences they perceive among themselves.

7. Curiously, although the movie, with its hand-turning-the-pages-of-a-book imagery, implies that the book begins in the same manner, it does not. In contrast with the movie, the book begins not with a sense of fantasy and illusion but with a sense of disillusion: "Cigars had burned low, and we were beginning to sample the disillusionment that usually afflicts old school friends who have met again and have found themselves with less in common than they ... believed they had." Another difference between the movie and the book is that in the book, the revolution that impels the characters to flee took place in "the third week of May," whereas in the movie, it took place on March 10th, the exact day the Lhasa Uprising is said to have occurred.

8. Bishop's (1989) project is to explain why no Western country assisted Tibet during the Chinese occupation. His explanation is that the idea of Tibet as Shangri-La eventually replaced the idea of Tibet as a real place in the minds of Westerners so that there was no interest any longer in saving the real Tibet (1989: 241). As Westerners already had the myth, he asks, why did they need the place? The subsequent development of a multitude of friends of Tibet organizations demonstrates, however, that the relationship between Tibet-as-Shangri-La and Tibet as a real place is much more complicated. Tibet-as-Shangri-La did not replace Tibet as a real place. Tibet, and the Tibetan exiles, continue instead as real-world referents for Tibet as Shangri-La.

9. See, for example, "China: New Year Bombs," *The Economist*, February 6, 1999; "China Fears for its Wild West," *The Economist*, November 15, 1997.

10. Ted Anthony, "A Return to Shangri-La–With an Intriguing Real-World Twist," *World Tibet Network News*, June 30, 1996.

11. U.S. Senate Foreign Relations Committee (1993).

12. The address for the site is ⟨www.engagedpage.com⟩.

13. Emma Amyatt-Leir, "A Story of Tibetan Courage," Tibetan On-Line Resource Gathering Site, September 1996. The Tibetan myth of Shambala is widely considered to be the origin of the idea of Shangri-La.

14. Speech before the Tibetan Alliance of Chicago, July 28, 1996 (Steve Kloehn, "Dalai Lama Offers Simple Answers To Complex Questions" *Chicago Tribune*, July 29, 1996).

15. Prebish (1979: 125) and Fields (1981: 273–338) also discuss the role Western Buddhists played in the development of a variety of friends of Tibet organizations.

16. *Time*, June 22, 1987, v. 129, p. 10–13.

17. The Dalai Lama's exile administration promotes its International Campaign through offices it maintains offices in the United States, the United Kingdom, Canada, Australia, Switzerland, France, and Japan.

18. "Address to members of the European Parliament by His Holiness the Dalai Lama," Strasbourg, 15 June 1988 (Dharamsala: Department of Information and International Relations, 1993). The zone of peace theme may derive from a speech delivered by Nepal's

King Birendra in the 1970s in which he argued that Nepal should become a zone of peace between India and China.

19. In his memoirs, the Fourteenth Dalai Lama recounts a meeting he had with Mao Zedong in 1954 in Beijing. He and Mao had discussed a number of issues related to development in Tibet, when according to the Dalai Lama, Mao leaned over to him and whispered: "I understand you very well. But of course, religion is poison. It has two great defects: It undermines the race, and secondly it retards the progress of the country. Tibet and Mongolia have both been poisoned by it" (Dalai Lama of Tibet 1962: 117–118). Shakya (1999: 140–141, 252–253, 266–268) analyzes how the Chinese government, at different phases of its engagement with the Tibetans, managed the issue of the monasteries. Although the government conceded to the Tibetans on a number of minor issues related to the existence and continued operation of the monasteries, generally, its long-term aim remained disbanding the monasteries and eradicating the monks as a social group (Shakya 1999: 267).

20. The Information Office of the Dalai Lama (1981: 136) estimates 80,000 Tibetans fled into exile in the late 1950s and early 1960s.

21. Tibet, prior to its incorporation into the People's Republic of China, had no system of public schools. Tibet's educational system consisted of monastic institutions; two government-run schools intended to train aristocrats for government service; and a handful of short-run experimental private schools (Bass 1998: 1–2). Some Tibetan elite hired private tutors for their children; others sent them to British schools in India (Bass 1998: 2). Most Tibetan children received no formal education whatsoever. Tibet's illiteracy rate was estimated to be 90 percent in 1951 (Bass 1998: 2).

22. According to the Tibetan Women's Delegation (1996), the friends of Tibet organizations that participated were: Australia Tibet Council; Bay Area Friends of Tibet (U.S.); Canada Tibet Committee; International Campaign for Tibet (U.S.); International Committee of Lawyers for Tibet (U.S.); Norwegian Tibet Committee; Swiss-Tibetan Friendship; Tibet Association in Sweden; Tibet Support Group (UK); Tibetan Association of Northern California (U.S.); Tibetan Rights Campaign (U.S.); Tibetan Women's Association, East Coast (U.S.); Tibetan Women's Organisation (Switzerland); U.S.-Tibet Committee (U.S.); Utah Tibet Support Group (U.S.).

23. Statistics I compiled from Tibetan identity card applications indicate that there are at least forty-five monasteries in Kathmandu with at least 795 monks and 138 nuns. Monks and nuns in most monasteries usually come from the same place in Tibet and arrive in Nepal in the same year or in proximate years. The reason seems to be that monks and nuns follow their principal lama into exile and resettle with him.

24. Photos of Steven Seagal Rinpoche with his Tibetan Buddhist teachers can be seen at www.stevenseagal.com.

25. The Karmapa Lama, for example, established 358 monasteries and dharma centers in 38 countries with 131 in the Americas; 130 in Europe; 85 in Asia; 7 in Australia and New Zealand; and 5 in Africa.

26. Another story follows that a student from the University of Wisconsin was studying Tibetan Buddhism in Boudha. As the story goes, he had a lot of problems and was always nervous. He cried sometimes. Some Tibetan friends suggested Tibetan medicine because in Tibetan medical belief, if you are very nervous, eating a little meat from the heart of a rabbit might help. The student replied that he had not tried Tibetan medicine but that studying Tai Kwon Do helped. Sometime later, as the story goes, the student jumped off the roof of a three-story house.

27. The importance of the sexual aspect of these practices to some Western Buddhist practitioners is particularly evident in an article about Tibetan Buddhism published in the United States. The author flaunts his sexuality and argues that it is empowered by Tibetan Buddhist practice. He writes that there are "four instances during which we all momentarily lose control of our minds … [when] 'sneezing, falling asleep into a dream, moving from dream to dream during sleep, and during sex' … [By] training practitioners to gain

clear, compassionate control over their minds during such extreme circumstances, they usually retain enough control … that keeping Buddhist vows … on a day to day basis becomes a piece of cake. Needless to say, as a 'fully qualified yogi' practicing since 1981, I'm familiar with all this. I would love to tell you how to use some of the Annatara Yoga practices but it's one of those things you have to get an initiation for. If I tell you anything, I will return as a snail" (Laurence O. McKinney, "A Dream Is a Wish Your Heart Makes," *Cybersangha*, September 1996).

28. Other Tibetan exiles also argue for non-participation in friends of Tibet relationships. One Tibetan, identified to me only as a "Khampa from Varanasi," in an audio-taped statement that circulated throughout the Tibetan exile community, argued that if other countries really want to help Tibetans, they should stop sending money to Tibetan exiles; help to develop Tibet instead; and expel all of the Tibetans who have settled in their countries so as to force them to return. As long as there are schools and monasteries and settlements for Tibetans in exile, he argued, Tibetans will remain in exile. Only if Tibet is developed will Tibetans want to return.

29. Samdong Rinpoche first published these ideas in a booklet entitled "Den-pai U-tsug," in Tibetan, and "Satyagraha" in Hindi and English. This translation is from the *Tibetan Bulletin*, July–August 1997.

The Southwest Corner of the Jawalakhel Camp

The Main Gate of the Jawalakhel Handicraft Center

Children from Nyalam, Tibet

Atisha School Students

Tibetan Shop Owners

Nepali Weavers Producing a Modern Design Carpet

Wool Dries on the Roof of a Tibetan House Located Just Outside the Jawalakhel Camp

Residents of the Old Age Home Administered by the Snow Lion Foundation

Adult Tibetan Weavers Employed by JHC

Tibetan Monks Symbolize Sacred Wisdom of the Tibetan Past

Tibetan Children Symbolize Hope for a Better Future

The Dorji School, the Largest Tibetan Exile School in Nepal

4

Weapons of Weak States

The relationships the Tibetan exiles maintain with the many international organizations that assist them affect not only the way in which the Tibetan exiles define and understand themselves as Tibetan, they also affect the way in which the Tibetan exiles participate in their host state of Nepal. International organizations advocate on behalf of the Tibetan exiles in Nepal. They pressure the Nepal government into favorable treatment. International organizations are in a position to do so, as the same states and international organizations that advocate on behalf of the Tibetan exiles also help Nepal finance its government expenditures. International aid finances some 70 percent of Nepal's development-related expenditures as well as much of its regular budget.[1] International organizations exercise considerable influence over the government of Nepal.

This chapter examines how the relationship between the Tibetan exiles and the many international organizations that assist them affects Nepal's efforts to govern Tibetans and ethnic Tibetans in its territory. It does so through the issue of state sovereignty. It argues that Nepal's government officials use various "weapons of the weak," such as administrative delays, false compliance, and feigned ignorance, to maintain state sovereignty in a context of multilateral intervention. Weapons of the weak are everyday forms of resistance that lack coordination or planning and avoid direct symbolic confrontation (Scott 1985: 29). Scott (1985) developed the concept to analyze how peasants resist capitalist agricultural development and its human agents. I use the concept to analyze how officials from smaller, less powerful states resist intergovernmental intervention. Because of the role intergovernmental organizations play in financing Nepal's government, Nepal's officials are not in a position to disagree openly with them about how the Tibetan exiles ought to be treated. Two events demonstrate the use of weapons of the weak as an alternative to overt disagreement.

The first involves Nepal government efforts, from April to November of 1995, to return to Tibet as many as three hundred Tibetans newly arrived in Nepal. Tibetans have been arriving as exiles in Nepal continuously since the 1950s (See Table A.1 for statistics on their dates of arrival). The 1995 deportations were neither the first nor the last in a series of efforts to return them. UNHCR, other intergovernmental organizations, and many non-governmental organizations argued that the deportations were a violation of human rights that must be stopped. The suggestion that financial assistance to Nepal could be compromised stopped them for a time, yet as the crisis passed, the deportations continued.

The second event involves a project intended to register all Tibetan exiles in Nepal with the Home Ministry to issue refugee identity booklets (blue books) to them.[2] The project had been discussed off and on for many years, and King Birendra's government even issued blue books to about one-fourth of all Tibetan exiles in Nepal in 1974. Successor governments failed to follow up on the project until 1994, when the newly elected United Marxist-Leninist (UML) government began to issue blue books again. Again, after only one-fourth of the books were issued, the Home Ministry stopped the process. The Nepal government provided no official explanation, claimed its policies had not changed, and promised the project would continue.

Both events demonstrate that Nepal's government officials, in a context in which overt disagreement with intergovernmental organizations is not possible, maintain state sovereignty through weapons of the weak. Weapons of the weak enable Nepal's officials, without compromising foreign aid, to demonstrate to Tibetans, and to the many states and organizations that intervene on behalf of Tibetans, that they will act to maintain Nepal's sovereign status.

This chapter proceeds in four parts. The first examines how Nepal defines state membership. It does so to help explain why the Nepal government has never officially acknowledged the presence of the Tibetan exiles in its territory, why the government, in the words of one Tibetan exile in Nepal, "sees us but does not see us." Nepal has no legal category that includes the Tibetans, yet it does extend certain rights to them. The second part focuses on the status of the Tibetans. It argues that the Tibetans have ambiguous status. Just as other people with ambiguous status are perceived as a potential threat to the social order (Douglas 1966; Malkki 1989, 1994, 1995b), so the Tibetan exiles are perceived as a potential threat to Nepal. The third part explores the parameters of the potential threat the Tibetan exiles pose. It argues that the Tibetan exiles are implicated in two kinds of threats to Nepal. They are implicated in the potential for internal rebellion against a Hindu-dominated state, as well as in the potential for external aggression by various other states that claim the Tibetans as their own. Nepali officials, as a result, would like to contain the economic and political influence of the Tibetan exiles, if not rid themselves entirely of the responsibility for hosting them. The fourth part examines how Nepali officials respond to intergovernmental organizations that advocate on behalf of the Tibetan exiles. It argues that they use weapons of the weak to resist pressure to grant the Tibetan exiles more favorable treatment. It explores how Nepali officials used weapons of the weak to maintain state sovereignty throughout the 1995 deportations and the Tibetan blue book project.

The Nepal State and Its Norms of Membership

Nepal is governed by a lineage of kings who trace their ancestry to Prithvi Narayan Shah. Shah was an eighteenth-century military leader who conquered the lands surrounding his home territory, the kingdom of Gorka, to consolidate and create the Nepal state (Sever 1993: 3–22). The Nepal state, since its consolidation in 1769, has transformed many times in terms of its political organization and membership structure. The present king rules over a constitutional monarchy, which since 1990 has been undergoing a series of democratic reforms that guarantee a broad range of rights to Nepal's citizen subjects. These reforms are changing the way in which the Nepal government relates to its citizen subjects and to the many other peoples resident within the borders of Nepal.

Nepal today defines and regulates state membership through a principle of citizenship. It has done so since 1962 when it adopted its first constitution. Prior to 1962, Nepal defined state membership not in terms of citizenship but in terms of landholding arrangements. The differential rights and responsibilities of members of the state depended upon what type of land they held, whether *rajya, birta, jagir,* or *kipat* (Regmi 1965). Non-landholders had no direct relationship with the state; whoever held the land on which they lived maintained complete authority over them. Nepal, through its 1962 constitution (article 7), however, defined citizenship for the first time to include all people born in Nepal, all people whose parents were born in Nepal, and all women married to male Nepali citizens. It also provided for citizenship through naturalization or through the bequest of Nepal's king. Compared with many other states worldwide, Nepal maintained a very inclusive definition.[3]

From the 1964 Citizenship Act to the 1992 Citizenship Amendment Act, however, Nepal's citizenship laws have become much more restrictive. Birth in Nepal no longer provides unqualified access to citizenship. Nepal now grants unqualified access only to the descendants of male Nepali citizens. Citizenship through naturalization is now much more restrictive as well. In accordance with the Citizenship Amendment Act of 1992, citizenship by naturalization can be requested only by people of good conduct and character, engaged in some occupation in Nepal, who are able to speak and write Nepali, who have renounced any previous nationality, who have either married a male Nepali citizen or have lived in Nepal for fifteen years, and who are from a country where Nepali people can apply for naturalized citizenship. Nepal's king may still grant honorary citizenship to anyone at any time, as he did for a number of Tibetans at the end of the Tibetan guerrilla war.

Nepal considers anyone who is not a citizen to be a foreigner. Unlike many European states, but similar to all other South Asian states, Nepal maintains no intermediary legal category for non-citizen residents.[4] People are either citizens or foreigners. Nepal has no formal legal category even for refugees; it has neither signed any of the international legal instruments that define refugee status nor developed its own nationally defined refugee law. Nepal may allow a group of refugees (people who have fled their own country out of a well-founded fear of persecution) to remain within state borders, yet it provides them with no formal legal status.

Nepal guarantees a range of rights to both citizens and to foreigners resident within state territory. In 1962, Nepal guaranteed to all citizens rights to equal protection (article 10 of the 1962 constitution), free speech, expression, assembly, movement and residence in Nepal (article 11), rights to acquire and sell property (article 11), and not to be exiled (article 12). It guaranteed to all persons resident in Nepal rights to freedom (article 11), religion (article 14), not to be punished arbitrarily (article 11) and not to be exploited (article 13). With the passage of the 1990 constitution, the range of rights expanded for both citizens and residents. In 1990, Nepal guaranteed to all citizens rights to equality (article 11), information (article 16), property (article 17), and the right not to be exiled (article 21). To all persons resident in Nepal, it guaranteed rights to freedom, opinion, expression, assembly, free movement and residence (article 12); rights to press and publication (article 13), to religion (article 19), to privacy (article 22), and to form political parties (article 112); rights against arbitrary punishment (article 14), preventive detention (article 15), and exploitation (article 20). The 1990 constitution also, for the first time, guaranteed rights to communities. These include the right to preserve and promote the language, script, and culture of any community in Nepal and to operate schools up to the primary level in the community's own mother tongue (article 18).

Legislation enacted separately from these constitutional provisions further defined the rights of individuals and communities in Nepal. The 1961 Industrial Enterprises Act, for example, restricted to Nepali citizens the right to own small-scale cottage and village industries in Nepal. The 1964 Land Reform and Ukhada Land Tenure Acts, likewise, restricted to Nepali citizens rights to own and inherit land in Nepal. The 1950 Nepal-India Treaty of Peace and Friendship extended to Indian citizens the same rights to industrial and economic development (article 6), residence, property ownership, participation in trade and commerce, and free movement (article 7) as citizens of Nepal. The Nepal government has been trying for years to renegotiate the treaty.

The Ambiguous Membership Status of the Tibetan Exiles in Nepal

The Tibetan exiles, as both a community and as individuals, are ambiguous members of the Nepal state. As a community, the Tibetan exiles are ambiguous members, as the Nepal government has accepted their presence yet has never officially defined their legal status. It has never officially recognized them as refugees; it has no formal legal category through which to do so. As individuals, the Tibetan exiles are equally ambiguous. Although many Tibetan exiles have acquired Nepali citizenship, most have done so illegally, so that the citizenship status of all Tibetan exiles, even those with a legitimate legal claim, remains in doubt. This ambiguous membership status poses problems for both the Nepal government and the Tibetan exiles themselves. For the Nepal government, it raises issues of sovereignty and security. Nepali officials implicate the Tibetan exiles in the potential for internal rebellion as well as external aggression. For the Tibetan exiles, their ambiguous membership status raises issues of loyalty and identity. (I explore these issues briefly here, as they relate to Nepal's efforts to govern the Tibetan exiles. I discuss them further in chapters five and six).

Throughout the Tibetan exile, successive governments in Nepal have accepted the presence of Tibetan exiles yet have avoided formal definition of their status. In the early years of the Tibetan exile, from 1950 to 1960, King Mahendra unofficially accepted the presence of Tibetan exiles in Nepal, yet never defined their status. King Birendra granted honorary citizenship to 200 to 300 Tibetan exiles and issued refugee identity booklets to approximately 4,000 others, yet he too never officially clarified their status. The refugee identity booklets, although they used the term "refugee," failed to clarify their status, as Nepal neither accepts any of the international legal instruments related to refugees nor has its own refugee law. Issued to demilitarized guerrilla fighters, the booklets were meant primarily to monitor their movements not to clarify their status. The refugee identity booklets the United Marxist-Leninist (UML) government issued to Tibetan exiles in 1995 have the same problem. After the UML government issued booklets to only about one-fourth of all Tibetan exiles in Nepal, moreover, the UML government stopped the process. The Tibetan exiles remain undefined.

Without formal recognition of their legal status as a community, many Tibetan exiles, as individuals, have acquired citizenship in Nepal. Estimates of the number of Tibetans with citizenship range from a low of 10 percent, when only those with "good citizenship" (i.e., acquired through legal means) are considered, to a high of 90 percent, when all Tibetans believed to possess Nepali citizenship documents are considered. Most estimates, which assume that all Tibetan exiles with land or a business in Nepal have citizenship documents, average 60 percent, approximately twelve thousand Tibetan exiles.

More definitive estimates are unfeasible, even with Nepal government records, as many Tibetan exiles use Nepali names when they acquire citizenship documents illegally.

Most Tibetan exiles with citizenship documents have acquired them illegally. As a result, the citizenship status of all Tibetan exiles remains in doubt. One Tibetan businessman explains: "Even though I am a citizen, Nepalese do not accept my citizenship. They think that I am a 'lama,' which means that they can give me a hard time. In all government offices, if a 'lama' comes in for anything, that is someone to ask for bribes.... Tibetans are known for taking shortcuts to get work done quickly. Although wealthier Tibetans can do this, they raise the price for everyone else. It is harder for Tibetans who are not wealthy" (personal communication, August 29, 1995).

There are two principal legal means through which Tibetan exiles have acquired citizenship in Nepal. The first involves the 200 to 300 former guerrilla fighters to whom King Birendra granted honorary citizenship in 1974 for surrendering to the Nepal army. The second involves 100 to 150 children of Tibetan-Newar marriages (*khatsara*) who acquired Nepali citizenship with the assistance of Nepal consular officers in Tibet before the exile. The history of this latter group is very interesting. Up until the time Tibet was incorporated into the PRC, the Newars maintained a large trading community in Lhasa, Shigatse, and other trade centers in Tibet estimated to have numbered about 20,000 people (Nepali 1965). Many Newar traders in Tibet married Tibetan women, even when they had Newar wives at home. Under Nepali law, until recently, male children of Tibetan-Newar marriages were considered to be Nepali citizens and female children were considered to be Tibetan citizens (Nepali 1965). When the Chinese incorporated Tibet into the PRC, Nepal's consular officers in Tibet provided both male and female *khatsara* children, and their families, with the documents they needed to acquire citizenship in Nepal.[5] One Tibetan woman, who acquired citizenship in this manner, explains:

> After my father was imprisoned [in Tibet], my grandmother went to Shigatse and applied at the Nepal consulate for a visa. Someone in our family intermarried with a Newar, and so she was able to get this paper, and with this paper, we were able to get citizenship. I got citizenship just before I got married by taking the paper to the CDO [chief district officer] and applying. There are 100 to 150 families in Nepal who were in the same situation and we all applied like this at the same time.... If there is a chance to make your life better and to do something for yourself, then why not do it? (personal communication, August 1, 1995)

There are many other means, both illegal and quasi-legal, through which the Tibetan exiles have acquired citizenship in Nepal. Some who are not descended from Tibetan-Newar marriages, for example, have applied for citizenship under the pretense that they are. As one Tibetan in Nepal explained, when an old Nepali man dies, following his death, neighboring

Tibetans may go to the CDO and claim to be his heirs. They say that their Newar father has died, and they use documents obtained from the family of the deceased to claim descent. Other Tibetans claim that their fathers were former guerrilla fighters who had honorary citizenship. As another Tibetan explains: "My brother had to get Nepali citizenship to be able to go to the US.... My uncle [from Boudha] thought of how to get it. One man from the Jorpati camp [where former guerrilla fighters were resettled] had just died. My uncle acquired his papers, and my brother applied at the CDO as his son." Other Tibetans simply purchase their citizenship documents. Another Tibetan explains: "In the CDO, there is always one or more men who can be bought. When that is discovered, many people go to get citizenship.... Sometimes a mistake is made and a Tibetan is caught offering money for papers and is arrested.... It costs only about 1,500 rupees for citizenship ... it is not that expensive. The process is even easier now because of democracy. During *panchayat* times [under the government of the king], the authorities could do whatever they wanted and there was no way to argue. No one had any rights. Now, at least, if something happens, you can hire a lawyer" (personal communication, August 30, 1995).

In the high borderland regions of Nepal, Tibetans explain, it is easier to purchase citizenship documents than in Kathmandu. The ethnic Tibetan peoples who inhabit the borderlands share not only the same religion and customs as the Tibetan exiles but also have many of the same grievances toward the Nepal government. Issuing citizenship documents to Tibetans, for them, is not only a way through which to help people with whom they feel a sense of affiliation, but is also a way through which to express disagreement with the government in Kathmandu. Another Tibetan explains: "It is easy for Tibetans to get citizenship certificates from Sherpa officials. The CDO in the Chialsa district is Sherpa. Tibetans can get citizenship papers from him by saying that their name is, for example, 'Tenzin Namgyal Sherpa' ... It is the same for the Tibetans in Tserok [Mustang] and Dhorpatan. They say that their names are, for example, 'Samten Dorje Lama' or 'Karma Yeshe Gurung'" (personal communication, April 23, 1995). The names they use (Sherpa, Lama, or Gurung) imply that they are members of the Sherpa, Tamang, or Gurung ethnic Tibetan communities, all of which can claim citizenship in Nepal.

There is another way in which Tibetan exiles in the high borderland regions have been able to acquire citizenship documents. "Every once in awhile," a Tibetan exile from the Everest region explains: "The district officers assemble a team to go out and register people for citizenship because it is difficult for some Nepali people in remote villages to go to the district office. When the team registers Nepalese for citizenship, they often also register Tibetans.... In general, it has been very easy for Tibetans living in Nepal to acquire citizenship. It is difficult only for Tibetans who have come from India" (personal communication, April 23, 1995).

Among themselves, Tibetan exiles struggle with what it means for them to acquire citizenship in Nepal. How does being the citizen (*yulmi*) relate to the issue of political loyalty (*zhen-pa*)? Is it possible to maintain loyalty to more than one state? Does the acquisition of citizenship in any state necessarily imply the abandonment of the Tibetan political cause? The changes in the policies of the Dalai Lama's exile administration complicate the issue further. Throughout most of the Tibetan exile, the exile administration maintained that the acquisition of citizenship in any state necessarily implies disloyalty to Tibet. In 1990, with the ratification of the Charter for the Tibetan Exiles, however, the exile administration permitted Tibetans to acquire citizenship in other states provided that they also fulfill a number of qualifications. They include maintaining loyalty to Tibet, observing the rules of the Charter, paying taxes to the exile administration, maintaining the Tibetan political cause, and performing obligations imposed by the exile administration in the interest of Tibet.[6] The change was intended both to reflect political reality, as many Tibetan exiles had already acquired citizenship in other states, and to facilitate the resettlement of Tibetan exiles emigrating to the United States under the U.S.-Tibet Resettlement Project.

Some Tibetan exiles, in accordance with the logic that loyalty is possible toward only one state, argue that citizenship in Nepal necessarily implies disloyalty to Tibet and the Tibetan political cause. Nepali citizenship, they argue, causes Tibetans to "forget and stop loving their own motherland," to "sell their country, bring poison, chaos and conflict to their people and nation," and "break laws just for personal benefit and interest." Nepali citizenship, they argue, "weakens the spirit of the Tibetan national cause," "weakens international support for the Tibetan cause," "causes the Tibetan culture and Tibetan festivals to disappear," "causes the Tibetan language to disappear," and creates a "great risk of losing our precious religion."[7]

Other Tibetans, more pragmatically, argue that loyalty is more flexible and that citizenship in Nepal may actually help the Tibetan political cause. Nepali citizenship, they argue, not only leads to a happy and secure life, but it also helps preserve the Tibetan religion, by enabling Tibetans to build monasteries in Nepal; preserve the Tibetan culture, by enabling Tibetans to build schools in Nepal to educate their children "as Tibetans"; and preserve Tibetan traditions, by enabling Tibetans to live in their own way with greater "human rights." Without Nepali citizenship, they argue, Tibetans would not have the opportunity to preserve their religion, culture, language, and traditions, the basis for their claim to an independent Tibet.

The acquisition of Nepali citizenship, still other Tibetans argue, is unrelated to their loyalty to Tibet. As one Tibetan businessman argued, there are two kinds of citizenship—real citizenship and citizenship that facilitates business. Only real citizenship implies political loyalty, as citizenship that facilitates business is only a practical arrangement. Another argued:

In general, people can have citizenship of Nepal and still be committed to the Tibetan cause. Some people who have citizenship work very hard for the Tibetan cause. Others who do not have citizenship, even still, their minds are somewhere else ... like in America. (personal communication, November 4, 1995)

Loyalty and identity are the principal issues that emerge among Tibetan exiles when discussing their ambiguous citizenship status in Nepal. For Nepal's officials, issues of sovereignty and security are more prominent. Nepali officials implicate the Tibetan exiles in both internal and external threats to Nepal. We may view their concerns in terms of the issues they themselves raise–the threat of internal rebellion; the threat of Chinese aggression–or we may view them in structural terms. Mary Douglas (1966) has demonstrated that people in ambiguous structural positions are often perceived as potential threats to the social order. She argues:

> Consider beliefs about persons in a marginal state. These are people who are somehow left out of the patterning of society, who are placeless. They may be doing nothing morally wrong, but their status is indefinable. Take, for example, the unborn child. Its present position is ambiguous, its future equally... It is often treated as both vulnerable and dangerous. The Lele regard the unborn child and its mother as in constant danger, but they also credit the unborn child with capricious ill-will which makes it a danger to others. (1966: 95)

Malkki (1989, 1994, 1995b) applies the argument to the position of refugees, migrants, and other stateless peoples. We may also apply the argument in the particular case of the Tibetan exiles. Part of the reason they are perceived as a threat to Nepal, I argue, is that they are structurally ambiguous.

Sovereignty, Security, and the Status of the Tibetan Exiles

Nepali officials regularly concede that the Tibetan exiles have done much to benefit Nepal. They often cite the role of the Tibetan exiles in developing the carpet industry. The carpet industry, by 1995, employed an estimated 200,000 Nepali citizens and earned more foreign exchange for Nepal than any other industry. Nepali officials also regularly cite the role of the Tibetans in the construction of numerous schools and monasteries in Nepal. Some even discuss the cultural contributions Tibetan exiles have made, such as introducing *mo-mos* (Tibetan dumplings) into the Nepali diet.

Beneath the surface, however, Nepali officials harbor suspicions about the Tibetan exiles and their political intentions. They implicate the Tibetan exiles in the potential for internal rebellions as well as for external aggression. The similarities the Tibetan exiles share with other ethnic Tibetan populations in Nepal, combined with their organizational capacity, is the basis for the perception of an internal threat. The potential for other states or international organizations to intervene in Nepal to act either on behalf of or against the Tibetan exiles is the basis for the perception of an external threat.

Tibetan exiles share many similarities with Nepal's other ethnic Tibetan peoples. They include people as diverse as the Sherpa, the Tamang, the Gurung, and the Limbu. All of these people have two aspects in common. First, Nepal's high-caste political elite consider them all to be low-caste "bhote." They consider them, in other words, to be dirty, backward, uneducated hill-dwellers who cannot be trusted. The second is that, since Nepal's 1990 democratic reforms, they all have been organizing politically as never before to protest years of discrimination under a nation defined in terms of Hinduism, the Nepali language, and the monarchy (Shah 1993). Nepal's ethnic Tibetans comprise nearly one-fourth of the sixty ethnic groups defined by the 1991 census.[8] Taken together, they constitute approximately 12 percent of Nepal's total population.

The Tibetan exiles are the most economically powerful and politically organized of all of Nepal's ethnic Tibetan peoples. As the director of the Tibet Office explains, the Tibetan exiles are "very powerful" and the Nepal government is concerned:

> Any Tibetan event automatically becomes the talk of the town.... Tibetans are very visible in the business community and all over Kathmandu.... They [the government] can see that we have tremendous organizational capacity and that we have the ability to sway the opinions and the actions of many people in Nepal.... The government would like to put us all in one place where they can watch us closely. Either that, or they would like to disperse us widely throughout Nepal so that we cannot organize easily. The government does not have the same organizational capacity [as we do] ... they insist we maintain a low profile. (personal communication, July 28, 1995)

Tibetan exiles demonstrate their organizational capacity through the public events they sponsor, such as the Tibetan New Year and the Dalai Lama's birthday party. During any of these events, Tibetan exile leaders must assure the Nepal Home Ministry that they will take personal responsibility for whatever occurs.

Despite the similarities the Tibetan exiles share with Nepal's other ethnic Tibetan peoples, and despite their organizational capacity, the Tibetan exiles are unlikely, in the present political context, to organize politically with any of them against the Nepal government. Tibetan exile leaders give two principal reasons why this is so. First, although high-caste Nepalese may consider all of Nepal's ethnic Tibetans (including the Tibetan exiles) to be all more-or-less the same, the Tibetan exiles perceive significant differences between themselves and other ethnic Tibetans. They categorize Nepal's ethnic Tibetan peoples along a continuum of similarities and difference from themselves. Tibetan exiles consider themselves most similar to the Manangi, Lopa, and Sherpa people, as they all use the same script, speak similar languages, follow the same religion, wear similar clothing, and permit intermarriage. Tibetan exiles consider themselves less similar to Tamang, Magar, Gurung, and Thakali, whose languages, customs, and religion are similar, yet who often speak Nepali and wear Nepali clothing.[9] They consider themselves even less similar to Rai, Limbu, and Kirati, who follow many Nepali customs in addition to speaking Nepali and wearing Nepali clothing.[10] Tibetan exiles, in some contexts, use the same term, "Tibetan" (*pö-ba*), to refer to both themselves and all of Nepal's other ethnic Tibetans. In most contexts, however, they make a distinction between themselves as "Tibetan exiles" (*kap-chol-wai pö-ba*) and other Tibetan-like peoples in Nepal (*pö-mi rig-pa*).

The second reason the Tibetan exiles are unlikely to organize politically with any of Nepal's other ethnic Tibetans is that they do not consider themselves to have the same political interests. It is better for them, they argue, to support the government in power, as it enables them to conduct business. If they supported Nepal's other ethnic Tibetans, they argue, they would undermine their ability to conduct business and would ultimately advance the interests of no one. A prominent Tibetan businessman explains why:

> First, many Tibetans do not have genuine naturalized citizenship, and the falsehood of their papers would be exposed immediately if they became involved politically. Second, many Tibetans in Nepal do not speak Nepali well enough. We know how to speak it for business purposes but Nepali people know we are really Tibetan as soon as we start to speak. Third, most Tibetans in Nepal hold real feelings for Tibet and its future. We think about the problems in Nepal as other people's problems. (personal communication, September 11, 1995)

Another Tibetan concurs:

> There are many "all-Mongol" parties in Nepal, but we do not belong to them.... Nepal is trapped between India and China and is always looking at them to decide what to do. We do not want to get involved in that. (personal communication, July 9, 1995)

Tibetan exiles may be unwilling, in the present political context, to become involved in Nepal's ethnic Tibetan politics, yet it is unknown when they may consider it in their interest to become involved. Tibetan exiles have, in the past, become involved in Nepali politics as a means to protect their own interests. There are many Tibetan exiles, for example, who donate to political parties. One Tibetan businessman, a contributor to the Nepal Congress Party, for example, explained his involvement with: "We know how terrible it is to live under communist rule. We know how terrible communists can be. We do not want communism to take hold in Nepal" (personal communication, August 30, 1995). As it is unknown when Tibetan exiles may become involved politically in Nepal, Nepali officials remain concerned about their potential to pose an internal threat.

Nepali officials also express concern about the external threats they perceive the Tibetan exiles to pose. The potential for other states, or for intergovernmental organizations, to intervene in Nepal either on behalf of, or against, the Tibetan exiles is the basis for the perception of an external threat. Nepali officials most often implicate the Tibetan exiles in the potential for Chinese aggression against Nepal. For that reason, Nepal has requested that the Tibetan exiles not engage in pro-independence activities in its territory. Nepal responded with force in the 1970s when Tibetan guerrilla fighters did engage in pro-independence activities in Nepal. Nepal deployed its army against the Tibetan guerrillas for refusing to surrender their weapons and disband their camps at the end of the guerrilla war (upon the withdrawal of U.S. support for them). Nepal responds with force whenever Tibetan exiles organize explicit political protests against China. One such example occurred in September 1995 when a group of Tibetan exiles staged a demonstration in front of the Chinese embassy to protest the thirtieth anniversary of the establishment of the Tibetan Autonomous Region of China. Tibetan exiles blamed China, not Nepal, for their detention. As one Tibetan exile explains, "It is not in Nepal's interest to have Tibetans in jail because then it costs money to feed them" (personal communication, September 3, 1995). Just how likely it is that China would intervene militarily in Nepal is difficult to determine. The threat is enough to influence Nepal's policies, however. Nepali historians discuss a long-term strategy among Nepali officials of balancing the interests of India against the interests of China to maintain Nepal's sovereignty and security (Rose 1971; Uprety 1980, 1984; Subba 1993; and Dahal 1995).

Nepali officials also implicate Tibetan exiles in the potential for intervention by the Republic of China on Taiwan. A recent court case in Nepal illustrates their concerns. It also reveals that some Tibetan exiles maintain citizenship simultaneously in many countries besides Nepal. The case involves Chu An Tsujen, a citizen of Taiwan who was accused of applying for, and receiving, Nepali citizenship "based on false particulars," with his Tibetan name Chede Tshering. As reported in Nepal's press, the case was brought to trial in 1993, yet before it could be heard, the government of Taiwan requested in a letter to Nepal's Foreign Ministry that the case be dismissed. In order to protect the job security of the many Nepali people who work in Taiwan, the Nepal government complied with the request. Without going to trial, Chu An Tsujen's citizenship was revoked and he was barred from entering Nepal for ten years. Nepali officials interpreted the case to represent a threat the Tibetan exiles pose to its external security. The press made a point of saying that the Nepal government has no way of knowing how many more Tibetan exiles in Nepal are also citizens of Taiwan.[11]

Nepali officials implicate the Tibetan exiles in both internal and external security threats. For that reason, Nepal would like to contain the economic and political influence of the Tibetan exiles as much as possible. The relationship the Tibetan exiles maintain with the many international organizations that assist them, however, complicate Nepal's ability to govern them as they wish. International organizations that intervene in Nepal on behalf of the Tibetan exiles include the U.S. Agency for International Development, the Swiss Development Corporation, and in the cases I discuss below, the United Nations High Commissioner for Refugees (UNHCR).

The Normative Dynamics of UNHCR Assistance to Tibetan Exiles in Nepal

Intervention by UNHCR in Nepal on behalf of the Tibetan exiles has a long history. During the initial exile, UNHCR intervention remained largely unpublicized, as the U.N. took the position that the Tibetan situation was to be considered China's internal affair. Holborn's (1975) history of the UNHCR describes its involvement in Nepal on behalf of Tibetan exiles both in the 1960s and in the 1970s, however. UNHCR also assisted in the demilitarization of the Tibetans at the end of the guerrilla war. In 1989, when the Nepal government allowed UNHCR to establish an office to coordinate assistance to the Bhutanese in Nepal, UNHCR resumed interventions on behalf of the Tibetans. On occasion, as during the deportations and the Tibetan blue book project, Nepali officials interpret UNHCR intervention as a violation of Nepal's sovereign status. They respond through the use of weapons of the weak.

Deportations and Diplomacy

The 1995 deportations are intricately interrelated with the operation of the UNHCR-Tibetan reception center system, the principal point of contact among Tibetans, UNHCR officials, and Nepal's immigration officials. It was through the reception center system that the deportations were discovered both to have occurred and to have ended. The deportations demonstrate Nepal government resistance to the reception center system.

The Dalai Lama's exile administration began the reception center system first in India. It expanded the system into Nepal in 1983 to facilitate the emigration of increasing numbers of Tibetans out of Tibet after the Chinese government relaxed its border controls in the 1980s.[12] UNHCR became involved with the reception center system in 1989, soon after it was invited into Nepal to coordinate assistance to the Bhutanese. Prior to UNHCR involvement, the Dalai Lama's exile administration managed the reception center system on its own.

UNHCR's participation in the reception center system is governed by separate agreements it signed with the Nepal government and with the Tibet Office. UNHCR's agreement with the Nepal government permits UNHCR to finance the reception center system and to administer assistance to Tibetan exiles in exchange for two concessions. The first is that Nepal is to serve as a transit country only. The second is that the reception center system, and all its activities, are to remain quiet. UNHCR's agreement with the Tibet Office, the implementing partner for the reception center system, specifies the various categories of expenses UNHCR will cover and grants responsibility for managing the reception center system to the Tibet Office.

Since 1989, when UNHCR became involved, approximately 2,500 Tibetans have arrived in Nepal through the system each year. Most new arrivals find their way to the main reception center building on their own, as the details of the center are well known among Tibetans. Occasionally, Nepal's police arrest newcomer Tibetans before they arrive at the center. When that occurs, what usually happens is that the police notify UNHCR of their arrival, UNHCR sends a protection officer to conduct status determination procedures, and most Tibetans are released to UNHCR for documentation and for transport to India through the reception center system. All parties involved in the management of the system attest that it generally works as planned, that the police generally cooperate, and that the system alleviates some of the more serious problems new Tibetan arrivals face in Nepal, such as a need for emergency medical attention (mostly to treat frostbite).

In April 1995, however, the Nepal police began to arrest and to return to Tibet groups of Tibetans newly arrived in Nepal. Fifty at one time, thirty-three at another, more than three hundred Tibetan exiles were reported returned during an eight-month period.[13] One of the first groups to be returned, a group of twenty-five, had been brought all the way from the border at Kodari to the Immigration Office in Kathmandu before being transported back to Tibet. UNHCR officials in Kathmandu had been notified of the arrival of the group so they could arrange for status determination procedures. The sudden disappearance of the group was the first indication that the reception center system was no longer working as planned.

News about the deportations spread quickly throughout the expatriate community in Kathmandu as ambassadors and other intergovernmental officials began to speculate on why they had begun. No one really knew why, as the Nepal government denied any change in policy. U.S. embassy employees said only that they found the deportations "confusing." Given that "Nepal receives significantly more aid from Western countries than from China," they suggested that "Maybe Nepal is deporting Tibetans in order to get more aid from China next year."[14]

As discussions about the deportations continued, however, a dominant interpretation emerged. The expatriate community began to see the deportations as indicative of a new, hidden but powerful, anti-Tibet conspiracy, which developed soon after the ideologically communist UML party was elected into power in Nepal. The London-based Tibet Information Network (TIN) picked up on the story and reported that the deportations signaled an "apparent shift in policy towards Tibetan escapees" that began "only days after the Nepalese Prime Minister Man Mohan Adhikari ... told Party leaders [in Beijing] that Nepal recognized China's claim to Tibet."[15] TIN neglected to mention that all other governments that have ever come to power in Nepal—communist or otherwise—have also recognized China's claim to Tibet and that it has been standard policy since 1956.[16] They explained the deportations in terms of a new Nepal-China communist alliance intent to victimize the Tibetans.

An alternative interpretation of the deportations is that they represent the ongoing use of weapons of the weak by members of the Nepal government, and by the Nepal police, to resist the reception center system. The reception center system allows UNHCR and the Dalai Lama's exile administration to control the Nepal-Tibet border. Control over state borders is a powerful symbol of state sovereignty that governments do not relinquish easily. The deportations represent efforts on the part of the UML government, newly elected in 1995, to regain control over the border and to reclaim sovereign status.

There are many reasons why it makes sense to view the deportations in this manner. The first is that it helps to account for a more general pattern of Tibetan deportations from Nepal. The 1995 deportations were neither the first nor the last in a series of efforts on the part of successive Nepal governments to return newly arrived Tibetan exiles to Tibet. The 1995 deportations, as they occurred under the ideologically communist UML government, may have invited more publicity than others, yet they differed in no other way from those which occurred under Congress-party or RPP-coalition governments or even under the government of the king. Tibetan exiles themselves suggested the idea to me that the deportations represent a reassertion of Nepal government control over its borders, rather than a new Nepal-China conspiracy. As one Tibetan observer, soon after the deportations began, commented:

> Just as they do with gold smugglers, the Nepal government goes through periods of squeezing and periods of relaxing. The government allows smuggling to go on and on and then one day customs officers seize a couple hundred kilograms of gold and express shock that smuggling occurs. When everything is normal again, smuggling starts again. So as with the refugees, it happens sometimes that immigration officers arrest and deport a couple hundred Tibetans and express shock at the idea that Tibetans are coming into the country. As time passes, they start to allow them in again. The trick is to determine when the government will start to squeeze and when it will start to relax. (personal communication, July 3, 1995)

The second reason it makes sense to view the deportations not as a new threat but as a general pattern of resistance is that it enables a more nuanced consideration of Nepal's and China's interests. The view that the deportations represent a new communist conspiracy against Tibet suggests that China requested them, possibly in return for increased aid to Nepal. It is important to ask, however, why China would request the deportations in the first place. Chinese officials must have known that preventing the Tibetans from leaving Tibet would invite more negative publicity than a few hundred exiles from a forty-year-old conflict would otherwise receive. China benefits in no way from the deportations. Nepal, however, does benefit. Nepal is already host to a large and growing expatriate Indian population as well as an estimated 86,000 Nepali-speaking Bhutanese. Nepal faces perpetual problems controlling its borders. It reasserts control when it can.

Tibetan exiles in Nepal also found it hard to believe that China requested the deportations, for the deportations contradict what they interpret China's main interest to be. If China's main interest is to secure control over Tibet, they asked, why would they stop Tibetans from leaving? As one Tibetan explained:

> Maybe the Chinese premier did say to him [Nepal's Prime Minister Adhikari] that he should stop Tibetans from coming and maybe the prime minister did make a comment to the Immigration Office. But in my own personal opinion, I think that the Chinese government prefers it when Tibetans leave.... Then Tibet becomes open for the resettlement of more Han Chinese and one day, with so many Han Chinese in Tibet, Tibetans will lose any claim they have to Tibet at all. (personal communication, July 3, 1995)

The director of the reception center system, well positioned to speculate on China's interests, supported the idea that the Chinese government prefers it when Tibetans flee into exile. He, too, wondered why China would support the deportations. "The Chinese do not stop Tibetans from leaving," he once commented. "They are happy to see them go because then they think that there will be more land for them" (November 9, 1995).

The third reason it makes sense to view the deportations as part of a general pattern of resistance is that they occurred concurrently with a growing recognition that the reception center system was not working as planned. The reception center system, although it was supposed to remain unpublicized, is now well known. Use of the system by non-governmental human rights organizations to gather information exposed its existence. Foreign embassy staff, TIN reporters, and representatives from other friends of Tibet organizations now target the center as a site at which to protest events such as the arrest of Tibetans at the China-Nepal border. A UNHCR protection officer complained: "They never understand the real situation, and they always understand an offense against a Tibetan to be a personal offense against themselves. They always take it personally. The Nepal government is trying to prevent such activities from occurring" (personal communication, April 27, 1995). Nepali officials started to view the system as a political embarrassment.

In addition to the publicity, the reception center system also started to assist Tibetans who cannot, under even the most liberal interpretation of international refugee law, be considered refugees, yet who suffer instead from the same basic problems as Nepal's own population.[17] Independence demonstrations in Lhasa from 1987 to 1989 did result in the arrival of some bona-fide refugees in Nepal, but in the words of the reception center staff themselves, those Tibetans constitute "only the smallest percentage of cases." Poverty in Tibet and better opportunities in exile are the reasons most Tibetans give for leaving Tibet. That raises the question of why the Nepal government should commit efforts and resources to alleviating poverty and a basic lack of opportunity among Tibetans rather than among its own population. The deportations represent Nepal government resistance against a requirement to assist foreigners who are no worse off than their own citizens. UNHCR continues to help Tibetans to emigrate due to their poverty and basic lack of opportunity anyway. They do so, as they consider Tibetans to be "persons of concern," not "refugees." They consider poverty and a basic lack of opportunity to be legitimate enough to keep the system going. A UNHCR protection officer explained:

> Some people might argue that the Tibetans are only economic migrants, but then other people might argue that the Chinese are implementing discriminatory policies that cause economic deprivation. Because we do not use the term "refugee" when we do status determination procedures, we do not adhere to the definitions very strictly. We can apply more liberal criteria when admitting people. (personal communication, April 27, 1995)

The reception center system also started to facilitate Tibetans' efforts to travel back and forth between China, Nepal, and India to conduct trade and to go on pilgrimage rather than to escape into exile as initially planned. In 1993, when nearly 3,700 Tibetans traveled through the reception center system, a 48 percent increase over 1992, many of them used the system to finance their travel to a Kalachakra initiation the Dalai Lama performed in India that year. After the initiation ceremony, many returned to Tibet. Tibetans use the system for this purpose because it is easy to do so. As part of the system, all newly arrived Tibetan exiles in Nepal, if traveling alone, receive 2,500 Nepali rupees, twice the amount of most monthly office salaries in Nepal. If traveling together as a family, the head of the family receives 2,500 Nepali rupees and 1,000 Nepali rupees for each additional family member. All Tibetan exiles also receive a free one-way bus ticket to Delhi. The system subsidizes Tibetan travel.

The reception center system was no longer working as planned. It had become well known; it was facilitating the emigration of people who cannot be considered refugees; and it was subsidizing cross-border travel. In addition, as Nepali officials began the Tibetan blue book project, described below, they became aware that, contrary to the terms of the UNHCR-Nepal agreement, there were many Tibetans in Nepal who had arrived after 1989. The general perception was a loss of control over the border. The deportations represent a reassertion of control.

In response to the deportations, the U.S., British, and Australian embassies sent a joint communiqué to the Nepal foreign ministry to pressure the government to stop them. That foreign aid to Nepal was at stake was suggested. As the U.S. ambassador to Nepal explained:

> Tibetans have a lot of support in Washington, and with Jesse Helms, who is both anti-communist and anti-aid, as the chairman of the foreign relations committee, the Nepal government should be very, very careful about what it does. Actions against the Tibetans could easily be used as an excuse to make even deeper cuts into [Nepal's] aid package. (U.S. Ambassador Sandy Vogelgesgang, personal communication, September 9, 1995)

The U.S. ambassador expressed disapproval by attending the Dalai Lama's birthday celebration. It was the first time a U.S. ambassador accepted the invitation to attend. The ambassador herself explained that her attendance, "aside from being a tribute to a nationally-recognized world religious leader on his birthday," was meant: "To signal to the Nepal government that the U.S. does not approve of the policy of deporting Tibetans.... How can they criticize Bhutan for its human rights violations against Nepali-speakers and then turn around and deport Tibetan refugees from their own country? It is a serious human rights violation that must stop."[18]

UNHCR, likewise, responded to the deportations by hiring a new protection officer, an American with a background in human rights issues in China, both to patrol the Nepal-China border and to monitor police treatment of Tibetans.[19] To assist its new officer, UNHCR also hired a Tibetan. Both men traveled throughout northern Nepal for several months to make connections with border police and Tibetan communities. By November, thirty-eight Tibetan newcomers found at the border at Kodari arrived in Kathmandu without any problem.[20] Another group found in Pokhara, well south of the border, arrived in Kathmandu on the next morning's bus.[21] Reception center staff interpreted the safe arrival of both groups to indicate an end to the deportations, at least for the time being. A Tibet Office staff member commented: "It seems that the Nepal government is no longer sending anyone back to Tibet. That group of thirty-eight made it to Kathmandu and were able to travel to India. After them, other groups were able to come and go as well."[22]

Tibetan exile leaders were pleased with the support they received from the U.S. ambassador and from UNHCR throughout the deportations. They interpreted it as legitimation for their claims over Tibet. Nepali officials interpreted their support, however, as intervention in their own internal affairs. Nepali officials are in no position to disagree openly with U.S. or UNHCR policy, however. Nepal's dependence upon foreign aid to finance its government expenditures prevents overt disagreement. Weapons of the weak (in this case, denial of any change in policy throughout the deportations) provide an alternative to overt disagreement. They enable Nepal to reassert control over its borders and reassert state sovereignty without compromising foreign aid.

Blue Books and Border Controls

The Tibetan blue book project demonstrates further use of weapons of the weak among Nepal's government officials to resist UNHCR intervention on behalf of Tibetan exiles. Tibetan exile officials had been requesting for years that the Nepal government issue refugee identity booklets (blue books) to all Tibetans. Successive Nepal governments had been promising for years to implement the project. It was only in 1994 that the newly elected United Marxist-Leninist (UML) government followed up on its promises. It did so only after UNHCR agreed to provide the necessary funds. Even with UNHCR involvement, however, after only one-fourth of the blue books were issued, the Nepal Home Ministry stopped the process. Home Ministry officials provided no official explanation, claimed their policies had not changed, and promised the project would continue. Without overt resistance, the Home Ministry effectively prevented the completion of the project and rendered the blue books ineffective.

Ever since King Birendra's government issued the first blue books to Tibetan exiles in 1974, the Dalai Lama's exile administration has been arguing for all Tibetan exiles in Nepal to receive them. Exile officials seemed to believe that the blue books would define them officially as "refugees" under international law. They argued that the books "demonstrate that the Nepal government accepts each individual Tibetan as a refugee... make staying in Nepal more legal for each Tibetan [and] ... make it illegal for Nepal to deport Tibetans."[23] Tibetan exiles also believed that the blue books would facilitate their application for business licenses, drivers' licenses, bank accounts, and travel documents in Nepal. They appealed to UNHCR to pressure the Nepal government to issue blue books to them.

In September 1994, the newly elected UML government agreed to issue the blue books. A Nepali lawyer suggested three reasons why government officials may have considered it in their own interest to issue them at that time:

Perhaps it is related to the problem of the Bhutanese refugees. As the government is trying to handle the Bhutanese problem, it may also be trying to handle the problem with the Tibetans. Or it may be related to the problem with Indian migration. The government has been contesting the 1950 treaty with India and has been discussing registering Indian merchants with the government. The Tibetan project is easier and may intend to send a message to Indian merchants that they may be next. Or, it may be related to the UML government and its relationship with China. Registering Tibetans may be a concession to China that could help the Chinese know exactly who the refugees are. (personal communication, June 4, 1995)

A UNHCR protection officer explained, however, that it was the "Tibetan community" (i.e., the Tibet Office) that expressed the need for the blue books. UNHCR convinced the Home Ministry that the project was in Nepal's interest: "The needs of the Tibetans were met with needs on the Nepal side. The goal of UNHCR is to get to a position in which there are no undocumented people in Nepal" (personal communication, November 9, 1995).

The project, as planned by UNHCR, the Nepal Home Ministry, and the Tibet Office in Nepal, involved collecting documentation on all Tibetan exiles in Nepal and then issuing blue books to four groups of Tibetans only: Tibetans who held blue books from 1974; dependents of blue book holders from 1974; Tibetans who were born in Nepal; and Tibetans who were not able to obtain blue books in 1974 yet who have lived in Nepal since before December 31, 1989 (Government of Nepal 1994). All Tibetans arriving in Nepal after 1989, in accordance with UNHCR-Nepal agreements, were considered ineligible for blue books. They were supposed to be transported to India through the reception center system.

Nearly eight thousand Tibetans in the Kathmandu Valley, an estimated 90 percent of the population, applied for blue books.[24] One reason for the high percentage of applicants is a rumor that spread throughout the Tibetan community that the blue books could be used like passports to facilitate international travel. Another is that many Tibetans included all of their relatives, even those who live in India, on their application forms.[25] Tibetans explained that if the blue books could be used like passports, they wanted their relatives in India also to receive them. "If you count all of the people who applied for blue books," one Tibetan explained, "There will be many more than those actually in Nepal."

By February of 1995, Tibet Office representatives had collected all of the applications and documentation, from even the remote settlements, and were working with the Nepal Home Ministry to issue the blue books. The last step in the process was considered the most difficult, as it involved asking the chief district officer in each district to sign the books. "The district officer may take one hour every day to sign books, and in that hour, he may sign maybe only twenty-five books," a Tibet Office representative explained. The delays led to a sporadic and inefficient distribution process. They made it more likely that the process would be interrupted before it was completed.

Before the process stalled completely, about one-fourth of all Tibetan exiles in Nepal received blue books. The first Tibetans to receive them were those who already held blue books from 1974, as the Nepal Home Ministry had already approved their presence in Nepal. The only other group to receive them were the Tibetans who live in the Swiss-Tibetan settlement camps. Two factors may explain why. The first is the potential for Swiss intergovernmental organizations to intervene on their behalf. The second, specific to the Jawalakhel camp, is the close relationship the Jawalakhel Handicraft Center maintains with the local district office. Their relationship has value that transcends the specifics of the blue book project.

In July of 1995, the blue book project stalled completely. UNHCR and Tibetan exile leaders approached the Nepal government for an explanation. The Nepal government maintained the position that its policies had not changed and that the project would continue. Some Nepali officials suggested that the project may be too expensive. That led UNHCR to grant additional funds to the Home Ministry. By December of 1995, however, the project still had not continued. It became clear that the remainder of the blue books would not be issued at all.

The blue book project ended, I argue, because Nepali officials perceived a loss of control over their borders. Tibet Office representatives themselves suggested that interpretation to me, as they themselves could see that most of the applicants did not have adequate documentation to demonstrate that they had been living in Nepal since before 1989.[26] Did UNHCR intervention not just permit, but invite, Tibetan exiles into Nepal? Comparison with the Bhutanese situation was inevitable.

In 1989, the Nepal government invited UNHCR into its territory to help manage a situation involving, at the time, some three hundred Nepali-speaking Bhutanese who were requesting asylum (Baral 1994; Dixit 1994). UNHCR, through agreements with a number of other organizations, established camps where asylum claims could be processed, in accordance with international refugee norms, and where food, clothing, and shelter could be provided. Whether intentionally or not, the camps operated at a standard of living that far exceeded that of either Nepal or Bhutan. Soon, many more Nepali-speakers started to arrive at the camps and to claim asylum. By 1994, there were an estimated 86,000 people living in eight camps in two of Nepal's eastern districts. The United States, Japan, UNHCR, the World Food Program, Lutheran World Services, Save the Children, OXFAM, CARITAS International, and many other international organizations were providing them with assistance. By that time, which of the many asylum-seekers could make a legitimate claim to refugee status had ceased to be the principal issue. Far more important became the issue of who had the right to decide. The governments of Nepal and Bhutan could not agree how to proceed. Neither wanted to accept responsibility for the camp inhabitants. In the meantime, the inability of UNHCR to resolve a problem that it had, in part, created became another example Nepali political elite could cite of the way in which international organizations violate the sovereignty of Nepal and contribute to its social problems.

Just as UNHCR-supported camps in eastern Nepal transformed a 300-person refugee problem into an 86,000-person refugee problem, by providing greater resources than could be found in either Nepal or Bhutan more generally, was the UNHCR-Tibetan Reception Center system attracting Tibetan exiles into Nepal? The Director of the Tibet Office suggested how important it was to Nepali officials to determine when each Tibetan exile had arrived:

> The Home Department has made many different requests ... yet many of them are impossible. For example, they have asked for recommendation letters from the VDCs [village development committees] testifying that each Tibetan has lived in the district for many years, but that is impossible, because many of the VDC commissioners have been newly appointed in the last year. Also, Tibetans move around a lot, and many of them haven't been in any one district for a long time even though they have been in Nepal for a long time. (personal communication, July 28, 1995)

With the cessation of the Tibetan blue book project, even the Tibetan exiles who were able to obtain blue books questioned what the project had intended. As Tibetan exiles tried to use their blue books, they found that the books guaranteed none of the rights they had expected and may actually have caused them greater difficulties. Most disappointing for them was the realization that the blue books could not be used like passports. Tibetan exiles explained that whenever they travel to India, whether to conduct business or to visit relatives, they are stopped at the border for not having proper documents. Many Tibetan exiles believed that the blue books would prevent them from being stopped. As one Tibetan explained: "The Tibetans in India have been issued passports. I thought the blue books were the same. You should ask the UNHCR representative if passports will be issued to the Tibetans.... I thought that is what we would receive."[27]

As a Nepali lawyer explained, however, the blue books were never intended to be used like passports: "The Nepal government does not want to be responsible for Tibetan activities that occur outside of Nepal." A UNHCR protection officer supported his assessment with: "The I.D.s do not guarantee any of the privileges of citizenship [and] ... cannot be used like passports.... Not in themselves. But they can help in applying to the Home Ministry for travel documents. Whether or not a particular applicant will get travel documents still depends upon the mood of the particular official that day. Mostly the I.D.s are useful to the government to be able to keep track of the movements of the refugees" (personal communication, April 24, 1995).

Tibetan exiles also began to worry that the blue books not only guaranteed no rights but also created greater difficulties. In the blue books themselves, there is a list of regulations that states that the blue books have to be renewed every year. Three pages of spaces for renewal stamps precede the regulations. Each renewal stamp, Tibetan exiles explained, will cost them bribe money. That the blue books could be renewed only in the district in which they were issued was also interpreted to be a problem as it was expected to restrict the movements of Tibetan exiles within Nepal. One Tibetan described how much of a problem such a requirement can cause:

A friend of mine used to live in Jawalakhel but now lives in Swayambhu. When he tried to renew his [1974] identity book, because he lives in Swayambhu, the Lalitpur district officer would not do it. My friend went to the Kathmandu district office to see if he could get it renewed there, but they told him that he would have to go to Lalitpur because that is where it was issued. My friend went back to Lalitpur and they told him again they would not renew his book because he now lives in Swayambhu. My friend came to me to ask me to interpret for him and we went to the Lalitpur district office again. Again they said that they would not do it, so I asked what can be done? If they will not renew it in Kathmandu and they will not renew it in Lalitpur, what can be done? The assistant district officer wanted us to give him some money, but we did not want to.... Why should we have to do that when what we are doing is legal? (personal communication, February 26, 1995)

As the Tibetan exiles compared the 1995 blue books with the 1974 blue books, two additional problems emerged. One is that the 1995 books require Tibetans to re-register with local authorities every time they change residence and every time the composition of their household changes. Another involves the deletion of the word "Tibetan" from the cover. As one Tibetan exile explained, the deletion of the word "Tibetan" signifies Nepal's denial that Tibet ever existed:

Look at this. The identity books issued in 1974 say "Tibetan Refugee Identity Card" and the ones issued in 1995 say only "Refugee Identity Card" ... In the same way, on the 1974 application form, it says "Tibetan Refugee Identity Certificate Application Form" and on the 1995 form, it says only "Refugee Identity Certificate Application Form." On the 1974 form there is a line to write "What country are you from?" On the 1995 form there is no line ... and there is only "Where were you born?" For those Tibetans who were born in Nepal or in India, the form does not carry the word "Tibetan" even once. (personal communication, February 26, 1995)

Despite the disappointments of the Tibetan blue book project, Tibetan exiles interpret their ability to negotiate with the Nepal government as generally greater now than in the past. They interpret Nepal's efforts to delay compliance as only temporary. Some Tibetan exiles argue that Nepal's resistance efforts may actually help them, as it invites intergovernmental officials to become involved on their behalf. As one Tibetan exile, following the arrest of a group of Tibetan demonstrators, argued:

During panchayat times, when the king was in power, people were afraid of the king. If anyone did anything wrong, or if anyone spoke against the king, that person would disappear.... It is said that people were taken up into the Nagarjuna hills and shot there for their crimes.... During those times, whenever the Tibetans wanted to get together, as for the Dalai Lama's birthday, the Nepali police would show up ... they would tell us that we could not get together, and we would argue back and forth for a long time until finally they would let us..... If they were going to let us do it anyway, why didn't they just let us do it?... These days, when the Nepali police do things like take "Free Tibet" stickers out of the shops, that is no problem. How much do stickers cost? Things like that might even help us, because then foreigners see what is happening and want to help us. Maybe the Nepal government will make everyone put "Free Nepal" stickers in their shop or something. That is no problem. (personal communication, September 3, 1995)

As the deportations and the Tibetan blue book project demonstrate, however, weapons of the weak do have some effect and can provide a means through which Nepali officials can resist multilateral intergovernmental intervention. In Nepal, weapons of the weak enabled the Nepal government, without direct symbolic confrontation, to end the Tibetan blue book project and to continue to deport Tibetans without compromising foreign aid. Nepal reasserted control over its borders and its Tibetan population and reasserted its status as a sovereign state. Tibetan exiles remain ambiguous members of the Nepal state. The government continues to see them but not see them, to acknowledge their presence but avoid formal recognition of their status. It continues to resist formal recognition of the Tibetans and international advocacy on their behalf.

Notes

1. Nepal defines "development-related" in such a way as to include much of its regular budget (Guru-Gharana 1995: 11). The Nepal Aid Group, founded under the auspices of the World Bank, provides much of the funding.
2. Tibetans refer to them as "blue books" because of the color of their covers. In a similar manner, they refer to the identity booklets the Dalai Lama's exile administration issues as "green books" and the travel documents the overseas Chinese Security Bureau in Delhi issues as "white passes."
3. Most states define citizenship through either a *ius soli* principle, based on birth within state territory, or a *ius sanguinis* principle, based on direct descent from a present citizen of the state (Brubaker 1989). Nepal's 1962 citizenship laws are unusual in that they provide for citizenship through either principle. Nepal, in 1962, had very inclusive citizenship laws.
4. Hammar (1990) uses the term "denizen" for long-term residents without citizenship status. Although it is not, in itself, a formal legal category, it facilitates the analysis of the rights and responsibilities people acquire through long-term residence in a state. Hammar (1990) uses the term, for example, to analyze the rights and responsibilities of guest workers in Europe. Soysal (1994) analyzes the role international organizations play in enforcing denizen rights.
5. I heard this story from many Tibetans in Nepal. Prem Uprety, professor of history at Tribhuvan University, further confirmed it (personal communication, December 4, 1995).

6. Articles 8 and 13 of the Charter for the Tibetan Exiles outlines these qualifications.
7. The points of view expressed here and in the next paragraph derive from essays I received in May 1995 as part of an essay contest I sponsored among seventh-grade Tibetan exile students on the advantages and disadvantages of taking citizenship in Nepal.
8. Shyam Thapa, "Unity in Diversity," *The Kathmandu Post,* December 3, 1995.
9. Some Tibetans argue that because the term "Tamang" can be translated as the Tibetan *ta-mag* (horse fighters) or *ta-mang* (people with many horses), Tamangs are Tibetan. Others consider Tamangs to be more similar to Nepali people (*rong-pa*). A preference for cross-cousin marriage among Tamangs, which makes intermarriage between Tibetan exiles and Tamangs unusual, reinforces the perception of difference. One older Tibetan described Tamang people as "all mixed up.... Their *popo-las* and *momo-las* [grandfathers and grand-mothers] are Tibetan and so they wear Tibetan clothes and practice the Tibetan religion. But they are also like Nepalese. They dance like Nepalese by crashing cymbals together and they also wear red color on their scalps and *tikka* on their foreheads" (personal communication, May 31, 1995).
10. Tibetan exiles in Kathmandu consider intermarriage with people who are clearly "ethnic Tibetans" (*pö-mi rig-pa*), such as the Sherpa, Lopa, and Manangi, to be no stranger then marrying other Tibetans from outside their own region (*lung-pa*) in Tibet. They consider intermarriage with Thakali, Magar, and Gurung also to be acceptable. With Rai, Limbu, and Kirati, they consider intermarriage to be a bit strange. They consider intermarriage with Brahmin, Chhetri, and Newar also to be strange, although, as Tibetans have an exog-amous marriage rule, not unacceptable. To the Brahmin, Chhetri, and Newar themselves, however, it is unacceptable, as they practice caste endogamy.
11. The particulars of the case derive from an article entitled "Tibetan refugees not to get cit-izenship: Minister Deupa" published in *The Rising Nepal,* August 12, 1993.
12. Prior to 1980, two international agreements enabled the Tibetans to cross the border into Nepal as religious pilgrims and petty traders. The 1956 Nepal-China Treaty on Friendship and Trade granted religious pilgrims license to cross the border without documents as long as they registered at border check posts. The 1964 Nepal-China Trade Agreement granted border inhabitants license to travel as far as thirty kilometers into state territory without documents to conduct trade. Nepal and China renewed the agreements repeat-edly with few changes until 1986 when they signed the "Agreement on Trade, Intercourse and Related Questions between Nepal and the Tibet Autonomous Region of China." It required petty traders and pilgrims to carry "border inhabitant certificates" when travel-ing within thirty kilometers of the border and passports with visas for any distance beyond that (Bhasin 1994: 555, 1347–1349, 1381).
13. UNHCR protection officer, personal communication, November 28, 1995.
14. U.S. Embassy intern, personal communication, July 11, 1995.
15. "Nepal Deports 53 Tibetan Escapees," *Tibet Information Network,* May 13, 1995. The deportations did begin soon after former Prime Minister Man Mohan Adhikari returned from a meeting with the Chinese premier in Beijing, yet there is no reason to believe that the two leaders ever even discussed Tibet.
16. Documents in Bhasin (1994: 556) demonstrate the continuity in Nepal's recognition of China's claim to Tibet since 1956.
17. The 1951 U.N. Convention Relating to the Status of Refugees, and its 1967 Protocol, define "refugee" based on "a well-founded fear of being persecuted" that renders one unable or unwilling to avail oneself of the protection of one's country of origin or habit-ual residence. The 1951 Convention restricted the definition to Europe and to events occurring before January 1, 1951. The Protocol removed the definition's geographic and temporal restrictions.
18. U.S. Ambassador Sandy Vogelgesgang, personal communication, September 9, 1995. No other ambassadors attended the celebration. Ambassador Vogelgesgang commented later that she was disappointed that she was the only ambassador there.

19. UNHCR protection officer in Nepal, personal communication, August 10, 1995. The officer was hired by the Geneva office. It was not a local-level decision. Given that UNHCR generally does not hire Americans, the choice of an American in this case was most likely meant to send a signal to China that the U.S. supports UNHCR's Nepal activities.
20. Assistant director of the Tibet Office, personal communication, November 11, 1995.
21. UNHCR protection officer in Nepal, personal communication, November 28, 1995. They were a group of 22 Tibetans, and they did arrive in Kathmandu at seven o'clock the next morning. The Tibetans who contacted UNHCR about their arrival also requested compensation for the cost of assisting the newcomers.
22. Assistant director of the Tibet Office, personal communication, November 11, 1995.
23. Tashi Namgyal, director of the Tibet Office, personal communication, July 28, 1995.
24. Statistics on the Tibetans who submitted applications are reported in Table A.1. I personally compiled all of the statistics using copies of the blue book applications housed in the Tibet Office and at the Jawalakhel camp. According to my count, there were 7948 Tibetans in the Kathmandu Valley who applied for blue books. The count is incomplete, however. The director of the Jawalakhel camp withdrew some of the application forms from the files before I was given access.
25. Applications were submitted by household, with all the members of each household listed on the same form. Relatives resident in India were freely listed among the others.
26. The Home Ministry considered only a letter from a chief district officer, birth records, school records, or refugee identity booklets from 1974 as adequate documentation. They did not consider medical records to be adequate. Most applicants had no documentary support whatsoever.
27. Tibetan exiles in India have not been issued passports. The International Committee for the Red Cross issued travel documents to people who work for the Dalai Lama's exile administration and other Tibetan exiles who travel frequently. ICRC documents are not passports, however.

5

Middlemen and Moral Authority

On July 6, 1995, an estimated ten thousand people, mostly Tibetan, gathered in Boudha to celebrate the Dalai Lama's sixtieth birthday.[1] Tibetan families, school friends, monks, and business partners talked and celebrated among themselves as they circumambulated the stupa, strung up prayer flags, burned incense, tossed barley flour (*tsampa*), and offered white scarves (*katah*), all in prayer for the Dalai Lama's health and well-being. Most then proceeded to the playground of the Srongtsen Bhrikuti School, a school affiliated with the Dalai Lama's exile administration, where a song-and-dance competition among Tibetan exile students was to begin. As they sat packed close together on their blankets and small carpets under six large overlapping tents, the Tibetans directed their attention to a large platform, festooned with microphones and speakers, raised before them. Representatives from the Dalai Lama's exile administration had also arranged to speak. The director of the Tibet Office, in particular, delivered a very long speech, in Tibetan. Most Tibetans listened to his reminders that the Dalai Lama's exile administration is the only organization with authority over "all Tibetans, inside and outside Tibet, monks and laymen, old and young," the only organization that represents the Dalai Lama, and the only organization working to return all Tibetans to an independent Tibet: "Tibetans need to stay united, as the Tibetan struggle is for the whole of the three provinces, all 2.5 million square miles and all six million people.... All Tibetans should always think about returning to Tibet, for why are Tibetans scattered throughout the world? Because Tibet was occupied by a foreign country. No one should forget."[2]

Tibetan exile officials frequently use public events like the Dalai Lama's birthday celebration to remind Tibetans that the exile administration is the only organization with authority over them all, that its authority derives from the Dalai Lama, and that its intent is to return to Tibet. The message is always the same, whether it is the Tibetan New Year, the Buddha Jayanti,

Democracy Day, or any other Tibetan holiday.[3] During all these events, Tibetan exile officials invariably invoke the name of the Dalai Lama and the myth of return to Tibet to legitimate their authority. The exile administration claims authority over all Tibetans.

This chapter analyzes how the Dalai Lama's exile administration both legitimates and exercises authority over Tibetans. It argues that exile officials may legitimate their authority through the charisma of the Dalai Lama and the myth of return, yet they actually exercise authority through their position as middlemen in the provision of international assistance. The chapter proceeds in five parts. The first uses Weber (1968) to differentiate between the exercise of authority and its legitimation. It argues that although political leaders may legitimate their authority through charismatic, traditional, or rational-legal means, they exercise it through control over economic resources or the threat of the use of force. The Dalai Lama's exile administration, I argue, exercises its authority through its control over economic resources; its access to economic resources derives from its position as middleman in the provision of international assistance. The second part analyzes how the Dalai Lama's exile administration used its position to expand into Nepal. The exile administration is headquartered in Dharamsala, India. It expanded into Nepal only in the 1970s, more than a decade after the initial exile. I examine three strategies the exile administration used to expand into Nepal and secure authority over Nepal's Tibetan exiles. The third part outlines the structure and functions of the Dalai Lama's exile administration in Nepal. It argues that the exile administration used its middleman position to become Nepal's largest and most well-organized Tibetan exile organization. The fourth analyzes the contingencies of the position of the exile administration in Nepal. It argues that although the exile administration maintains a dominant position, it continually negotiates with other Tibetan exile organizations to maintain it. The final part analyzes how the Dalai Lama's exile administration legitimates its position. It argues that it does so through the charisma of the Dalai Lama and the myth of return. Both strategies are limited, however. As a result, Tibetan exile officials may claim authority over all Tibetans, "inside and outside Tibet, monks and laymen, old and young," yet their claims should be viewed as performative rather than descriptive, as other Tibetan exile organizations also use the same strategies for legitimation.

The Exercise of Authority versus its Legitimation

Previous studies of the Dalai Lama's exile administration emphasize the role of the Dalai Lama in its ability to affect compliance with its decisions. Nowak (1984: 25) argues that the Dalai Lama serves as a key symbol that maintains the traditional Tibetan identity with the exile administration in control.

French (1991: 192) argues that the Dalai Lama is a typically charismatic leader whose personal qualities serve to affect compliance. Both of these arguments highlight the importance of the Dalai Lama to the exile administration, yet they overstate his role. The Dalai Lama is not a typically charismatic leader. Although the present Dalai Lama is, indeed charismatic, the office he holds has for so long been routinized (Weber 1968: 246–254) that there is no longer a direct connection between his own decisions and the day-to-day decisions of Tibetan exile officials.[4] To understand why Tibetan exiles comply with the exile administration, therefore, it is necessary to make two distinctions previous accounts do not make. The first is between the person of the present Dalai Lama, the institutionalized office of the Dalai Lama, and the Tibetan exile administration, all of which Tibetans themselves discuss quite cogently as distinct. The second is between the strategies Tibetan exile officials use to legitimate their authority and those they use to exercise their authority. Tibetan exile officials, I argue, may legitimate their authority in the name of the Dalai Lama, yet they actually exercise it through their control over economic resources.

Weber (1968) proposes a framework for distinguishing between the exercise of authority and its legitimation. Weber (1968: 212–245) proposes three ways in which political leaders legitimate their authority–through personal charisma; through traditional procedures, such as the hereditary transfer of power; and through intentionally established, rational-legal procedures, such as elections. All of these serve to confer legitimacy on those in power. How do those in power actually exercise their authority? Weber (1968: 941–948) proposes a continuum of ways. At one end of the continuum, they exercise authority through a control over economic resources so that those who obey "are motivated simply by the pursuit of their own interests." At the other, they exercise it through "patriarchal, magisterial, or princely powers," implicitly supported by the coercive apparatus of the state (the army, police, prisons, and courts), so that those who obey have an "absolute duty" to do so.[5]

The Dalai Lama's exile administration lacks the coercive apparatus of a state. As a guest of other states, it cannot raise an army or train a police force; it has been trying to develop a system of courts, yet for the most part, it cannot enforce its decisions through coercive means. What it does instead it to enforce its decisions through economic means. It makes access to the resources international organizations provide through its offices contingent upon compliance with its decisions. The Fulbright scholarships the U.S. government makes available through the exile administration's Department of Education illustrate. In order to qualify, Tibetan exiles must attend schools affiliated with the exile administration (where they learn the exile administration's particular view of Tibet's history), must pay all taxes they owe to the exile administration, and must ensure that their parents pay all their taxes as well. The exile administration thus uses the Fulbright scholarships to entice Tibetan exiles into its own school system as well as to ensure tax payments.

The Dalai Lama's exile administration is not the only exile organization to use economic resources in this manner. Shain (1989: 31) argues that exile organizations worldwide use economic resources in this manner to maintain their authority. He argues:

> Leaders try to promote participation in political acts through the manipulation of material rewards and by distributing a variety of collective symbols of solidarity. For example, they may provide jobs or health care, or finance children's education, or award other material benefits that reduce economic distress. All such efforts help preserve the national identity of exiles abroad and enhance the position and power of the exile organization itself.

Like many other exile organizations worldwide, the Dalai Lama's exile administration uses a control over economic resources to enforce its decisions. Its access to economic resources derives from its position as middleman in the provision of international assistance. The Dalai Lama's exile administration uses its middleman position to tax fellow exiles (thereby gaining access to additional economic resources) and to regulate schools, monasteries, businesses, health care centers, publishers, and research centers. In the early years of the Tibetan exile, it also used its position to expand into Nepal.

The Dalai Lama's Exile Administration Expands into Nepal

In the 1970s, the Dalai Lama's exile administration first expanded into Nepal. Prior to the 1970s, most Tibetan exiles in Nepal were unaware that an exile administration even existed. They organized themselves where they were, without assistance. The exile administration first expanded into Nepal through the Swiss-Tibetan settlement camp system. The general manager of the Jawalakhel Handicraft Center (JHC), the first of the Swiss-Tibetan businesses, became the first representative of His Holiness the Dalai Lama to Nepal. Most Tibetan exiles in Nepal today remain self-settled (*khator*), outside of any formal settlement camp, yet they know about the Dalai Lama's exile administration. They use it when it is in their interest.

The Dalai Lama's exile administration used three strategies to expand into Nepal. All of them involve the use of economic resources to build organizational connections and enforce regulatory compliance. The economic resources the exile administration used consisted, more often than not, in resources international organizations provided to help Tibetan exiles. In the process of helping Tibetan exiles, the exile administration also expanded its administrative control.

The first strategy involves the recruitment of individual Tibetan exile leaders into its service. We see this strategy in the appointment of the manager of the JHC as the first representative of His Holiness the Dalai Lama to Nepal.

We see it also in the way in which the exile administration expanded its control through the other Swiss-Tibetan and U.S.-Tibetan businesses in Nepal. The exile administration secured control over them by funding their general manager and assistant general manager positions. In 1995, the exile administration was trying to do the same with the Mustang Organization, and its affiliated businesses, as well as with the Snow Lion Foundation, with its network of schools, clinics, and old age homes in Nepal.

Once the exile administration provides the funds for a position, that position is thereafter called an appointed position (*sa-mig*). Those who hold such positions are called officially appointed staff members (*shung-kö le-che-wa*), as opposed to local-level staff members (*rang-khong le-che-wa*), funded by the organization itself. Officially appointed staff members must answer both to the director of the Tibet Office in Nepal (whose title, in Tibetan, means quite literally, "the decision maker," or *dön-chö*) and to the secretary (*drung-che*) of their respective department, whether Home, Finance, Education, or International Relations. The degree of control varies with individual personalities. Many Tibetan exiles in Nepal, for example, described the former secretary of the Finance Department as very strict. A former manager of the Boudha factory explains:

> There is very little flexibility for the general managers of Finance Department businesses. Even as general manager, I always had to ask for approval from the Finance Department to do anything. For example, if I had an expansion project, I could not just decide to do it. I had to ask the Finance Department.... The Finance Department actually has a sort of point system in which they count the number of letters and approval requests sent to them by their managers and then the people who have the lowest score at the end of the year do not receive their yearly bonuses.... I thought my job was to run a business not to write letters all the time.... I did not have a lot of leverage to act.

Tibetan exiles describe other department secretaries as relatively relaxed. One administrator, for example, referred to the secretary of his department as a "handkerchief" (*lag-pa chi-sa*), that is, someone not very powerful yet useful for "cleaning his hands" of unpleasant business.[6]

In 1995, I witnessed the creation of a new appointed position, as the exile administration's Home Department sought to bring the Jawalakhel Handicraft Center's production director into its service. The Jawalakhel Handicraft Center (JHC), at the time, already had two officially appointed staff members in its service. Both the general manager and assistant general manager were appointed by the Home Department. The Home Department wanted to transform the position of production director also into an appointed position. One reason was to secure greater control over JHC and its production process. Another was to entice the current production director to remain in JHC's employment despite his many offers from private factories in Kathmandu. The Home Department offered to make funds available to JHC to pay the production director's salary and benefits. For JHC, that was desirable, as it meant that it would no longer have to commit its own resources to his position. All that was left was to convince the production director to agree.

For the production director, accepting an appointed position had both advantages and disadvantages, and the decision whether or not to accept was not easy. The advantages included a higher salary, free education for his five children at schools affiliated with the exile administration, housing and medical benefits, and a pension.[7] The principal disadvantage was the possibility of a transfer into another appointed post. Transfers are a strategy that the Dalai Lama's exile administration uses frequently to manage its appointees. Transfers prevent appointees from developing local loyalties that might compete with loyalty to the exile administration. They also provide appointees with a broad base of experience to train them for higher administrative posts. Tibetan exiles consider some transfers, such as to a Tibet Office in the U.S., England, or Switzerland, as very desirable. They consider others, such as to a remote post in northern Nepal or the hot middle plains of India, as something to be avoided at all costs. They consider Kathmandu, like Delhi, to be a generally desirable place in which to work. What the production director wanted to avoid is a transfer out of Kathmandu. In the end, the production director accepted the promotion into an appointed position. He reasoned that he could avoid an undesirable transfer through resignation, or through a leave of absence, as many other official appointees have done. His position became an appointed position.

Recruiting individual Tibetan exile leaders into official service is only one strategy the exile administration used to expand into Nepal. Another involves a system of incentives it offers to Tibetan exile organizations. Organizational incentives enable the exile administration to enforce its more general rules and regulations among Tibetan exiles in Nepal. Schools provide an example. The exile administration views the school system as a means through which to cultivate loyalty to itself and the independence cause. Toward that end, its Department of Education formulated its own curriculum for all Tibetan exile schools. Its textbooks convey a particular interpretation of the Tibetan past and particular goals for Tibet's future that it would like all Tibetan exiles to learn as part of what it means to be Tibetan. The Department of Education would like all Tibetan exile schools in Nepal to use its curriculum. One way in which it entices schools to do so is to make access to Department of Education scholarships, or funds for capital expansion, conditional upon use of the curriculum and compliance with its more general rules and regulations.

We see this strategy in the relationship between the Department of Education and the Atisha School in Nepal. The Department of Education provides scholarships to Atisha's students. In turn, the Atisha School uses Department of Education textbooks in its classes and generally complies with Tibet Office requests (such as organizing students to perform songs and dances during events like the Dalai Lama's birthday celebration). In 1995, the director of the Atisha School wanted funds to build an Atisha high school. All of his efforts to solicit funds on his own had been unsuccessful. He approached the exile administration's secretary of education for funds, and after extensive negotiations, the secretary agreed, yet only in exchange for control over the school's land.[8] Control over the school's land would have provided the Department of Education with greater control over the school and its management than it exercises over any other school in Nepal. The agreement dissolved, however, when the secretary resigned from her post and the general manager of the JHC (whose support for the project was necessary, as JHC owns the land on which the high school was to be constructed) was transferred. With the dissolution of the agreement, the director of the Atisha School complained that the exile administration "needs to give us something if they want to call us a Tibetan government school." He believed himself entitled to funds in exchange for compliance with exile administration decisions. The Atisha School, in the end, remained affiliated with the exile administration, as it continued to depend upon Department of Education scholarships. As the director watched other schools obtain funds, he reframed his own situation as a matter of "luck" (*lung-ta*): "Different schools have different luck.... IM is spending a lot of money to build Namgyal Middle School and that will soon be finished. SOS is spending a lot of money to build Pokhara High School and that will soon be finished. As for Atisha School, we have no sponsor, and so we have no school."[9]

The third strategy that the exile administration used to expand into Nepal and exercise its authority over fellow Tibetan exiles involves the threat of total exclusion from affiliation with the exile administration, its reputation, and the resources international organizations provide through its offices.[10] The exile administration continues to use the threat of exclusion frequently as it continues to expand in Nepal. There are many examples of this strategy. The exile administration excluded the Tibetan guerrilla fighters who surrendered to the Nepal government in 1974 from all assistance. It excludes Tibetan organizations suspected of accepting funds from Taiwan from assistance. After telling a story about another man who had been excluded from exile administration assistance, for alleged fraud, one Tibetan commented: "Anyone who goes to China or Taiwan for money is also expelled from the Tibetan exile community. If the exile government keeps expelling people who do not follow them, there will be no one left for them to govern."

The relative poverty of the Jorpati camp, in comparison with other Tibetan settlement camps in Kathmandu, demonstrates the results of exclusion from affiliation with the Dalai Lama's exile administration. Jorpati camp inhabitants are among the many who surrendered to the Nepal army at the end of the guerrilla war. Their poverty was an issue that puzzled me, at first, because I thought at the time that Nepali citizenship was the most important factor in the Tibetans' economic success in Nepal. I expected

Jorpati camp inhabitants to be wealthier than most other Tibetan exiles in Nepal, as they acquired citizenship, legally, as far back as 1974. What their relative poverty demonstrates is that affiliation with the exile administration, and the access it provides to international resources, is far more important than citizenship.

In 1992, Jorpati camp inhabitants reconciled with the Dalai Lama's exile administration, yet they remained excluded from assistance.[11] "The Tibetan government gives us no help whatsoever," Baba Yeshe, the founder of the camp, for example, explained, "For sixteen years, they did not even recognize that we exist."[12] "The Tibetan government is doing nothing to help the factory or pay the children's school fees," a Jorpati camp administrator, likewise, explained, "The Tibet Office never even tells us the time and place of Tibetan celebrations." Publications produced by the Dalai Lama's exile administration, like the Project Support Needs Directory (a fundraising publication), routinely fail to mention the Jorpati camp. Tibetan exile officials, likewise, avoid all discussion of the issue. Only officials I interviewed regularly would agree to discuss the Jorpati camp with me. They admitted that the exile administration still does not assist them in any way.[13] Tibetan exile officials argue that the Jorpati camp still has not complied with the exile administration's policies. Four issues are involved.

The first involves their acceptance of an officially appointed Tibetan Freedom Movement representative. The Tibetan Freedom Movement is the organization that collects taxes among Tibetan exiles. Instead of accepting the officially appointed representative, Baba Yeshe appointed his own representative for the camp. The second issue involves the relationship between the Jorpati camp and the Neckermann organization. The Neckermann organization funded the construction of the Jorpati camp factory and school and purchased carpets from the factory until the 1980s. Tibetan exile officials, aware that a German organization sponsored the school, asked Jorpati administrators to disclose how much assistance they receive. Jorpati administrators argued that they no longer receive assistance from them. The director of the Tibet Office requested financial records to confirm their claim. Jorpati administrators refused to disclose the records, as they argued that the exile administration wants to use them to solicit funds for itself. The third issue involves the relationship between the Jorpati camp and Taiwan's Mongolian and Tibetan Affairs Commission. Tibetan exile officials for years have accused Baba Yeshe, the camp leader, of accepting assistance from Taiwan.[14] Exile administration policy requires non-association with anyone who does. The final issue involves accepting the exile administration's own interpretation of Baba Yeshe and his past. Tibetan exile officials have, for many years, portrayed Baba Yeshe as a traitor, as someone who works only to divide the Tibetan exile community. Jorpati administrators, in contrast, portray him as a good man. As one Jorpati administrator argued:

Many people say that Genla [elder] Yeshe is a bad person, but it is not true. Genla has established camps for Tibetans and has arranged for them to go to school.... He has helped even Tibetans who were not involved in the guerrilla war.... He has helped hundreds of Tibetans, and he is only one man. Is there any other man in the Tibetan community who has helped that many people? Even Gyalwa Rinpoche [the Dalai Lama], when Genla Yeshe met him, said that he is a good person who did nothing wrong. Why do Tibetans say he has done wrong?

Through the negotiation of all of these issues, Jorpati administrators discovered that exile administration assistance requires compliance. Jorpati administrators have been working to effect compliance, yet Tibetan exile officials are skeptical of their efforts. As a result, there has been no real change in policy. One Tibetan exile official, for example, explained: "Although there has been a change on paper, no one knows what the change will mean in implementation. It was only two or three years ago that the camps were recognized." It may require many years of compliance with the exile administration before the Jorpati camp ever receives assistance. The incentive for the Jorpati camp involves access to the resources international organizations provide through the exile administration.

Through all three strategies–the recruitment of individual leaders, the system of organizational incentives, and the threat of total exclusion from affiliation with the exile administration and its resources–the exile administration expanded into Nepal and continues to exercise authority among Tibetan exiles in Nepal. Its ability to do so depends on its position as middleman in the provision of international assistance. International organizations provide the exile administration with the resources it needs to entice fellow Tibetan exiles into compliance with its decisions.

The Structure and Function of the Dalai Lama's Exile Administration in Nepal

The Dalai Lama's exile administration is the largest and most well-organized Tibetan exile organization in Nepal. It controls many of Nepal's other Tibetan organizations. It uses its position to maintain a unified Tibetan community in Nepal, to maintain the independence cause, and to recruit support for itself and its efforts among fellow Tibetan exiles.

The exile administration's principal office in Nepal is the Tibet Office (*dön-chö khang*).[15] In 1995, it was located in Lazimpat, on a compound just north of the royal palace. The director of the Tibet Office (*dön-chö*), appointed by the exile administration's Cabinet of Ministers (*kashag*), manages all Tibet Office business. Eight full-time staff members, appointed by the exile administration's Public Service Commission, assist him with his work. Tibet Office business includes maintaining contact with all diplomatic missions in Nepal to promote the Tibetan independence cause; negotiating with the Nepal government to allow Tibetan activities to proceed unencumbered in Nepal; coordinating the plans for Tibetan festivals and other public celebrations; organizing and conducting elections; organizing and administering social welfare programs; managing the UNHCR-Tibetan reception center system; and representing the authority of the Dalai Lama's exile administration at all Tibetan events in Nepal.[16]

The Tibet Office works in cooperation with other Tibetan exile organizations in Nepal to accomplish its goals. There are many of these organizations in Kathmandu alone. The Tibet Office categorizes them as either "government" organizations (those directly affiliated with the Dalai Lama's exile administration) or non-governmental organizations (those with their own structure and administration). In 1995, the government organizations included five schools; five Tibetan Freedom Movement offices; thirteen affiliated for-profit businesses; four local assemblies; and a district election commission.[17] The non-governmental organizations included the Tibetan Youth Congress (TYC); the Tibetan Women's Association (TWA); and the Snow Lion Foundation. The Snow Lion Foundation is the largest Tibetan non-governmental organization in Nepal. It maintains its own network of schools, health clinics, and old age homes.

The Tibet Office convenes frequent meetings among these many affiliated organizations in its efforts to govern the Tibetan exiles in Nepal. It convenes meetings of the thirteen affiliated businesses, for example, to discuss issues such as salary disputes or the child labor issue. It convenes meetings of the five schools, plus the Snow Lion Foundation, to discuss issues such as changes to the Tibetan curriculum. It convenes meetings of all of the organizations together to plan public events such as the Dalai Lama's birthday celebration. During the meeting to plan the Dalai Lama's sixtieth birthday celebration, Tibet Office administrators convinced the thirteen affiliated businesses to finance the celebration. They convinced all Jawalakhel-based Tibetan exile organizations (the Atisha School, Jawalakhel Handicraft Center, Carpet Trading Company, et al.) to help set up, manage, and clean up after the celebration.

The Tibet Office maintains its closest relationship with Tibetan Freedom Movement offices (*pö rang-wang den-pai ley-gul*). The Tibetan Freedom Movement was founded in the 1970s in India; it expanded into Nepal along with the Dalai Lama's exile administration.[18] Its function is to collect taxes from fellow Tibetan exiles and to issue green books to them.[19] Green books facilitate individual compliance with the exile administration, its taxation policies in particular.[20] Whenever Tibetan exiles apply for resources from the exile administration (such as scholarships, sponsorships, or resettlement opportunities; admission into affiliated schools; or permission to vote in elections), they must submit their green books with their applications. Most Tibetan exile offices require applicants to keep their taxes up to date to become eligible for these resources. There are many taxes that Tibetan exiles are required to pay. All Tibetan exiles in Nepal are required to pay a standard two-rupee per month tax (*cha-tay*).[21] Employees of organizations affiliated with the Dalai Lama's exile administration are required to pay 2 percent of their salaries, as well as the standard two rupees per month. Business owners are required to pay 10 percent of their annual business income as well as two rupees per month.[22] The exile administration has no coercive means to force Tibetan exiles to pay their taxes. It encourages them to do so by making access to international resources contingent on tax payments.

The taxes that the Tibetan Freedom Movement collects do not provide enough funding to support the Dalai Lama's exile administration, much less its many activities. The exile administration continues to depend upon international support to maintain itself and its activities. It depends upon its middleman position to remain the largest and most well-organized Tibetan organization in Nepal.

Negotiations with Other Tibetan Exile Organizations in Nepal

The Dalai Lama's exile administration uses its middleman position to control other Tibetan organizations in Nepal. Other Tibetan organizations do not comply unquestioningly, however; some do not comply at all. The exile administration must continually negotiate with other Tibetan organizations to maintain its authority in Nepal and enforce its decisions.

The Dorji School, the largest Tibetan exile school in Nepal, provides an example of a Tibetan exile organization that continually challenges the exile administration in its decisions. The Dorji School is not affiliated with the exile administration, and since its establishment in 1983, it has been excluded from all exile administration assistance. The Dorji School is not without support, however. Various Taiwanese organizations provide funds. It also has the support of Nepal's Department of Education. The Dorji School, thus, also maintains a middleman position in the provision of international assistance. It also uses its middleman position to maintain authority over fellow Tibetan exiles. It uses its position to challenge the exile administration's decisions, and in particular, its decision about how to educate Tibetan exile children.

The Dorji School and the Dalai Lama's exile administration disagree over three issues. The first is the definition of who is Tibetan for the purpose of school admittance. The exile administration maintains a very strict definition, based on the possession of a Freedom Movement green book; its definition includes only those Tibetans who pay taxes to the exile administration. The Dorji School maintains a very loose definition, based on ethnic markers such as language, clothes, food, religion, and marriage rules; its definition includes all Tibetan exiles as well as numerous other ethnic Tibetan peoples, such as Lopa, Sherpa, and Manangi.

Tibetan exile officials defend their position with reference to the history of Jawalakhel's first school. Swiss intergovernmental organizations built a school for Tibetan exiles in Jawalakhel in 1966, yet the Nepal government nationalized it in 1971. Subsequent to nationalization, the school made the Nepali language the medium of instruction, forbid the use of the Tibetan language during normal school hours, allowed only people with Nepali citizenship to teach in the school, and admitted neighborhood Nepali children, who soon outnumbered the Tibetans. Only in 1982, when the Nepal government again permitted private schools to operate in Nepal, did the Jawalakhel Tibetans re-establish a Tibetan school (the Atisha School), intended for Tibetans only. Tibetan exile officials argue that Tibetan schools should be for Tibetans only, as Nepali people (people with Nepali citizenship) have schools of their own.

Lhundub Dorji explains the exile administration's position differently.[23] He argues that it has to do with foreign aid. He says that Tibetan exile officials are concerned that if they admit too many Nepali citizens in their schools, then international organizations will not want to fund them, as they will no longer consider them to be Tibetan refugee schools. Lhundub Dorji tells a story about a meeting the director of the Tibet Office called to discuss the issue. He claims that everyone except himself agreed that foreigners prefer to fund schools that administer only to Tibetan refugee children and that therefore it would be best not to admit people with Nepali citizenship.[24] The Tibet Office made a rule, then, that no more than 10 percent of the students in any Tibetan exile school could have Nepali citizenship. Lhundub Dorji is very critical about the decision. He attributes it to greed. "The parents who worked in the Boudha Handicraft Center did not want to have to pay school fees," he claimed, "That is the source of the rule."

Lhundub Dorji argues that all ethnic Tibetans are entitled to a Tibetan education, irrespective of their citizenship status, and irrespective of the willingness of international organizations to provide the necessary funds. The issue has acute personal significance for him, as he belongs to a category of Tibetans routinely excluded from exile administration schools. He is a Tibetan-Newar (*khatsara*), the child of a Tibetan mother and Newar father. Many Tibetan exile officials do not consider Tibetan-Newars to be Tibetan. The assistant director of the Tibet Office explained his position on the issue to me as follows: "Khatsaras take advantage of the Tibetan community. They claim they are Tibetan to get an education and then they claim they are Nepali to get work. Very few Khatsaras work for the Tibetan community. Khatsaras are not really Tibetan." Lhundub Dorji considers Tibetan-Newars to be Tibetan, entitled to a Tibetan education.

In 1983, Lhundub Dorji founded the Dorji School, the first school for Tibetans in Nepal deliberately not affiliated with the exile administration. In

1995, it had 375 students from nursery level to class twelve. Sixty percent of them were Tibetan-Newars. The school admits Tibetan exiles as well as ethnic Tibetans with Nepali citizenship. It survives without the support of the exile administration, as it has its own foreign sponsors.

Soon after Lhundub Dorji founded his school, many other Tibetans followed his example and founded schools of their own, separate from the exile administration. In 1995, there were at least fourteen other schools like the Dorji School in Kathmandu alone. They educate nearly two thousand Tibetan and ethnic Tibetan students. Lhundub Dorji organized them into the United Schools Association, an organization working with Nepal's Department of Education to develop a Tibetan curriculum for ethnic Tibetans in Nepal.

The second issue over which the Dorji School and the Dalai Lama's exile administration disagree is the Tibetan curriculum for Nepal. Tibetan exile officials want to use the curriculum, in part, to promote the Tibetan independence cause. Dorji School administrators, irrespective of their personal opinions about the independence cause, do not consider that to be an appropriate part of the curriculum. The Dalai Lama's exile administration, starting in 1986, developed a series of Tibetan-language textbooks based on its new curriculum. Tibetan teachers found the textbooks to be a vast improvement over what they had been using in the past.[25] In 1992, even the Dorji School started using them.

Soon after the Dorji School started using them, however, Nepali administrators on the staff protested that the textbooks contained statements that they could not support, like "Tibet is a completely free and independent country" and "Get the Chinese out of Tibet."[26] Nepal's Minister for Education, likewise, refused to allow the textbooks to serve as the basis for Nepal's Tibetan language curriculum. Nepal's Curriculum Textbook and Supervision Development Centre convened a meeting to discuss the issue.[27] At the meeting, Tibetan exile officials supported the use of their own textbooks. Nepali officials rejected the idea; they even raised the issue of whether or not Tibetans should have their own schools in Nepal. They argued that Tibetans are a minority community in China; would it invite Chinese aggression to consider them a minority community in Nepal as well? Tibetan exile officials decided, then, not to become involved in Nepal's curriculum projects and to go on using their textbooks anyway. Lhundub Dorji supported the idea of new textbooks, specific to Tibetans in Nepal, however. Nepal's Minister for Education appointed him chairman of the Tibetan-language curriculum development committee for Nepal.

The Tibetan-language curriculum development committee is expected to develop new Tibetan-language textbooks more appropriate for Nepal. Funding for the project is significant, as UNESCO, UNICEF, and many other international organizations support it. Once the committee completes its textbooks, all schools that teach the Tibetan language in Nepal, including the exile administration's schools, will be required to use them. The exile administration risks losing control over its curriculum through its non-involvement with the project.

The third issue over which the Dorji School and the Dalai Lama's exile administration disagree is the future of Tibetan exiles in Nepal. Tibetan exile officials promote the idea that all Tibetans in Nepal will one day return to Tibet, when Tibet achieves independence. They use their schools to prepare students for a return. The Dorji School, along with most other private Tibetan schools in Nepal, wants to prepare Tibetans to integrate into Nepali society instead. The Dorji School has developed a plan to facilitate integration.

The plan involves the construction of a new Dorji School, a boarding school for five hundred ethnic Tibetans, that teaches both "modern" subjects (English, science, math, Nepali, ethics and morals) and Tibetan subjects (Tibetan languages, religious traditions, and customs).[28] Modern subjects would be taught in the classroom; Tibetan subjects would be taught in housing blocks. Each housing block would contain students from one particular ethnic Tibetan group, such as Sherpa, Manangi, Tamang, and Tibetan.[29] Students in each block would eat their own foods, celebrate their own festivals, and speak their own languages. In this manner, students from all ethnic Tibetan groups in Nepal would learn to live together and respect each other's customs.

In contrast with the Dorji School plan, Tibetan exile schools promote the idea of a return to Tibet. They teach Tibetan students about all of the problems China has caused in Tibet, such as environmental degradation, population transfer, and religious oppression. They promote the idea that all Tibetans must work to get the Chinese out of Tibet.[30] One result I observed through my work at Atisha School, is that Tibetan children learn to hate the Chinese. Young boys at the Atisha School, in discussing the Chinese, would routinely stand up and, making the motion of driving a knife into someone, say that they just want to kill all Chinese.

The Nepal government supports the efforts of the Dorji School to promote the idea of a peaceful integration into Nepal. It opposes the exile administration's independence agenda. Its goal is for the Tibetan exile problem to end, not to be perpetuated across generations.

In the midst of these many disagreements, Tibetan exile officials have tried to discredit the Dorji School by accusing it of accepting financial assistance from Taiwan, thereby turning against the Tibetan independence cause (as Taiwan maintains the position that Tibet has always been a part of China). As the director of HIMS, the only private Tibetan school not accused, explains: "The Dorji School, in particular, is entirely funded by Taiwan. That is why its students are not invited to participate in Tibetan events. Why is Taiwan funding them? To create disunity among the Tibetan community."[31]

These accusations dissuade some Tibetan exiles from sending their children to the Dorji School. As one Tibetan, a neighbor of the Dorji School, for example, explains: "When Lhundub Dorji started his school, he asked me if I would send my son. With his school so close to my house, my son could come home for lunch, so I agreed. After a year, the Dorji School grew very quickly and everyone started saying that Lhundub Dorji was accepting money from Taiwan. All of my relatives and friends started to say that maybe my son should not attend the school. I heard that the discipline at the school was not very good, so I sent my son to another school instead." Lhundub Dorji explains, however, that his school has more students than it can accommodate. The accusation that he accepts financial assistance from Taiwan has not been so detrimental. He argues, in turn, that he has no interest in affiliating with the exile administration. "There are no advantages," he explains, "and there are many obligations."

The many conflicts between the Dorji School and the Dalai Lama's exile administration demonstrate that not all Tibetan exile organizations in Nepal follow exile administration decisions. Tibetan exiles often disagree with the exile administration and pursue their own plans when it is in their interest. Tibetan exile organizations with their own sources of international support are in a stronger position to disagree and may separate from the exile administration entirely if the relationship becomes too contentious. The exile administration may use its resources to entice Tibetans into compliance, yet its efforts are not always successful.

Strategies of Legitimation: The Dalai Lama and the Myth of Return

Despite the contingencies of its position, the Dalai Lama's exile administration continues to claim authority over all Tibetans, inside and outside Tibet, including all Tibetan exiles in Nepal. During public events, such as the Dalai Lama's birthday celebration, Tibetan exile officials perform the appearance of absolute authority. They legitimate their authority both in the name of the Dalai Lama and their ability to facilitate a return to an independent Tibet.

Both strategies the exile administration uses to legitimate its authority are limited, however. The charisma of the Dalai Lama is limited by the ability of other Tibetan exile organizations to use it as well. The myth of return is limited by increasing doubt among Tibetan exiles in Nepal that the exile administration can facilitate it.[32] The exile administration continues to legitimate its authority through the same strategies, nevertheless. Its position as the largest and most well-organized Tibetan exile organization requires it.

The Dalai Lama's charisma is critical to the exile administration.[33] Tibetan exile officials claim the Dalai Lama as the leader of their organization. They make all decisions in his name. The exile administration is not the only organization that legitimates its authority through the charisma of the Dalai Lama, however. The Tibetan Youth Congress, the Tibetan Women's

Association, Chushi Gangdruk (a Tibetan organization composed of former guerrilla fighters), and many other Tibetan exile organizations also legitimate their authority in the same manner. When these many organizations make conflicting decisions, each side defends its position in the name of the Dalai Lama and what he has said. With all of them simultaneously claiming legitimacy through the Dalai Lama, who among many claimants supports the Dalai Lama's actual position, is by no means clear. The Dalai Lama himself is often ambiguous about whom he supports. He claims to support all Tibetans and the idea of Tibetan unity.

A 1995 conflict between Tibetan exile officials and the leaders of Chushi Gangdruk illustrates. The leaders of Chushi Gangdruk, a Tibetan organization composed of former guerrilla fighters, signed an agreement in 1994 with Taiwan's Mongolian and Tibetan Affairs Commission concerning how jurisdiction over Tibet would be divided should the government of Taiwan ever return to control the Chinese mainland in the future. Tibetan exile officials were understandably upset over the agreement, as they had always assumed that they are the only Tibetans empowered by the Dalai Lama to sign agreements with foreign governments. They responded with a series of public attacks against Chushi Gangdruk as well as by founding a new Chushi Gangdruk to replace the old one. Both the old and new Chushi Gangdruk now claim legitimacy as representatives of the true objectives of the Dalai Lama.[34]

Tibetan observers of the conflict were very critical about which side they should support. They did not just accept the new Chushi Gangdruk as the only one with legitimacy. They instead discussed the criticisms the old Chushi Gangdruk made of the exile administration (that it does not do enough to facilitate Tibetan independence, that it works only for its own interests, that it does not represent all Tibetans). One Tibetan exile explained his position as follows:

> Tibetan officials often use the Dalai Lama's name to support their own personal goals.... And when these officials do something wrong and you try to criticize them, they always say that you are criticizing not them but the Dalai Lama.

Another Tibetan described the Dalai Lama as the leader of all Tibetans generally rather than the leader of the exile administration in particular. He argued that there are many decisions Tibetan officials make that he, in his own personal opinion, does not think the Dalai Lama supports. He argued:

> The Dalai Lama (Gyalwa Rinpoche) used to be the head of both the country (*gyal-khab*) and the government (*shung*). Now he is the head only of the country and is withdrawing from involvement with the government.... These days, the Dalai Lama calls himself "the person who represents all Tibetans generally" (*pö chi-way mi*).

What the conflict demonstrates, therefore, is that although the exile administration may legitimate its authority through the charisma of the Dalai Lama, that does not mean that Tibetans conflate the decisions Tibetan exile officials make with the Dalai Lama's own decisions. They are generally very critical about people's claims to represent the Dalai Lama, and they make their own decisions about whom to believe.

Another means through which the Dalai Lama's exile administration legitimates its authority, thus, is through the myth of return to an independent Tibet. Tibetan exile officials promote the exile administration as the only organization that can negotiate a return. They do so through speeches, publications, and political activities they organize among Tibetan exiles in Nepal. We see the myth of return, for example, in a speech the director of the Tibet Office delivered to the delegates of the 1995 Kathmandu Tibetan Youth Congress. He explained that, with the help of the United Nations, the Dalai Lama's exile administration would facilitate a return. He explained:

> The United Nations intervenes in many conflicts around the world. They helped free Kuwait after Iraq occupied their country, and they sent peacekeeping forces there to prevent Iraq from invading again.... It has happened everywhere. In Bosnia-Herzegovina, in Afghanistan, in Somalia, in Beirut.... The U.N. Security Council, which includes America, England, France, China, and Russia, has veto power over all U.N. decisions, and in the past, China has blocked the U.N. from helping Tibet. These days, however, many countries are splitting apart, like Russia, Czechoslovakia, Yugoslavia, and as they do, they form new countries that become members of the U.N.... Maybe in the future, they will become as strong as the Security Council.... Then, the United Nations would have to implement its resolutions on Tibet.... We need to try ways tried in the past as well as new ways to make Tibet independent.[35]

The Dalai Lama's exile administration maintains a myth of return through the many political activities it organizes among the Tibetan exiles in Nepal as well. These include political demonstrations, strategy meetings, and petitions in support of Tibetan independence. From 1995 to 1997, they also included a referendum (*mang-mö thag-chö*) that Tibetan exile officials conducted among all Tibetan exiles about the future of Tibet. Through the referendum, Tibetan exile officials asked Tibetans which of four strategies they should use as the focus for their efforts to achieve a return. The strategies were the middle path (*lam u-ma*), independence (*rangzen*), self-determination (*rang thag rang-chö*), and peaceful resistance (*den-pay u-tsug*). Tibetan exile officials claimed they would follow whatever strategy the Tibetans chose. At the time the referendum was first announced, Tibetan exiles in Nepal were confused as to its purpose. One Tibetan, for example, argued that:

Most Tibetans, if you ask which of the four methods is the best, are not able to answer. If they could, they would say to someone else, "Here, you choose for me." They just do not know. It is like asking my daughter which method she prefers. If you asked her, "Which do you want, the middle path, independence, or peaceful resistance," she would answer, "I want chocolate." The choice does not make sense. It is like asking Tibetans to choose between the Buddha, the dharma, and the sangha. How can they choose? All of them are good.

Tibetan exile officials proceeded in their efforts to educate Tibetan exiles about the referendum for almost two years. Their efforts prompted discussion about which strategy has any chance of success. In the end, however, Tibetan exiles in Nepal remained doubtful that they would ever be able to return to Tibet. They remained doubtful of the ability of the exile administration to facilitate a return.

Tibetan exiles in Nepal did indeed discuss the referendum. Advocates for the middle path proposed that only negotiation with the Chinese government for some form of autonomy, as a preliminary step toward independence, would work. They cited the Dalai Lama's Strasbourg Proposal as their model.[36] Advocates for independence, in contrast, opposed negotiation with the Chinese. They proposed the use of all means, violent if necessary, to achieve independence. Some Tibetan exiles in Nepal described it as a policy of terrorism. The Palestine Liberation Organization served as their model. Advocates for self-determination proposed the use of the United Nations, and other intergovernmental organizations, to pressure China to conduct a referendum in Tibet. They cited the legal right of the Tibetans, as a people under international law, to self-determination. They also cited the many resolutions state governments and international organizations have passed in support of Tibet as evidence that the strategy would work. Advocates for peaceful resistance proposed a campaign of active non-violent protest. They cited Mahatma Gandhi's campaign for Indian independence as their model. They advocated sending Tibetan exiles into Tibet to stage non-violent political demonstrations, group after group, so that through their arrest and political detention, the international community would be made continuously aware of China's denial of basic human rights in Tibet. Only through the attempt to exercise the rights of the Tibetans, they argued, would the denial of those rights by the Chinese government be revealed.

Tibetan exiles in Nepal discussed the advantages and disadvantages of these strategies. One Tibetan speculated that only the fourth approach, peaceful resistance, would work, because it is the only thing that Tibetans can do themselves. Another argued:

Peaceful resistance will never work.... The British, when they were in India, did not like to kill so many people because they are Christian. The Chinese have no religion. If they have to kill hundreds of people, they will kill them. If they have to kill thousands, they do not care. They have no guilt. The Chinese government killed and imprisoned its own people after Tiananmen. If they can kill their own people, they can kill Tibetans.

Another argued:

If the government tried to send people to Tibet to protest, who would go? No one I know would go. If my son wanted to go, I would not let him. Children are supposed to look after their parents when they are old.[37]

Other Tibetans speculated that China will just disintegrate like the Soviet Union, and after it does, the United Nations will help them become independent:

There are many places under Chinese jurisdiction—Mongolia, Tibet, Taiwan, Hong Kong—and they will all want their own countries. Certainly there will be problems with Hong Kong because it has been under the Injees [British] for so long. The people there will not stand to live under a communist system.

Again, other Tibetans disagreed:

Many people are hoping that China will fall apart like Russia did, and then maybe negotiation can happen, but in my own personal opinion, even if China does fall apart, that does not mean that Tibet will become independent.

Despite their discussions, after an initial round of votes, Tibetan exile officials concluded that most Tibetan exiles are still not educated enough to decide how the exile administration should proceed. They cited a preponderance of ballots that stated only that the Dalai Lama should decide as reason enough to postpone the referendum indefinitely. Their decision renewed doubt among Tibetan exiles in Nepal that they would ever be able to return to an independent Tibet. They remained doubtful that the exile administration is capable of facilitating a return.

The exile administration continues to legitimate its authority over the Tibetan exiles in Nepal through the charisma of the Dalai Lama and the myth of return, nevertheless. Its position requires some form of legitimation. Its efforts to legitimate its authority enable it both to govern fellow Tibetan exiles (although not without negotiation) and to maintain its middleman position in the provision of international assistance. International organizations fund the exile administration in part because it claims to represent all Tibetans; it claims to have full Tibetan support. As the largest and most well-organized Tibetan exile organization, its claims are credible enough to facilitate the assistance relationship.

Notes

1. To Tibetans, July 6, 1995 was the Dalai Lama's sixty-first birthday, as Tibetans consider children to be a year old at birth. In Tibetan, July 6 is referred to as *tung-kar du-chen*, an honorific term for birthday celebration.

2. The speech ended, very powerfully, with "Tibetans should always thank the Nepal government and the Nepali people by respecting their feelings, traditions, and customs.... There is no single Tibetan individual who can act without representing the whole of the Tibetan community. Everything Tibetans do, they have been able to do because they are Tibetan, so for the good name of all Tibetans, they should always be respectful." The reason for this last point, the director of the Tibet Office later explained to me, was that a fight had occurred the day before at a soccer tournament in honor of the Dalai Lama's birthday between the Tibetan team from Jawalakhel and a team of Tamang peoples. During the fight, Tibetans from the Jawalakhel camp threw rocks and bricks at the Tamang players, and the Tamangs, in turn, warned the Tibetans that if they showed their faces at the birthday celebration the next day, they would be killed. The director of the Tibet Office had personally promised Nepal's home minister that nothing would go wrong at the celebration. He worried that the fight might continue there. If that happened, he explained, it would be detrimental not only to his relations with the home minister but also to the Dalai Lama, as the event had been organized to honor the Dalai Lama during a year considered dangerous and uncertain for him in accordance with the Tibetan twelve-year calendrical cycle.

3. The exile administration's printing office annually publishes large, colorful wall calendars to indicate which days are Tibetan holidays. The calendars are enormously popular among Tibetans. Each year, they carry a different image representative of Tibetans, such as a mandala, the Buddhist wheel of life, or the Potala palace. Tibetans use them to decorate the walls of their homes long after the year has ended.

4. Goldstein (1968: 161) discusses the difference between the personal charisma of the Dalai Lama and the charisma the Dalai Lama is presumed to embody because of his office. There is a further distinction to be made as well. That is between the Dalai Lama's office and the Tibetan exile administration.

5. Only pure charismatic leaders both exercise and legitimate their authority in the same way—that is, through the influence of their individual personalities. Over time, as they establish bureaucratic organizations to maintain or pass on their leadership positions, they too begin to exercise their authority through other means, a process Weber refers to as the routinization of charisma (Weber 1968: 254).

6. I have heard Tibetans in many different contexts use "dirty hands" (*lag-pa tsog-pa*) as a metaphor to describe unpleasant business (business that is either politically or morally suspect or that makes unpleasant any personal relationships that would otherwise remain strong). To have "clean hands" (*lag-pa tsang-ma*) means to be free from unpleasant business. Thus, the metaphor of a handkerchief (*lag-pa chi-sa*) refers to people on whom unpleasant business can be blamed.

7. The information presented here derives from an interview I conducted with the production director himself on March 8, 1995.

8. I do not know how, exactly, the land would have been registered. Nepali law prevents foreign organizations from registering land. One possibility, pursued successfully by other schools, is to establish a school foundation, registered under the Association Registration Act, and to register the land in its name. Another is to find Tibetans with Nepali citizenship, employed by the Education Department, and to register the land in their name.

9. Luck (*lung-ta*) plays an important part in Tibetan explanations for the success or failure of their projects. Luck is often used in comparison with other concepts such as merit (*so-day; so-nam*); personal power or influence related to wealth (*wang-thang*); respect (*tong*); experience (*nyam-nyong*); and skill (*lag-tse*). Luck and merit seem similar in many ways.

Tibetans believe individuals can increase both through their actions. I once asked a Tibetan scholar to explain the difference between them. He explained it as follows: "Merit is the result of things people do, of their actions. If you do good deeds (*so-nam sag*), then you will have more merit. If you do bad deeds, you will have less merit. So there is the possibility of increasing or decreasing your merit depending upon what you do. Merit is not something that exists in the mind (*sem*) yet is external. The idea of merit comes from Buddhism. Luck is an idea that came from Bön or whatever else existed before Buddhism. Luck is something given by the gods. It exists in the mind (*sem*) and one definition of it might be 'power that is given in the mind' (*sem-la nü-pa che-gi-yö-ray*). If a person's level of luck is high, then they have a strong mind." Tibetans increase their luck by praying to gods (*monlam gyab*), raising prayer flags (*dar-chog tag*), and burning incense (*sang-pül*).

10. Weber (1968: 316) also discusses the importance of exclusion, and its threat, to effect compliance when violence, and its threat, are not available. The other options he cites include "magically-conditioned advantages and disadvantages" and "rewards or punishments in the next world."

11. In December 1991, Baba Yeshe, in hopes that the exile administration would help support his camps, traveled to Bodh Gaya, where the Dalai Lama was performing a Kalachakra ceremony, and arranged for an audience with him. According to Baba Yeshe, the Dalai Lama told him that he is a good person, that he did nothing wrong by surrendering to the Nepal army, and that the exile administration would, from then on, recognize his camps. In 1992, the director of the Tibet Office visited the Jorpati camp and extended it official recognition. Most of the information that follows derives from interviews I conducted with Baba Yeshe on August 18, 1995 and with Jorpati camp administrators on December 4, 1995.

12. Baba Yeshe, personal communication, August 18, 1995. Avedon (1984: 126) reports that there are thirteen settlements in India that are also unrecognized by the Dalai Lama's exile administration, as the leaders of those settlements sided with Baba Yeshe when he surrendered to the Nepal army. Devoe (1983: 158) reports that these settlements suffer the same relative poverty as the Baba Yeshe camps in Nepal, as they "were receiving minimal or no donor aid" in contrast with other settlements which had "experienced continuity, and in some cases, an increase in aid." Devoe (1983: 158) supports the idea of a deliberate policy of exclusion.

13. Most Tibetan exile officials I interviewed said only that I would have to speak with the director of the Tibet Office to discuss the Baba Yeshe camps. The director, although willing to discuss most other subjects with me, repeatedly evaded my questions about the camps. The assistant director of the Tibet Office admitted that the Jorpati camp receives no assistance from the exile administration but argued that it is their citizenship status that is the problem. Asked why other Tibetans with Nepali citizenship receive assistance, he responded: "The new [Tibetan] constitution allows people who are forced to take citizenship to remain in Tibetan society, but their [Jorpati residents'] citizenship is not that kind. If people take citizenship only to be able to work and set up factories, that is allowed, but taking the kind of citizenship they have is not allowed."

14. Avedon (1984: 126) reports that exile officials have also accused "easterners" in thirteen Tibetan settlement camps in India of accepting financial assistance from Taiwan. Many Tibetan lamas in Nepal, and most Tibetan school directors, have also been accused. Kunsang Lama, a Tibetan exile from South India, claims that even some Tibetan exile officials have accepted money from Taiwan (Takhla 1990; T. Norbu 1990; and *Tibetan Review* 25 [9]: 8).

15. Other Tibet Offices worldwide are located in Delhi, New York, Toronto, Sydney, Tokyo, Paris, London, and Geneva. Tibet Offices maintain contact with the host government and with foreign embassies to advocate on behalf of Tibetans and the Tibetan independence cause in addition to looking after the needs of the Tibetan exiles under their jurisdiction. Tibet Offices differ in that manner from the more numerous Tibetan welfare offices (*day-dön lay-khung*), located in all formal Tibetan exile settlements. Tibetan welfare offices look after

the needs of Tibetan exiles yet play no diplomatic function. For that reason, the Tibetan Cabinet of Ministers (*kashag*) manages the Tibet Offices whereas the Home Department manages the welfare offices; the Cabinet of Ministers, in the name of the Dalai Lama, appoints Tibet Office directors, whereas the inhabitants of the settlements elect their welfare officers.

16. Much of the information I present here derives from an interview I conducted with the director of the Tibet Office on July 28, 1995.

17. The schools include Atisha School, Srongtsen Bhrikuti School, Namgyal Middle School, Namgyal High School, and the Himalayan International Mountain School. Of the thirteen businesses, six are controlled by the exile administration's Home Department, four are controlled by the exile administration's Finance Department, and three are controlled by the semi-autonomous Mustang Organization. The five Tibetan Freedom Movement offices include those in Jawalakhel (*jo-khel*); Boudha (*chorten*); Swayambu (*p'agpa shing-kun*), Kathmandu city (*gye-sa*), and Jorpati (*jor-pa-ti*). The Tibet Office divides Kathmandu into these five districts (*sa-nay*) for administrative purposes.

18. The Tibetan Freedom Movement was initially founded to conduct political activities, such as organizing public demonstrations and otherwise advocating for Tibetan independence. Over time, its function has changed. Tibetan exiles in Nepal complain that now all it does is collect taxes. Freedom Movement representatives defend themselves by saying that they are not allowed to conduct independence activities in Nepal.

19. Tibetans call them green books only when talking about them in English. When speaking Tibetan, they call them freedom booklets (*rangzen lagteb*). Green books are about the size of a passport. They contain an information page with the bearer's name, father's name, mother's name, and birthplace, along with a unique identification number. They also contain a number of pages, with squares marked off for stamps, where tax payments can be recorded.

20. In the 1970s, when the Tibetan Freedom Movement was first established, some Manangi and Sherpa people, and even some Westerners, applied for and received green books to enable them to contribute to the Dalai Lama's exile administration. At first, this posed no problem, as the exile administration had few international sponsors and few resources to provide. Over the years, it has become a problem, however, as Sherpa and Manangi people now use their green books to apply for resources, such as scholarships for their children in schools affiliated with the Dalai Lama's exile administration. With the ratification of the 1990 Charter for the Tibetan Peoples, it became necessary to demonstrate Tibetan parentage to apply for a green book, yet some green books still remain in circulation among non-Tibetans from earlier years.

21. The standard tax rate is higher for Tibetans resettled in Western countries. In the United States, it is two dollars a month.

22. In addition to these taxes, one Tibetan also described paying an annual voluntary not-eating tax (*zay-cha-dö*) of five rupees per day for two days as a symbol of loyalty to the Dalai Lama's exile administration.

23. Lhundub Dorji, personal communication, November 29, 1995. The story that follows, unless otherwise noted, derives from interviews with Lhundub Dorji himself.

24. Snow Lion Foundation General Assembly minutes from 1982 to 1983 report only that a meeting about the Boudha School occurred. The logic behind the decision is unrecorded.

25. Prior to 1986, most Tibetan exile schools used an assortment of monastic-style Tibetan language texts as the basis for their curriculum. Students found these texts difficult to understand; teachers considered them inappropriate for a "modern" education. Sherab Gyatso, the director of the project to develop the new textbooks, describes the many problems with monastic-style texts in "Language Books that Scare Children Away," in "The Crisis of the Tibetan Language in Exile," *Tibetan Review* 28 (9): 16.

26. Lessons seven and eleven of the exile administration's sixth-grade Tibetan language textbook illustrates further. Lesson seven, entitled "Tibetan Heroes" (*pö-gi pa-wo*), commemorates Tibetans in Tibet who protested against China in September 1987. Lesson eleven, entitled "Potala," in describing the history of the Dalai Lama's palace in Tibet, depicts

Tibet as an independent state. The preface of all of the books, in addition, reports that the books were written to preserve the Tibetan language and culture from Chinese oppression.

27. The Nepal government founded its Curriculum Centre soon after its 1990 constitution guaranteed to "each community residing within the Kingdom of Nepal" the "right to preserve and promote its language, script and culture" as well as "the right to operate schools up to the primary level in its own mother tongue" (Constitution of the Kingdom of Nepal 2047 [1990], part 3, article 18, sections 1 and 2). The Centre's task is to develop curricula for all minority communities in Nepal. The account I report here of the Centre's meeting is a combination of stories told to me both by Lhundub Dorji and the Snow Lion Foundation representative who attended the meeting.

28. The information I report here derives from an interview I conducted with Lhundub Dorji on November 29, 1995.

29. The ten blocks would include: Sherpa; Tamang; Newar; Tibetan; Manangi; Gurung; Rai; Limbu; Chepang; and Thakali. It is interesting to note that Lhundub Dorji, in this context, considers Newars to be ethnic Tibetans. Many Tibetan exiles in Nepal consider them to be more Nepali instead.

30. The Tibetan language teacher at the Atisha School showed me materials the exile administration's Department of Information and International Relations had sent him to use in his classroom. They are the basis for the discussion I present here.

31. Ngawang Choechen, personal communication, May 17, 1995.

32. When compared with other exiles in similar situations, it seems unlikely the Tibetan exiles will ever be able to return to an independent Tibet. The Tibetan exiles may be classified, in accordance with a framework developed by Kunz (1973), as "anticipatory refugees," that is, former ruling elite and their associates who leave their country during a successful revolution, "provided that they have reasonable assurances of finding reasonable resettlement elsewhere." Anticipatory refugees, according to Kunz (1973), very rarely return. Zolberg, Suhrke, and Aguayo (1989: 250) provide further examples to support Kunz's framework.

33. Weber (1968: 241) defines charisma as "a certain quality of an individual personality by virtue of which he is considered extraordinary and treated as endowed with supernatural, superhuman, or at least specifically exceptional powers or qualities."

34. The conflict between Chushi Gangdruk and the Dalai Lama's exile administration erupted in the summer of 1994, while I was studying in Dharamsala. My information about the conflict derives from three sources: a document Chushi Gangdruk sent to the Cabinet of Ministers to explain its position, copies of which were posted publicly in Dharamsala; interviews with Chushi Gangdruk's leaders in *Sargyur*, a Tibetan news video tape; and interviews with both parties in *Mangtso*, a Tibetan-language newspaper.

35. Tashi Namgyal, director of the Tibet Office, speech delivered at the 1995 Regional Tibetan Youth Congress meeting in Kathmandu, October 21, 1995. I recorded the speech and translated it with the help of my Tibetan language teachers.

36. The Strasbourg Proposal is a set of five points the Dalai Lama offered as the basis for negotiation with China, during a speech he delivered to the European Parliament on June 5, 1988. It proposed that all ethnic Tibetan areas in China should become a single province; that the province should be governed democratically; that China would remain responsible for Tibet's foreign policy; that China could maintain a limited number of troops in Tibet until Tibet could be transformed into a demilitarized zone; and that Tibetans would have to ratify all plans through a nationwide referendum.

37. Her explanation continued with: "The only people who ever protest are monks and nuns. They have no children to look after and no family connections. If they die, there is no family that suffers. When protests take place in Lhasa and the Chinese start shooting, other people always run away and the monks and nuns are left standing by themselves. Only the monks and nuns ever stand up for anything."

6

Conflict and Consciousness

"There are several different legends about the first human beings in Tibet," lesson one of a sixth-grade textbook written by the Dalai Lama's exile administration begins. "It is said that the enlightened father monkey, the Great Bodhisattva Chenresig, and the mother rock demoness mated in a cave in the area of Yarlung Tsethang. From their union, many children were born. The children gradually multiplied to produce the ancestors of the Tibetan people. Six lineages came into being: Se, Mu, Dong, Tong, Dra, and Dru."[1]

The lesson, "The Origin of Tibet and the Tibetans," goes on to describe Tibet as its own country, situated north of India, Nepal, and Bhutan, east of Pakistan, south of Mongolia, and west of China. It portrays Tibet as a "perfect ecosystem" (*yul-jong gi kö-pa pun-sum-tsog*) with much to offer to the world. The story's intent is to educate young Tibetans in a number of political claims–that the Tibetans are a people unto themselves (that they did not derive from some other ethnic or national group); that they are the indigenous owners of the Tibetan plateau; and that Tibet is its own country. These claims counteract China's claims that the Tibetans are (and have always been) one of China's national minorities and that Tibet is a part of the "great motherland" of China.

"The Origin of Tibet and the Tibetans" is an example of mythico-history. A mythico-history is a story that defines the collective past of a people in order to make present-day political claims (Malkki 1989: 125). Liisa Malkki developed the concept to analyze how refugees living in camps versus those living in town discuss their lives. She argues that refugee camps provide fertile ground for the development of mythico-histories, that they promote the development and maintenance of collective national consciousness. She uses the example of Hutu from Burundi living in Tanzania to demonstrate that camp refugees, far more often than town refugees, identify with a collective national past.

The Tibetan exiles in Nepal resemble the Hutu in Tanzania in that they can also be divided into camp residents and town residents. Of the Tibetan exiles in Nepal, less than half live in camps; the others live self-settled throughout Nepal. In my interviews with both camp Tibetans and self-settled Tibetans, I noticed a similar pattern to what Malkki (1989, 1995b) observed whereby camp residents demonstrated a greater commitment to the idea of a Tibetan national past than non-camp residents. Unlike Malkki (1989, 1995b), however, I attribute the difference not to the structure of the camp itself yet to the political strategies of the camp leaders. Tibetan exile leaders use the camp structure to cultivate and maintain the idea of a collective national past among the Tibetan exiles. One such strategy involves the use of mythico-histories, like "The Origin of Tibet and the Tibetans," to encourage young Tibetan exiles to maintain Tibet's political cause.

This chapter analyzes how the Dalai Lama's exile administration cultivates and maintains a collective national consciousness among the Tibetans in Nepal. It argues that the exile administration faces two simultaneous challenges in its efforts. The first derives from the relationships the Tibetan exiles maintain with the many international organizations that assist them. International organizations in some ways help the exile administration. They provide the funds, for example, that maintain Tibetan exile schools. International organizations, in other ways, challenge exile administration efforts, however. They encourage the Tibetan exiles to accommodate their own norms and values, thereby influencing how the Tibetan exiles view themselves, their collective past, and their political future.

The second challenge derives from the relationships the Tibetan exiles maintain with local, regional, or sectarian communities. These communities include, for example, Khampa (eastern Tibetan), Amdowa (northeastern Tibetan), Kagyupa (follower of the Kagyu sect of Buddhism), and Bönpo (follower of the Bön religion). Tibetan exiles, at times, identify more with these sub-national groups than with the Tibetan nation. They also at times disagree with the exile administration's definition of the Tibetan nation and its membership.

The efforts of the Dalai Lama's exile administration to promote a distinct Tibetan national identity, as a result, may succeed in international contexts—being Tibetan carries considerable cultural capital, for example, when soliciting international assistance—yet it is not as successful in local contexts. Among the Tibetan exiles themselves, there is considerable debate about what it means to be Tibetan. As Tibetans negotiate their way through their everyday lives, they read different meanings into the Tibetan identity than what the exile administration promotes. The exile administration's definition of what it means to be Tibetan, far from being hegemonic, is only one of many interpretive options.

The Exile Administration's Efforts to Promote a Tibetan National Identity

The Dalai Lama's exile administration cultivates and maintains a distinct Tibetan national identity to promote its political cause, maintain unity among the Tibetan exiles, and educate the next generation in its own version of what it means to be Tibetan. These efforts have two principal audiences. One consists of an international audience composed of state leaders and officials from international organizations. Tibetan exile officials promote the idea of a Tibetan nation among them to claim political ownership over Tibet and to raise funds to support that claim. The other audience consists of Tibetans themselves, both those who live in Tibet and those in exile. Tibetan exile officials promote the idea of a Tibetan nation among them to maintain unity and to educate the next generation as Tibetans. These efforts are highly interrelated. In order to maintain their political claim to Tibet, Tibetan exile officials promote a unified Tibetan community. In order to maintain unity, they promote their political claims. Tibetan exile officials pursue different strategies with their different audiences, however. The goal—to promote and maintain the idea of a common Tibetan nation—may be the same, yet the strategies, and their frames of reference, differ.

The frame of reference for the exile administration's international audience is international law. To its international audience, the exile administration promotes the idea that the Tibetans are indeed a "people," as defined in international law, with a claim to indigenous ownership over Tibet. Its claim is based on the principle of self-determination, as defined and outlined in such instruments as the Covenant on Economic, Social and Cultural Rights and the Covenant on Civil and Political Rights. Both state: "All peoples have the right of self-determination. By virtue of that right they freely determine their political status and freely pursue their economic, social and cultural development."[2] Tibetan exile officials claim that the Tibetans are a people who qualify for self-determination. Cabinet Minister Tashi Wangdi's most recent statement on the issue uses UNESCO criteria to argue that Tibetans are a people due to their common historical traditions, cultural homogeneity, linguistic unity, religious and ideological affinity, territorial connection, and common economic life (Wangdi 1996).[3]

Tibetan exile officials maintain their claim to be a people under international law, entitled to self-determination, through a number of efforts. They lobby foreign governments and international organizations. They publish articles outlining their qualifications as a people. They make speeches about the Tibetans' status as a people at international conferences, such as the 1995 U.N. Conference on Women in Beijing. Their efforts are almost always in the English language, composed with due attention to the norms of international legal discourse.

These efforts have led to a number of resolutions in support of the Tibetans' right to self-determination. They include resolutions adopted by the U.N. General Assembly in 1959, 1961, and 1965; by the Australian Parliament in 1990; by the German Parliament in 1996; and by the European Parliament in 1997. These efforts have also helped to recruit financial and administrative support from such organizations as Amnesty International, the International Committee of Lawyers for Tibet, the U.S.-Tibet Committee, and the Tibet Information Network. All of these groups support the exile administration's claim that the Tibetans are a "people," entitled to self-determination.

Tibetan exile officials use different strategies and a different frame of reference for promoting the idea of a common Tibetan nation among Tibetans themselves. The frame of reference they use among Tibetans themselves is Tibet's mythico-historic past. Tibetan exile officials promote the idea among Tibetans that Tibet has always been its own country, that Tibetans are its indigenous people, and that Tibetans have maintained a continuous history as a unified people since the primordial era.

It is a paradox that despite the primordial nature of their claims, Tibetan exile officials use relatively modern strategies to promote them. Their strategies resemble those that Anderson (1983) cites as typical of national political elite worldwide. Anderson (1983: 67) proposes the idea that there are common strategies that national political elite worldwide use to help people to imagine themselves as members of the same national community. He proposes that, at base, these strategies rely upon (1) the use of national print languages; and (2) the "piracy" of other nations' models of nationalism (Anderson 1983: 67). Tibetan exile officials use both of these strategies to promote the Tibetan nation.

When Tibetans first arrived in exile in the 1950s and 1960s, they had no standardized Tibetan national language. Exiles from different regions in Tibet spoke their own mutually unintelligible dialects. They shared a script, used principally for religious texts, yet they shared no common referent for the idea of a Tibetan national language. As with the problem of language, the Tibetan exiles shared little by way of a common national history. History, in pre-1950 Tibet, consisted mostly of biographies of Buddhist teachers, the Dalai Lamas among them; records of the founding of important monasteries; and retrospective chronicles of the first Tibetan kings. The Tibetans had no national history, or "history in the Enlightenment mode" to use Duara's (1995: 33) phrase for it. They had only Buddhist histories.[4] Tibetan exile officials promoted a common Tibetan language and common national history through a number of strategies. They established schools with standardized textbooks that teach Tibetan language and history; founded libraries, archives, and museums to exhibit the textual and material evidence of Tibet's history; and published books, pamphlets, calendars, and maps to illustrate Tibet's national past. Anderson (1983: 67) categorizes all of these strategies as examples of the use of a national print language to promote the idea of the nation.

Tibetan exile officials also "pirate" other nations' models of nationalism in their efforts to promote the Tibetan nation (Anderson 1983: 67). The Constitution for the Future of Tibet, composed in exile in 1963, for example, was based on the U.S. model (Knaus 1999: 252). The Charter for the Tibetan Exiles, composed in 1990, was based on U.S., British, and Indian models. Symbols of the Tibetan nation imitate those used by national political elite worldwide as well. They include a national flag, national anthem, national costumes, and national landmarks. The content of these symbols derives from Tibetan sources. The flag, for example, has a mountain and two snow lions; national landmarks include the Potala palace (the Dalai Lama's palace in Lhasa) and the Yumbulhakhang (a building that marks the site of the first Tibetan kingdom in Tibet's Yarlung Valley). Their forms and functions, however, comply with what have become international norms.[5]

In addition to these strategies, Tibetan exile officials use a number of other related strategies Anderson (1983) does not mention yet that are important in the exile context for keeping people together to enable the promotion of national consciousness among them. These strategies are necessary to counteract the worldwide dispersal of the Tibetan exiles.[6] To counteract their dispersal, the exile administration provides incentives—such as employment, housing, educational opportunities, and health care—to encourage the Tibetan exiles to remain together, ideally in the exile administration's settlement camps. In addition, the exile administration makes access to other opportunities and resources, such as the scholarship funds it administers, contingent upon compliance with its policies, such as not taking citizenship in other countries.

The argument here—that Tibetan exile officials pursue a number of related strategies to keep the Tibetan exiles together and to promote national consciousness among them—is not to say that the Tibetans, prior to the Tibetan exile, did not have any sense of what they have in common. Tibetan exile officials did not create the idea of the Tibetan nation *de novo*. Tibetans, prior to the Tibetan exile, regularly distinguished themselves from Chinese (*gya-mi*) and Nepalese (*bel-po*), for example, based on such markers as clothing, food, and religion. Tibetans recognized each other as people who wore *chubas* (a type of wrap-around cloak, tied at the waist); people who drank butter tea and ate *tsampa* (a type of ground barley flour); and people who respected the Dalai Lama and his position. What Tibetan exile officials have done is to nationalize these characteristics, to promote them as the basis for particular nationalist claims. Tibetan exile officials use these common characteristics as evidence of the Tibetans' history as a nation so that today, in the present political context, they can claim the right of self-determination, under their leadership.

The 1990 Charter for the Tibetan Exiles provides an example of how Tibetan exile officials have nationalized Tibetan cultural characteristics. The Charter outlines what it means not just to be Tibetan, yet to be a Tibetan citizen (*yulmi*). It makes Tibetan citizenship contingent on the fulfillment of the following responsibilities (*lengen*):

1. Allegiance to Tibet
2. Compliance with the Charter and the laws of the Tibetan exile administration
3. Participation in the struggle for the Tibetan cause
4. Payment of voluntary taxes to the exile administration
5. Performance of all obligations imposed by the laws of the Tibetan exile administration[7]

The Charter conflates the idea of belonging to the Tibetan nation with loyalty to the exile administration and its political cause. It makes political loyalty to a nation and its leaders part of what it means to be Tibetan.

Exile administration efforts to promote and maintain a distinct Tibetan national identity among Tibetans are critical to its claims to national self-determination. Tibetan exile officials need to demonstrate that the Tibetans are unified as a nation under their leadership to be able to function internationally. They need to be accepted by the Tibetans themselves as their legitimate representatives to be able to assert their claims. Exile administration efforts to promote the idea of the Tibetan nation among Tibetans and among the leaders of states and international organizations are thus highly interrelated. They consist of different strategies, yet they are two sides of the same coin. Together they constitute Tibetan exile officials' nation-building efforts.

Support, among Tibetans, for the Exile Administration's Efforts

Exile administration efforts to promote and maintain a distinct Tibetan national identity have succeeded among certain groups of Tibetan exiles in Nepal. They include Tibetans educated in exile administration schools as well as Tibetans who work for the exile administration and its many affiliated projects. These Tibetans have organized to help the exile administration in its efforts. Their organizations include the Tibetan Youth Congress (*shonnu tsogpa*), the Tibetan Women's Association (*bu-may tsogpa*), and alumni associations (*lob-zur tsogpa*). What all of these organizations have in common is that they too promote the idea of the Tibetan nation. They argue against local, regional, and sectarian groups to promote Tibetan national interests above all others.

The Tibetan Youth Congress (TYC) was the first of these many groups to organize. It was founded in 1970 by young Tibetan exiles in India.[8] It expanded into Nepal soon after it was founded. By 1972, it had offices in each of the Swiss-Tibetan settlement camps in Nepal as well as in Kathmandu.[9] In 1995, it claimed a membership of 10,000 Tibetans, 1000 of them in Kathmandu. Its four principal objectives, as outlined in its constitution, are:

1. To promote national unity and integrity by giving up all distinctions based on regionalism, status or religion
2. To work for the preservation and promotion of the Tibetan religion, culture, and tradition
3. To struggle for the total independence of Tibet
4. To follow the guidance of His Holiness the Dalai Lama

The TYC works to achieve its objectives by organizing political demonstrations, debates, and petitions to international organizations. The TYC office in Kathmandu, in 1995, for example, helped to organize a peace march from Dharamsala to Delhi, India; sponsored a debate about the exile administration's referendum; and submitted a petition to the U.N. office in Nepal to ask the U.N. to implement its resolutions on Tibet and to include statements by the Dalai Lama in its fiftieth anniversary publications.[10] The TYC works closely with the exile administration to accomplish its goals. A TYC meeting I attended in Boudha in October 1995 illustrates. The stated purpose of the meeting was to celebrate the fiftieth anniversary of the founding of the United Nations. The meeting schedule included ample time for Tibetan exile officials to speak. Of the four main speakers, two were Tibetan exile officials. The schedule also included a speech contest, the topic of which was how to get qualified candidates into the exile administration's twelfth legislative assembly. The schedule, as I recorded it, was as follows:

1:45–3:00   Video from Dharamsala showing the celebration of the 25th anniversary of the founding of the Tibetan Youth Congress
3:00–3:15   Introduction and welcome speech by Sonam Gyaltsen, TYC's regional chairman for Kathmandu
3:15–3:45   Speech by Tashi Namgyal, representative of His Holiness the Dalai Lama to Nepal and director of the Tibet Office [The speech concerned the role the United Nations could play in bringing about Tibetan independence.]
3:45–4:30   Speech Contest
4:45–5:00   Speech by Khetsun Sangpo Rinpoche, representative to the exile administration's eleventh legislative assembly
5:00–5:15   Speech by Kunga Thinley, TYC's regional vice-chairman for Kathmandu
5:15–5:30   Tea and Food

The TYC not only works closely with the exile administration. It also serves as a training ground for exile administration service. Many members of the exile administration today are former TYC members.

TYC describes itself as a voice of opposition to the exile administration. Its members do, at times, disagree with exile administration decisions. Many TYC members protested vociferously, for example, against the Dalai Lama's Strasbourg proposal, in which he argued that he would accept some form of autonomy other than independence from China.[11] TYC made opposition to the Strasbourg proposal its official position. What TYC members share with the exile administration, however, is a commitment to Tibetan nationalism. TYC takes the nation as its organizing principle.

The Tibetan Women's Association (TWA), likewise, takes the Tibetan nation as its organizing principle. It was founded by Tibetan exiles in India in 1984, in memory of Tibetan women who died while demonstrating against Tibet's incorporation into China. Its principal objective, as outlined in its fundraising publications, is "to raise public awareness of the abuses faced by the Tibetan people, particularly women in Chinese-occupied Tibet." Toward that end, it works with various women's groups worldwide to publicize human rights abuses in Tibet. Its principal activity throughout the early 1990s was to prepare for the 1995 United Nations World Conference on Women in Beijing. The TWA sent nine Tibetan representatives to Beijing and nine non-Tibetan representatives from Tibet support groups around the world.

TWA expanded into Kathmandu in 1988. Its Kathmandu office, in addition to working with the exile administration to promote the Tibetan cause, also conducts social welfare projects.[12] In 1995, it was managing an old age home for fifteen elderly Tibetans, providing scholarships for Tibetan orphans to enable them to attend exile administration schools, and assisting Tibetan women recently divorced from their husbands to find work and child care. The Kathmandu TWA funds its social welfare activities through membership fees; fundraising events, such as a Tibetan food festival they sponsored in 1995; and through the sale of Tibet t-shirts, cups, and bags.

Kathmandu's TWA has also made plans to conduct a summer program to teach Tibetan customs and traditions to Kathmandu's Tibetan youth. As the president of Kathmandu's TWA office explained, she has become very concerned about Tibetan children in Kathmandu who act too much like foreigners and do not know good Tibetan manners. When Tibetans sit, she explained, they do not just fall down on their chair, but they fold back their *chuba* and sit with their legs straight, never crossed. When Tibetans hand someone something, they do it with two hands, not one, and they bow down low when they do it. When Tibetans pour tea, they do it with both hands and then they offer the tea to the person with both hands. She said that she is very worried about Tibetan children not learning these behaviors as part of the Tibetan culture.

Through these efforts, the TWA, like the TYC, promotes the idea of a unified and distinct Tibetan nation. It works to keep Tibetans united and to promote what it defines as Tibetan customs and traditions among them. The TWA, unlike the TYC, also works to promote the interests of women. Its efforts to assist abused women and recent divorcées are an example. The TWA also is the one political forum through which Tibetan women can rise to positions of political leadership in the exile communities. Unlike TYC's meetings, dominated by men, TWA's meetings enable women to speak about their concerns. Whereas TYC's meetings focus almost solely on political activism, TWA's meetings also deal with such topics as alcoholism among Tibetan men, drug abuse among Tibetan youth, ways to prevent the spread of tuberculosis, and ways to help Tibetan widows. The TWA is one way in which Tibetan women have been able to present these issues as a national concern.

Alumni associations are relatively new organizations among the Tibetan exiles. Graduates of India-based exile government affiliated schools who have since moved to Nepal founded them as an alternative to regional and sectarian organizations. Modeled loosely on *kyiduk*, discussed below, alumni associations gather to celebrate happy events, such as weddings, and to assist each other through unhappy events, such as deaths and illnesses. Alumni associations are not as formal in their organization as *kyiduk*, however, as they generally do not have contracts and do not function as sources of loans or investments. Alumni associations, like the TYC and TWA, work with the exile administration to promote the idea of the Tibetan nation among Tibetan exiles in Nepal. Asked what the purpose of their alumni association is, for example, members of the Mussoorie alumni association responded that its main purpose is to achieve Tibetan independence and to preserve the Tibetan culture in exile. The Mussoorie alumni association provides scholarships to Tibetan students who attend the Mussoorie School. As they provide their scholarships through the exile administration's Department of Education, they support exile administration efforts to keep Tibetans unified and to promote its political cause.

International Challenges to the Tibetan National Identity

The efforts of the exile administration to promote and maintain a unified and distinct Tibetan national identity face simultaneous challenges from both local and international organizations. International organizations challenge the Tibetan exiles to accommodate their own norms and values. We see this challenge, for example, in the way in which TYC and TWA members respond to the many international organizations that assist them. TYC promotes Tibetan nationalism, yet it does so within a framework of liberal democracy. One history of the TYC explains: "the Tibetan Youth Congress adopted and developed a political vocabulary. Democracy, elections, secularism, fundamental human rights, equality and the rest of the political rhetoric of liberal democracy set the tone and shaped the political culture of the youth organization."[13] An interview I conducted with the joint secretary of the Central Tibetan Women's Association at her home in Kathmandu illustrates the process even more clearly. I asked her what are the biggest problems facing women in Tibetan exile society today. She responded that whenever Westerners ask her questions like this, she never knows whether to answer what she thinks the biggest problems are or what we think their biggest problems should be. Without revealing which answer she was giving me, she responded that Tibetan women have so many responsibilities now that they did not have in Tibet. Now they have to earn money as well as take care of their families. As a result, not so many women can achieve their professional goals.[14]

International challenges to the exile administration's efforts to promote a unified and distinct Tibetan national identity can also be seen in the negotiation of three other issues in the exile communities. The first are business relationships. Tibetan exiles who work in the international carpet business, for example, often describe the Tibetan identity in terms that are quite different from what the exile administration promotes. Tibetan carpet entrepreneurs describe the Tibetan identity as one that lacks all restrictions, that is flexible and negotiable. Being Tibetan means that they can do what they like, unlike Nepalese and other Hindus, for example, who are forbidden, by their religion, from eating with certain people or going to certain places. Being Tibetan, they explain, means being able to attend Christian church or eat at people's houses, because what is most important about being Tibetan is "believing in humanity."

One Tibetan, for example, in describing how he started his carpet business, described how important the lack of restriction in the Tibetan identity was to his efforts. He described how, when he was a young man, he started eating in restaurants in Boudha for the purpose of meeting foreigners. One day, he met two Americans who agreed to sponsor his education at a business school in the United States. While he attended business school, in Washington state, he also worked at a lumber mill. He saved enough money to return to Nepal and start a factory. That experience, he explained, encouraged him to "believe in humanity," to think in terms of affiliation with all people rather than with only Tibetans.

Another Tibetan, in describing his travels to Europe to meet with prospective business partners, emphasized how important it is to demonstrate respect for their beliefs. Although he considers himself Buddhist, he explained, he considers it important to learn about Christianity and to attend church. When he is in Nepal, likewise, he explained, he considers it important to show respect for the Hindu beliefs of his Nepali employees. Being

Tibetan has been very useful for his business, he explained, as it allows him to affiliate with humanity.

Resettlement opportunities, like business relationships, also encourage Tibetan exiles to be more flexible about their identities. International organizations have been providing Tibetan exiles with resettlement opportunities since the 1960s, when a number of Tibetan children from Kathmandu were resettled in Switzerland. The 1990 U.S.-Tibet resettlement project, described in chapter 2, is only the most recent of these opportunities. Many Tibetans I interviewed in Nepal mentioned at least one family member who had emigrated to Europe or the U.S. through a formal resettlement opportunity. To use a phrase coined by Harrell-Bond (1986: 118) in her study of Ugandan refugees in the Sudan, Tibetan exiles "deploy themselves like chessmen" to take advantage of the resettlement opportunities international organizations provide. One Tibetan describes the problems that the dispersal of Tibetan families causes. He compares his own situation with the situation of the Tibetan children he observes around him today: "I had the good fortune of being brought up in a family in which there were three generations together, unlike many children in exile today.... There are things lacking in the character of those brought up today. They lack the care of their mothers and they do not learn age-old values and responsibilities" (personal communication, September 19, 1995). The dispersal of Tibetan families, in his view, makes it difficult for children to learn Tibetan customs and manners.

The third issue that encourages Tibetan exiles to be more flexible in their identities involves intermarriage prospects. Unlike other exile communities, such as the Jewish Diaspora, Tibetans do not have an endogamous marriage rule based on identification with a national group. They have only an exogamous rule that prevents the intermarriage of people with the same bone (*rü*) or the same "flesh and blood" (*sha-trag*) within seven generations. "Bone" represents the patriline; "flesh and blood" represents the matriline. Only after both "bone" and "blood" have been separated for seven generations can Tibetans intermarry.[15]

Tibetan exiles do express a preference for intermarriage with someone from the same village or region (*lung-pa*) in Tibet, yet if no one suitable is available, they consider intermarriage with foreigners just as acceptable as intermarriage with someone from some other region in Tibet. Decisions about marriage among Tibetans are made at the level of the household. As one Tibetan explains: "Anything that concerns marriage is not the concern of 'Tibetan society' (*pö-bay chi-tsog*) but only of particular households (*mi-tsang*). If the households accept the marriage, then Tibetan society has to accept it.... It is always through a household that people have connections."

There are many Tibetan exiles, including members of the Dalai Lama's family, who have intermarried with foreigners. Tibetan exiles generally discuss these marriages as beneficial for the Tibetan household involved. One example I heard about concerns a Tibetan woman who married a Swiss man and moved to Switzerland with him. The Tibetan household involved was concerned, at first, that the couple might not maintain Tibetan practices in their new home. As soon as the couple started to send money to help the household, however, they started talking freely about how happy they were about the marriage. Another example involves a Tibetan man who married an Austrian woman and moved to Austria. The man's parents in Kathmandu expressed how happy they are about the marriage and how successful their son has become. Still another example involves a Tibetan woman and an Australian man. At first, the members of her household were very upset and said that she must marry a Tibetan man, but when they too started to help the household, they considered the marriage acceptable.

Some Tibetan exiles are very critical about intermarriage with foreigners. They are most concerned about intermarriages between Tibetan women and foreign men. Tibetan women are very important for the preservation of the Tibetan culture in exile, one Tibetan argued, because they maintain the household: "In raising children, women are more important because it is always the mother who takes care (*champa chay*) of the children and teaches them what they need to know to grow up well." He argued that Tibetan women should never intermarry with foreigners because that would encourage them not to raise their children as Tibetans.

Intermarriage encourages Tibetan households and families to affiliate not just as Tibetans but also as some other national identity group. The cumulative effect of many such intermarriages is a challenge to the efforts of the exile administration to cultivate and maintain a distinct Tibetan national community.

Local Challenges to the Exile Administration's Efforts

In addition to the many challenges international relationships pose to the exile administration's efforts, there are also many challenges created by the Tibetans' local, regional, and sectarian relationships. Unlike the international challenges, local-level challenges were not created by the exile context; they certainly changed in the exile context, yet we can see their foundation in Tibet's history. Tibet, prior to its incorporation into the PRC, was plagued by persistent regional and sectarian factionalism. Goldstein (1989) and Shakabpa (1967) document some of these conflicts, such as between eastern Tibetans (*khampa*) and central Tibetans (*u-pa*); between the Gelugpa and Kagyupa sects of Tibetan Buddhism; and between Buddhists and Bönpos. Tibetan exile officials promote the idea that the Tibetan nation can exist despite these conflicts. They portray the Tibetan identity (*pö-ba*) as larger and stronger than any regional or sectarian identities. We see this idea, for example, in the following song, performed by the Tibetan Institute of Performing Arts, an organization sponsored by the exile administration. It proceeds:

> We are all Tibetan peoples (*nga-tso pö-rig pun-da*);
> Tibetans of one flesh and blood (*sha-trag chik-gi-pö-rig*) ...
> Tibetans from all three regions (*chol-ka sum-gi-pö-rig*);
> Tibetans from all five religions (*chö-lug nga'i-pö-rig*) ...
> United as one (*dok-tsa chig-dril nang-nay*) ...
> Will return to Tibet (*de-nay pö-la lo-dro*).

The song conveys a message of national unity despite regional and sectarian differences. It conveys also a particular political agenda—to return to an independent Tibet.

Local, regional, and sectarian differences persist in the exile context despite exile administration efforts. We see these differences, for example, in the following comments. One Tibetan exile, from south-central Tibet, explains a myth about the origins of the six different peoples of Tibet. The myth resembles "The Origin of Tibet and the Tibetans," cited at the beginning of this chapter. Rather than promoting the idea of commonality among Tibetans, however, it promotes the idea of regional difference. My informant explains:

> Tibetans have a belief about the origin of the character of the six different peoples of Tibet: Khampas, Amdowas, Upas, Tsangpas, Ngaripas, and Töpas. It is sometimes said that these six peoples represent each of the six realms of existence: gods, demi-gods, humans, animals, hungry ghosts, and hell-beings. Khampas are demi-gods because they have a very argumentative nature. They are jealous of the gods [people from his region] and are always fighting with them.

Another Tibetan related the following saying. It divides Tibet into three regional groups. It follows:

> Amdo is the region of horses (*do-may ta-i chol-ka*);
> Utsang is the region of religion (*u-tsang chö-ki chol-ka*);
> Kham is the region of people (*do-dö mi-i chol-ka*).

My informant explained that it means that people from Amdo, in northeastern Tibet, are very gifted with the management of horses; people from U-tsang, in central Tibet, are very knowledgeable about religion; and people from Kham, in eastern Tibet, are very brave.

Local, regional, and sectarian differences persist also because they have been institutionalized in the exile context. They serve as the basis, for example, for the allotment of seats in the exile administration's Assembly of Tibetan People's Deputies. Out of its forty-seven seats, thirty are reserved for regional communities (ten each for people who represent Kham, Amdo, and Utsang) and ten are reserved for religious communities (two each for people who represent the Sakyapa, Gelugpa, Kagyupa, and Nyingma schools of Buddhism as well as the Bön religion). Candidates campaign for election to particular Assembly seats, whether as representatives of Kham, Amdo, or Utsang, for example. To do so, they emphasize the interests of the people they represent. The exile administration promotes the idea that all representatives share a common commitment to the Tibetan nation despite their different regional or sectarian interests. Some Tibetan exiles criticize that idea, however. They claim that apportioning Assembly seats by region and sect only emphasizes differences among Tibetans. One Tibetan exile explains:

> There are a lot of people who believe that the Tibetan [exile] government works only for the interests of Utsang people [central Tibetans]. This idea is very strong poison (*dug-wa*) in the Tibetan community. Yet who in the Assembly really works for the good of all Tibetans? Maybe two or three people, but no more.... Assembly representatives (*thu-mi*) may look to the idea of unity, but it is like a chart on the wall. Their real concern is the people of their region or sect, for they are like the chair beneath them.

Local, regional, and sectarian differences have been institutionalized also in the form of mutual aid societies or *kyiduk*. Kyiduk are non-kin related organizations of mutual assistance. They are composed of approximately fifty households that join together for many different purposes—to celebrate happy events, such as weddings, births, and holidays; to assist each other through unhappy events, such as deaths and illnesses; to pool resources for investments, loans, or insurance; and to settle disputes. Kyiduk have a long history in Tibetan society. Miller (1956) observed them in Darjeeling and Sikkim even before the Tibetan exile. She describes them as a formalized system of mutual aid that become important especially during life cycle rituals and prolonged illnesses (Miller 1956: 160). She mentions their existence also in Tibet proper—in Lhasa, Gyantse, Shigatse, Chamdo, Derge, and Phari—and speculates that they arise only in areas with a highly concentrated Tibetan population (Miller 1956: 165). Aziz (1978) notes their existence in northeastern Nepal during the early years of the Tibetan exile. She describes them as highly formal organizations that serve economic and business purposes (Aziz 1978: 70).

Kyiduk are very important organizations for Tibetan exiles in Nepal. Their members assist each other not only during life cycle rituals yet also in business ventures. Kyiduk are a significant source of investment capital, for example, much like the *dhikur* associations Messerschmidt (1978) describes among the Gurungs, Thakalis, and Bhotias of Nepal. Kyiduk members also help each other expand their network of business contacts. Some kyiduk have even founded carpet factories in Nepal. Kyiduk are formal economic organizations. Their members pay annual dues. Kyiduk supplement their dues through voluntary donations, fundraising events, and business investments.

Kyiduk have their own rules and regulations, outlined in the form of formal written contracts. They are managed by administrative committees (*genzin lhentsog*), elected from among the membership every one to five years. Some kyiduk are wealthy enough even to maintain separate offices. Many also maintain storerooms filled with tables, chairs, and other furniture that kyiduk members can borrow for ceremonial events.

Tibetan exiles in Nepal have organized their kyiduk primarily on the basis of place of origin.[16] In Kathmandu, for example, I observed kyiduk for people from Ngari, Dingri, Nyalam, Kyirong, Porong, Shigatse, and Lhasa. Members organized and managed their kyiduk as if they all came from the same place in Tibet, although some kyiduk contained members from other places as well. The Shigatse kyiduk, for example, contained some families from Lhasa, yet Tibetans still referred to it as the Shigatse kyiduk and looked to it to represent the interests of people from Shigatse, such as during the search for the next Panchen Lama.

Some Tibetan exiles in Nepal have organized kyiduk on the basis of other principles besides place of origin. Two of these, the Bönpo Foundation and the Muslim Society, are organized on the basis of religious affiliation. Another represents the interests of Tibetan-Newar descendants. Still another, the Srongtsen Bhrikuti Samasta, maintains three criteria for membership. The first is the possession of significant wealth; the society charges higher membership dues than any other kyiduk in Nepal. The second is dual status as a Tibetan exile and a Nepali citizen. The third is non-affiliation with the exile administration; members of this particular kyiduk, composed mostly of wealthy carpet factory owners, disagree with the exile administration's approach to Tibet's political cause and do not want to be associated with it.[17]

Kyiduk encourage the Tibetan exiles to identify more with local, regional, or sectarian communities on a daily basis rather than with a Tibetan national community. We see the results of this local identification, for example, in how Tibetan exiles discuss charitable funding. Some Tibetan exiles contribute only to their own families, kin, and kyiduk rather than to the Dalai Lama's exile administration. As one Tibetan exile, in response to a question about why he does not contribute to the exile administration, explains: "I give money to Tibetan organizations only when I know the money goes to the people it is meant to help. Sometimes where the money goes is not so clear." Another Tibetan exile explains: "If someone asks me to donate for one particular event, and that person can explain exactly what I am supporting, then I will donate to them. I do not believe in institutions and I do not support institutions because there is no way to know where institutions spend their money."

When Tibetan exiles contribute to their own kyiduk, they have more control over what happens to their contributions and can direct them to the goals they themselves believe are most important. One kyiduk, for example, contributes only to the development of their home region in Tibet. They built a hospital in their region that they personally inaugurated on their first visit home since they fled into exile in 1959. Their next project, they explained, involves a school. As one member of the society explains: "If we have the opportunity to do some good ... we should do it. The children in Nyalam need education. That is their greatest need."

Another kyiduk also has plans to build a school in their own home region in Tibet. One member of the society explains that the school is intended to educate girls as well as boys and is intended to prevent girls from their region from marrying Chinese men:

> In Kham, men are very dominant in the family, and sons always get preference over daughters.... Daughters do not get the chance to go to school. Young girls need to be educated too.... [Also], many young men from Kham flee into exile to be able to go to school. That leaves no one but Chinese to marry Khampa girls at home. If Khampa girls marry Chinese, they will lose their religion and culture. It is better to try to keep the young men at home.

Another kyiduk works specifically for Tibetan exiles in Nepal. They complain that the exile administration neglects Tibetans in Nepal, that they only want to collect taxes from them. One of their goals is improve the relationship between Tibetan exiles and Nepali peoples. They have organized an ambulance service for all of the people, Tibetan and Nepali, in their community. They also organized a blood drive for local hospitals. They contribute to Nepali political parties to maintain their support for Tibetan businesses in Nepal. Their concern is with their own local community rather than with the Tibetan exiles as a national community.

Local, regional, and sectarian relationships, like the Tibetans' international relationships, challenge the efforts of the Dalai Lama's exile administration to promote and maintain national consciousness. These relationships encourage the Tibetan exiles to identify with communities alternative to a Tibetan national community. They encourage the Tibetan exiles to extend economic and political support to organizations other than the exile administration. One can argue, therefore, that the exile administration, as a result, is much more successful at promoting the idea of the Tibetan nation at the international level than at the local level. The idea of the Tibetan nation has more cultural capital at the international level than among Tibetan exiles themselves.

Tibetan as an Internationally Recognized Identity

The success of Dalai Lama's exile administration in promoting a distinct Tibetan national identity in international contexts is evident from many events. The Nobel Peace Prize was awarded to the Dalai Lama in 1989. Reebok Human Rights Awards were presented to Phuntsok Nyidron, a

Tibetan nun, in 1995, and Lobsang Jinpa, a Tibetan monk, in 1988, for their participation in Tibetan independence demonstrations. The exclusion of the Dalai Lama from the 1993 Vienna Conference on Human Rights made international headlines. And one Tibetan, Lodi Gyari, co-founded, in 1991, the Unrepresented Nations and Peoples Organization (UNPO), a non-governmental organization of thirty-nine "diplomatic outcasts," political elite whose nations have no states, to argue for their right to representation within the U.N. system.[18] All of these events demonstrate recognition by the international community of the existence of a Tibetan nation with a legitimate claim to self-determination.

The success of the exile administration in promoting a distinct Tibetan national identity in international contexts is demonstrated further by its success in maintaining its relationships with Swiss intergovernmental organizations, U.S. intergovernmental organizations, and international friends of Tibet organizations. For more than forty years, these many organizations have provided the Tibetan exiles with financial, administrative, and moral support. Part of the reason they do so is because they want to participate in the idea of the Tibetan nation themselves. Tibetan exiles have come to depend upon this international support as they make their life choices. As one young Tibetan in Nepal commented, if the United States does not sponsor his education, then some other organization will. "There are always many opportunities."

The success of the exile administration in promoting a distinct Tibetan national identity in international contexts challenges Malkki's (1994) characterization of the international position of migrants, refugees, and other stateless peoples. Malkki (1994) proposes that all of these peoples are best defined as "liminal," as people who are in-between categories and, as such, are perceived as a dangerous form of matter out of place, a challenge to the system of nation-states to which they do not belong. Her analysis is based on models of liminality developed by van Gennep (1960), Douglas (1966) and Turner (1969) who use the concept to analyze rites of passage. Liminal people, according to Turner (1969: 95), are separated from the normal structures of everyday life as they learn the responsibilities of their new role in the community. During the liminal phase, they are ambiguous and indeterminate, dark and invisible, associated with death and rebirth (1969: 95). Liminal people, according to Douglas (1966: 95), are sacred, polluted, and dangerous. In their position in between categories, they pose a challenge to the very idea of categorization. They are viewed as dangerous to the system from which they are separated.

Malkki (1994) defines migrants, refugees, and other stateless peoples as liminal, as she defines the international only as a system of nation-states. Nation-state representatives create the international, she argues, through their participation at common worldwide events, such as meetings of the United Nations or the Olympic Games. The international, by her definition, is a set of nationally defined symbolic forms displayed at common world-wide events that allow us to imagine ourselves as part of a shared human community. Through the identification of ourselves as representatives of our own distinct national communities, she argues, we become members of the "family of nations" and "citizens of humanity."

Tibetan exiles are, indeed, liminal when defined in terms of an international community composed of nation-states alone. They do not have a seat in the United Nations or a place marked "Tibet" on the Rand-McNally world map. They cannot send a team to the Olympics or a contestant to the Miss World pageant. "It's a Small World" is not sung in Tibetan during the Disney amusement park ride as it is done for so many other national communities.[19] Tibetans do not mint their own coins, print their own stamps, or issue their own passports and visas. As a result, there are many Tibetan exiles, particularly within the Dalai Lama's exile administration, whose principal occupation for more than forty years has been to make performative claims to membership in the family of nations, through internationally recognized symbols of nationhood, and to argue for Tibetan participation at common worldwide events.

Tibetan exiles are far from liminal when they are defined in terms of the many other organizations that comprise the international community, however. Tibetan exiles enjoy an internationally recognized high-profile national identity that enables them to maintain international assistance and to publicize their political cause. Being Tibetan is highly valued in international contexts.

The international, as a result, I argue, should be defined as more than just a system of nation-states, as more than just the contexts in which national representatives make performative claims to membership in the family of nations. The international should be defined in such a way as to accommodate the complete set of organizations that comprise the international community. Intergovernmental organizations, non-governmental organizations, and multinational corporations; organizations that provide refugee assistance, development assistance, human rights advocacy, or religious guidance, all together constitute the international. It is through all of these organizations that international resources are allocated and claimed. The Dalai Lama's exile administration has made effective use of these many organizations to cultivate and maintain the Tibetans' claim to international resources. Its efforts have sustained the Tibetan exile community for more than forty years.

Notes

1. The story, "The Origin of Tibet and the Tibetans," constitutes lesson one from a Tibetan-language textbook entitled "History and Religious History," published by the Education Department of the Dalai Lama's exile administration. The translation is my own.
2. Article 1, section 1 of both covenants is identical.
3. There is a long history to the idea of the self-determination of peoples. Its origin can be traced back to the idea promoted in the American Declaration of Independence (1776) and during the French Revolution (1789) that government should be responsible to its people (Cassese 1995: 11). Vladimir Lenin promoted self-determination as a principle of socialist class struggle (Cassese 1995: 17). He championed the right of ethnic or national groups to secede from the powers that governed them or, alternatively, to demand autonomy from them (Cassese 1995: 16) on the idea that such a principle is necessary for the expansion of the socialist world. Cassese (1995: 17) quotes Lenin's 1916 *Theses on the Socialist Revolution and the Right of Nations to Self-Determination* as follows: "In the same way as mankind can arrive at the abolition of classes only through a transition period of the dictatorship of the oppressed classes, it can arrive at the inevitable integration of nations only through a transition period of the complete emancipation of all oppressed nations, i.e. their freedom to secede." U.S. President Woodrow Wilson also promoted the idea of self-determination, yet he interpreted it much more through the lens of Western democratic theory (Cassese 1995: 19). Wilson interpreted self-determination as the right of each people to choose the form of government under which it would live (Cassese 1995: 20). His particular concern involved settling the competing territorial claims that emerged in 1918, at the end of World War I. The principle of self-determination became a part of the U.N. Charter in 1945. Article 1 (2) of the Charter states, in part, that one of the purposes of the United Nations is "to develop friendly relations among nations based on respect for the principle of equal rights and self-determination of peoples..." The U.N. further championed the principle when it made it part of the Covenants on Civil and Political Rights (1966) and Economic, Social, and Cultural Rights (1966). The principle further served to legitimize the end of colonial rule. It is important to note that throughout its long history, the principle of self-determination has taken on different meanings. Cassese (1995: 316) delineates five distinct meanings. They are: (1) a principle through which the territorial changes of sovereign states may be settled; the population concerned should choose through plebiscites or referendums; (2) a principle through which the population of any sovereign state, irrespective of territorial changes, can assert the right to choose its own rulers; (3) an anti-colonialist principle meant to restructure relationships among states; (4) a principle of freedom for national minority groups enabling them to choose their internal or international status, including the right to secede; and (5) a principle prohibiting invasion and foreign occupation. Arguments for self-determination for the Tibetans tend to discuss the principle in terms of the fourth interpretation, as a right of minority groups to choose their internal or international status. That interpretation accords the Chinese Communist Party's initial position on the matter. Article 14 of the 1931 CCP constitution states that the Party "recognizes the right of self-determination of the national minorities in China, their right to complete separation from China and to the formation of an independent state..." (Gladney 1998: 17). Once the PRC was founded, however, the CCP changed its position and insisted instead on the integrity of China's borders and the sovereign authority of the new communist government over the minority populations, including the Tibetans (Gladney 1998: 17).
4. What constitutes pre-1950 Tibetan history can be discerned from the list of Tibetan sources in Shakabpa (1967: 334–339), Tibet's first modern political history. It is the first Tibetan example of what Duara (1995: 33) refers to as "history in the Enlightenment mode." Biographies of Buddhist teachers dominate in Shakabpa's (1967: 334–339) list, followed by records of the founding of important monasteries, followed by retrospective chronicles of the first Tibetan kings.

5. Some of Tibet's national symbols pre-date 1950. The project to promote the idea of a common Tibetan nation seems to have started with the Thirteenth Dalai Lama, based on his observations of China's nationalist movement and on his experiences living in India. The Thirteenth Dalai Lama lived in India under British protection from 1910 to 1913. Upon his return to Tibet, he issued a Tibetan declaration of independence (Shakabpa 1967: 246), minted Tibetan coins, printed Tibetan money, and issued Tibetan postage stamps (Shakabpa 1967: 249). He may even have commissioned the Tibetan flag and the Tibetan national anthem (Klieger 1992: 68). His models included British, Russian, American and Chinese symbols of nationhood (Klieger 1992: 68).

6. The many countries that host Tibetan exiles include India, Nepal, Bhutan, Taiwan, Switzerland, Canada, and the United States.

7. Charter for the Tibetan Exiles, Article 13, "Responsibilities of Citizens."

8. The date reported here for the founding of the Tibetan Youth Congress derives from "The Fly versus the Mountain: How the Tibetan Youth Congress Contributed to Nationalism," *Tibetan Bulletin*, January-February 1996. Information about TYC membership derives from a TYC publication entitled "What is Tibetan Youth Congress" and from the petition the Kathmandu TYC office submitted to the United Nations in October 1995.

9. The Kathmandu office was closed in 1972 and revived only in 1991. Each of the founding members of the Kathmandu office tells his own version of the incident that led to the closure of the office. What happened is that the Nepal police heard news about the founding of a Tibetan Youth Congress in Kathmandu. Nepal, at that time, had banned all political parties. The police arrested the founding members. Their principal concern was any potential connection between the Tibetan Youth Congress and the Nepal Congress Party. The founding members of the Kathmandu office had to spend several weeks in prison translating their party materials into Nepali to demonstrate they were not affiliated with any political party in Nepal. They remember the incident as important both to their own lives and to their friendships with each other.

10. I have a copy of the petition. It is entitled "An Open Letter to the U.N." from the "Tibetan Youth Club, Kathmandu." It is addressed to Mr. Boutros Boutros Ghali, Secretary General of the United Nations. It is in English.

11. TYC's disagreement with the Strasbourg proposal was a frequent topic of discussion among Tibetan exiles throughout the period of my research. It is one of the factors that contributed to the decision to hold the 1995 referendum among the Tibetan exiles to determine how the exile administration should approach Tibet's political struggle. The topic emerged repeatedly in a TYC meeting I attended in Boudha on October 21, 1995. It was also reported widely in the Tibetan press.

12. The information reported here on TWA's Kathmandu activities derives from an interview I conducted with the president of TWA's Kathmandu office on August 1, 1995 as well as from observations I recorded during the Kathmandu TWA's annual meeting on November 18, 1995.

13. "The Fly versus the Mountain: How the Tibetan Youth Congress Contributed to Nationalism," *Tibetan Bulletin*, January-February 1996: 10.

14. Personal communication, November 11, 1995.

15. See Levine (1988) for a more extensive analysis of the Tibetan kinship system.

16. Miller (1956: 163) argues that kyiduk in Tibet before the exile were organized principally on an occupational basis. She describes kyiduk for painters, carpenters, tailors, silver smiths, and other craftsmen. She notes also that in Tibet before the exile, there were a number of religious kyiduk, each representing a different sect of Tibetan Buddhism (1956: 164). In Darjeeling, she argues, kyiduk were organized either on the basis of occupation or place of origin (1956: 162). She mentions a kyiduk for rickshaw drivers, for example, yet also mentions kyiduk for Sherpa, Khampa, and Amdowa. In my research among Tibetans in Nepal, I observed mostly place of origin kyiduk. Place of origin, I would argue, becomes more salient in the exile context.

17. This information derives from interviews I conducted with several members of the Srongtsen Bhrikuti Samasta. The name of this organization symbolizes the dual status of the organization's members as Tibetan exiles and Nepali citizens by combining the name of a seventh-century Tibetan king, Srongtsen Gompo, with his Nepali bride, Bhrikuti.

18. Hornblower (1993) calls the UNPO "a kaleidoscopic cross section of the oppressed, the colonized, the neglected and the rebellious" with "all the trappings of a mini-United Nations." She quotes Michael van Walt, UNPO Secretary-General, with: "There are some 5,000 distinct peoples in the world, but fewer than 200 states are recognized. Many groups want only basic human rights and their cultural identity. But others, perhaps 50, have the historical and political legitimacy to form new separate states." Among them, he includes the Tibetans.

19. In a similar manner, Tibetan exiles were unable to prevent a miniature version of the Potala, the Dalai Lama's winter palace, from being included in the newly built "Splendid China" theme park, two miles from Disney World in Florida. For various accounts of the controversy, see *Tibet Press Watch* (December 1993: 4); *Tibet Press Watch* (1994: 7); *The Economist* (May 14, 1994: 92–93); and *The New York Times* (January 9, 1994: 8; February 5, 1994: 14).

Conclusion

This project began as an inquiry into the factors that enabled the Tibetan exiles to develop and maintain control over Nepal's largest industry, the manufacture and export of hand-woven woolen carpets. Along the way, it developed into a project analyzing international assistance, and in particular, the normative dynamics of international assistance relationships. The relationships the Tibetan exiles maintain with the many international organizations that assist them enabled them to develop and control Nepal's carpet industry as well as to develop a network of settlement camps, monasteries, schools, and administrative organizations in Nepal. These relationships facilitated the ability of the Tibetan exiles to develop significant economic and political power in Nepal.

There are two further questions that arise from the Tibetan exiles' experience with their international patrons that I wish to pursue here. The first is practical, the second theoretical. On a practical level, I ask what lessons the Tibetan case has for other displaced peoples worldwide. The Tibetan exiles in Nepal have maintained their assistance relationships for more than forty years, long past their need for emergency or life-sustaining assistance. Even the organizations that assist them acknowledge that they are now self-sufficient. How have the Tibetan exiles maintained their assistance relationships? Could the Tibetan case serve as a model for other displaced peoples?

On a more theoretical level, I ask how to describe and analyze the social system through which the Tibetan exiles in Nepal live their lives. Tibetan exiles in Nepal make their major life decisions within a context that is shaped by local, national, and international relationships. One of my goals with this book was to develop a way in which to analyze how all of these levels of interaction interrelate. I proposed the entitlement model of global-local relations as a solution. It analyzes the international transaction of norms and values through the mechanism of aid. It explores, in particular, how the normative dynamics of aid relationships affect issues of sovereignty, authority, loyalty, and identity. One of my concerns, here, is to discuss the implications the entitlement model has for the analysis of the world as a global system. The entitlement model is essentially a transactional model; it does not address the larger world system within which the international transaction of norms and values occurs. I consider it useful, therefore, to discuss the issue of the larger world system and to address the model's implications.

Tibetan Success: To What Extent Is It Replicable?

Many scholars in the past have cited the Tibetan exiles as an example of successful resettlement due to their economic integration into their host countries, constructive interaction with their host communities, and psychological adaptation to the exile context (Goldstein 1978; Devoe 1983; Saklani 1984; Gombo 1985; von Fürer-Haimendorf 1990; Norbu 1994). Part of the reason for their success, I argue, is that international assistance organizations have helped the Tibetan exiles to resettle in a relatively peaceful and productive manner. International organizations support the Tibetan exiles' resettlement efforts.

If we consider, in particular, the case of the Tibetan exiles in Nepal, we see, for example, that Swiss intergovernmental organizations helped the Tibetan exiles to establish settlement camps with carpet factories. The Swiss themselves serve as guarantors over the settlement camp lands and the shares of the settlement camp businesses. U.S. intergovernmental organizations, likewise, supported the development of settlement camps and carpet businesses. In addition, they continue to provide the Tibetan exiles with scholarship opportunities, business connections, and public relations assistance. Friends of Tibet have helped, and continue to help, Tibetan exile monasteries and schools. Friends of Tibet funded more than 60 percent of the Snow Lion Foundation's budget from 1975 to 1995, for example. The Snow Lion Foundation manages twelve Tibetan exile schools in Nepal in addition to a number of medical clinics, social service centers, and an old age home. International organizations, in short, support the Tibetans' activities.

To acknowledge the role that international organizations play in the Tibetans' resettlement efforts only moves the question of the Tibetans' success to a different level, however. It raises the question of why the Tibetan exiles have been so successful at recruiting and maintaining international support. Why, in other words, do international assistance organizations consider them worthy of assistance? Part of the reason involves the narratives that international organizations maintain about the Tibetan exiles. Swiss intergovernmental organizations portray them as a humanitarian concern. U.S. intergovernmental organizations emphasize their efforts to develop a democracy. Friends of Tibet discuss them as an issue of cultural survival. In the words of Richard Gere, "This 1,200 year old heritage has much to offer our increasingly impersonal world."

The narratives that international organizations maintain about the Tibetan exiles are only part of the reason, however. These organizations would not be able to sustain their interpretation of the Tibetan exiles without some support. The question therefore becomes why the Tibetan exiles are so successful at sustaining the narratives that international organizations maintain about them. How do they sustain their international assistance relationships?

There are a number of factors involved. They influence the extent to which the Tibetan exiles may serve as a model for other displaced peoples worldwide. The first is, quite simply, the number of people involved. The Tibetan exiles are a relatively small group of displaced people. They number only about 130,000 worldwide with only about 20,000 in Nepal. Their situation is qualitatively different from displaced groups that number in the millions, if not tens of millions, such as the estimated 1.25 million Ethiopians in Sudan and Somalia; the five million Afghans in Pakistan and Iran; and the estimated ten million Bengalis who fled into India during Bangladesh's secession from Pakistan (Zolberg et al. 1989: 103, 128, 144). The resources and organizational skills necessary to assist millions of displaced people are just on a different scale than what was necessary to assist the Tibetans.

A second factor involves Nepal as a host state to Tibetan exiles. Nepal has maintained relatively liberal policies toward the Tibetans and the international organizations that assist them. Hagen (1994: 206) notes that Nepal's principal concern when he began Switzerland's assistance program to Tibetans in Nepal was that Nepali people should benefit from whatever assistance Swiss officials provide. Once he assured them of that, he was free to do as he pleased. U.S. intergovernmental organizations have likewise extended whatever assistance they saw fit with little interference from Nepal's government. The U.S. even extended military assistance to the Tibetan exiles with relatively little interference. Nepali officials denied any knowledge of their activities. Nepali officials, as I explain in chapter four, do occasionally resist intergovernmental intervention on behalf of the Tibetan exiles, yet they rarely express overt opposition. Nepal is too dependent on intergovernmental organizations to finance its own budget to express overt resistance.

A third factor involves the role of the Dalai Lama's exile administration in coordinating assistance to the Tibetan exiles. Exile administration officials, trained in part by the U.S. CIA, are effective middlemen in the maintenance of the Tibetans' assistance relationships. They advocate for the Tibetan exiles at international meetings. They publish books, pamphlets, and project needs directories to direct international organizations to appropriate projects. They help to sustain the Tibetans' international reputation as spiritual, vulnerable, non-violent refugees, worthy of international assistance. The exile administration, the Department of Information and International Relations (DIIR) in particular, helps to sustain the narratives that international organizations maintain about the Tibetan exiles. Tibetan exile officials are effective at impression management.

A fourth factor involves the activities of the Dalai Lama himself. The Dalai Lama is a powerful advocate for the Tibetan exiles. He promotes their reputation for spirituality, vulnerability, and non-violence. He attracts potential supporters to the Tibetan cause through the strength of his personality and through his message of peace for all of humanity. He has become a symbol of what the "Tibetan way of life" can offer the world. Through his charisma, the Dalai Lama legitimates the activities of the exile administration and promotes the Tibetan cause.

It would be difficult for any other displaced group to replicate the factors that contribute to the Tibetan exiles' ability to sustain their international assistance relationships. The relatively small number of Tibetan exiles, Nepal's liberal policies toward them, the narratives international organizations maintain about them, the middleman position the exile administration plays, and the charisma of the Dalai Lama are a rare combination, indeed.

Other displaced groups could learn, however, from the strategies the exile administration uses to publicize the Tibetans' situation. Exile officials periodically repackage the Tibetan cause to sustain international attention. As I argue in chapter three, exile officials have reinterpreted the Tibetan cause through the language of environmentalism, multiculturalism, cultural survival, and most recently, in honor of the U.N. World Conference on Women, women's rights. Exile officials promote the Tibetan cause through whatever language has the most symbolic capital at the time thereby maintaining international attention on the Tibetans' situation. Exile administration efforts to reinvent the Tibetan cause in this manner may not lead the Tibetans any closer to Tibetan independence. It may do little to help the Tibetans in Tibet. What it does do, however, is to maintain support for the Tibetan exiles, to maintain their assistance relationships. Other displaced groups worldwide could learn from the Tibetans' ability to maintain their assistance relationships in this manner, by accommodating the norms and values of those with the means to assist them.

There is one caveat, however. Tibetan exiles themselves have become very critical of the extent to which the exile administration accommodates others' values. In the words of Nawang Dorjee, director of education for the Tibetan Children's Village Schools in India, "We pride ourselves [in] establishing one of the most successful resettlement programmes in modern history, as if the final goal were to live as 'proud refugees.' Our goal is to regain freedom for Tibet. Or have we changed our course?" (1992: 11). Similarly, in the words of Tsering Shakya, "The tendency is to promote the Tibetan political struggle in terms of the populism of the West rather than in the daily concerns of [the Tibetan] people... If the Tibetan issue is to be taken seriously, Tibet must be liberated from both the Western imagination and the myth of Shangri-La" (1992: 15–16). There are limits, in other words, to the extent to which the Tibetan exiles themselves are willing to accommodate others' values for the sake of sustaining international assistance. As the debate about Western reinterpretations of Tibetan Buddhism, recounted in chapter three, illustrate, there are some aspects of Tibetan society and culture that are not infinitely flexible. There are some norms and values the Tibetan exiles claim as their own.

Should other displaced groups use the Dalai Lama's exile administration as a model for recruiting and maintaining international assistance, they too will likely have to address issues of authenticity and cultural ownership as they too accommodate the norms and values of those who assist them. They will have to decide how far they are willing to adapt to others' expectations for the sake of sustaining their assistance relationships. The Tibetan exiles may describe themselves as bats, as creatures that accommodate others' expectations only on the surface while maintaining an identity as Tibetan at the core, yet the reality is far more complex. Tibetan exiles continually renegotiate what it means to be Tibetan at the core. The Tibetan identity is a site of ongoing contestation.

International Assistance as Part of a Larger World System

There are many different groups involved in the ongoing contestation of the Tibetan identity. They include Tibetans in Tibet, Tibetans in exile, the communities that host Tibetan exiles, and the organizations that assist Tibetans, among many others. All of these groups are involved in various levels of interaction, from the local face-to-face level to the national level to the international level. We may use the entitlement model of global-local relations to analyze the normative dynamics of their interactions, yet that leaves unanswered the question of how to describe and analyze the social system through which these interactions occur. What, in other words, is the world system? What model of the world system is most appropriate for analyzing the normative dynamics of international assistance?

The analysis of international assistance, I argue in the introduction, requires a model of the world system that accounts for both organized social action and the transaction of global norms and values. It requires a model that analyzes how organized action and global norms and values interrelate. Economic approaches to global-local relations, such as Wallerstein's (1975) capitalist world system, I argue, overemphasize organized action to the detriment of the analysis of global norms and values. Cultural approaches, such as Malkki's (1994), Appadurai's (1996), and Hannerz's (1987, 1992), overemphasize the transaction of global norms and values to the detriment of the analysis of organized action. Institutional approaches to global-local relations, such as those proposed by Meyer et al. (1987), Boli (1987), and Ramirez (1987), come the closest to the approach I have in mind, as they analyze how global norms and values become institutionalized for the purpose of organized action. The one shortcoming I see in the application of the institutional approach to the analysis of international assistance is that it privileges the state as the principal actor in the institutionalization of global norms and values. States, in the institutionalist model, develop and promote global norms and values through their relationships with each other, such as through their interactions in the United Nations or the World Trade Organization. They then apply these norms and values in the formulation of policies toward their own citizens.

Relationships of international assistance do, at times, involve states. Organizations that assist the Tibetan exiles, for example, include Swiss and U.S. intergovernmental organizations as well as Taiwan's Tibetan and Mongolian Affairs Commission. Relationships of international assistance are also often mediated by states. States retain the right to decide which international organizations to allow to operate in their territory. States are not the only organizations that provide international assistance, however. Privately funded voluntary organizations, such as the friends of Tibet organizations I discuss in chapter three, are also involved. Among the Tibetan exiles, they are just as influential as intergovernmental organizations in both the promotion of global norms and values and the organization of social action. The U.N. World Conference on Women in Beijing provides an example. Although the U.N., an intergovernmental organization, sponsored the conference, many of the participants were voluntary non-governmental organizations. Voluntary organizations, such as the Canada Tibet Committee, the International Campaign for Tibet, and the International Committee of Lawyers for Tibet, among others, were the most influential in enabling Tibetan exiles to participate in the conference. Non-governmental organizations were also very influential in setting the agenda for the conference. They negotiate with states and intergovernmental organizations in setting the global moral agenda.

States use various strategies for promoting norms and values among their own citizens. They include the use of state welfare programs to promote such values as social equality, social integration, solidarity, and stability (Goodin et al. 1999: 22). I see international assistance as an equivalent strategy at the international level. Both state welfare and international assistance programs involve the transaction of resources simultaneous with a transaction in norms and values. Both also, at times, make the continuation of assistance contingent on the accommodation of certain norms and values. For that reason, I refer to both as entitlement systems. State welfare is a membership entitlement system, as its beneficiaries are limited to a closed and bounded group, defined in terms of citizenship. International assistance is a non-member entitlement system, as its beneficiaries are not members of the organizations that provide assistance.

The depiction of the world system that I advance here, therefore, is that of two principal types of organizations. The first are characterized by their closed and bounded membership. States are a primary example, but smaller membership groups, such as unions, clubs, lineages, or mutual aid societies, are also included. Their members transact resources, along with norms and values, among themselves. They constitute membership entitlement systems. The second are characterized by a much more open concept of community. International assistance organizations are a primary example, but other organizations, such as missionary religious organizations, are also included. Their members extend resources specifically to non-members as a way in which to promote their norms and values among them. They constitute non-member entitlement systems. Both types of systems compete over such issues as sovereignty, loyalty, authority, and identity as both seek to promote their norms and values among local communities worldwide.

Implications for Anthropology as a Discipline

The image of the world system advanced here, as one characterized by both membership and non-member groups that transact norms and values along with the transaction of resources, has significant implications for anthropology as a discipline. Anthropologists typically take membership groups, whether villages, lineages, or nation-states, as their unit of analysis. Anthropological research typically involves the analysis of such groups at the local level. Local level analysis is only a partial picture of the total social system through which most local communities worldwide today live their lives, however. Local communities worldwide today increasingly interact with various other groups that seek to promote alternative norms and values among them. They include international assistance organizations, transnational corporations, and missionary religious organizations, among many others. It is important to account for these various other organizations and the influence they have on local communities. Anthropologists, as a result, need to devise research methods to analyze these various other organizations as well. For me, those methods involved interviews and archival research within international assistance organizations as well as site observations at local institutions where international organizations conduct their work. It is a challenge for anthropologists to develop other methods as well to account for the many local, national, and international interactions that shape our increasingly interconnected world.

Appendix

TABLE A.1 Statistics on Kathmandu Tibetans from Refugee ID Applications

Gender Distribution

Male	4497
Female	3451
Total	7948

Age Distribution

81–90	20
71–80	180
61–70	514
51–60	677
41–50	656
31–40	933
21–30	2017
11–20	1751
0–10	1143
unreported	57
Total	7948

Place of Birth

Nepal	3741
Tibet	4038
India	160
Bhutan	3
unreported	6
Total	7948

Monks	795
Nuns	138

TABLE A.1 Statistics on Kathmandu Tibetans from Refugee ID Applications *(cont.)*

Year of Arrival in Nepal

Year	Count
1993	10
1992	4
1991	9
1990	10
1989	99
1988	275
1987	288
1986	192
1985	376
1984	210
1983	152
1982	118
1981	105
1980	281
1979	111
1978	81
1977	69
1976	48
1975	159
1974	59
1973	33
1972	32
1971	15
1970	89
1969	16
1968	23
1967	13
1966	17
1965	57
1964	27
1963	47
1962	75
1961	64
1960	329
1959	689
1958	0
1957	0
1956	1
1955	2
1954	1
1953	1
1952	0
1951	0
1950	1
1949	1
unreported	56
Born in Nepal	3703
Total	7948

TABLE A.1 Statistics on Kathmandu Tibetans from Refugee ID Applications *(cont.)*

Number of People in Household

Eleven	4
Ten	13
Nine	37
Eight	71
Seven	89
Six	171
Five	197
Four	285
Three	345
Two	350
One (female)	277
One (male)	1086
Total	2925

Heads of Household
(households with one member excluded)

Male	1155
Female	407
Total	1562

Household Composition

Husband/Wife	87
Husband/Wife/Extended Family	30
Husband/Wife/Children	518
Husband/Wife/Children/Extended Family	184
Single Father/Children	169
Single Father/Children/Extended Family	37
Single Mother/Children	234
Single Mother/Children/Extended Family	42
Brothers	77
Sisters	26
Brothers and Sisters	50
Sisters and Children	14
Brothers/Sisters/Children	14
Uncle and Nephew	10
Grandmother and Grandchild	7
Other	63
Total	1562

Refugee ID Book Holders from 1975   564

Glossary

Phonetic Approximation	Transliteration	Translation
bel-po	bal-po	Nepalese
bu-may tsogpa	bud-med tshogs-pa	Tibetan Women's Association
cha-tay	dpya-khral	standard tax
champa	byams-pa	love, physical caring for a person
champa chay	byams-pa byed	to take care of a person, such as a child
chö-yön	mchod-yon	priest/patron
chorten	mchod-rten	stupa; used also for Boudha, site of a very large stupa
dar-chog tag	dar-lcog-rtags	raising prayer flags
day-dön lay-khung	bde-don las-khungs	Tibetan welfare offices
den-pay u-tsug	bden-pa'i u-gtsugs	peaceful resistance, satyagraha
dön-chö	don-gcod	director of the Tibet Office
dön-chö khang	don-gcod khang	Tibet Office
drung-che	drung-che	secretary of a department in the exile administration
dug-wa	dug-wa	poison
genzin lhentsog	'gan-'dzin lhan-tshogs	administrative committee
geshe	dge-bshes	the highest degree in the Gelugpa school of Buddhism
gomshi	goms-gshis	habit, inherent nature
gu-shab	gus-zhabs	respect, as in the negotiation of deference
gya-mi	rgya-mi	Chinese
gyal-khab	rgyal-khab	country

Phonetic Approximation	Transliteration	Translation
Gyalwa Rinpoche	rgyal-wa rin-po-che	a respectful title for the Dalai Lama
gye-sa	rgyal-sa	capital city; in this case, Kathmandu
jindag	sbyin-bdag	patron or sponsor
jo-khel	'jo-khel	Jawalakhel
jor-pa-ti	'jor-pa-kri	Jorpati
kap-chol-wai pö-ba	skyabs-chol-wa'i bod-pa	Tibetan exiles
kashag	bka'-shag	Tibetan exile administration's Cabinet of Ministers
katah	kha-btags	white scarf, an offering
kha mangpo	kha mang-po	talkative, mouthy
kha-tor	kha-gtor	self-settled; outside of any formal settlement camp
khampa	khams-pa	eastern Tibetan (e.g., from Derge, Batang, Litang, etc.)
khoryug	khor-yug	the environment
khyampo	khyam-po	hippie, someone who just wanders from place to place
kugpa	lkugs-pa	stupid people
kyiduk	skyid-sdugs	mutual aid society
kyön	skyon	faults
lag-pa chi-sa	lag-pa phyid-sa	handkerchief
lag-pa tsang-ma	lag-pa gtsang-ma	to have clean hands (be free of unpleasant business)
lag-pa tsog-pa	lag-pa btsog-pa	dirty hands (a metaphor for unpleasant business)
lag-tse	lag-rtsal	skill, as in manual skills
lam u-ma	lam dbu-ma	the middle path
lengen	las-'gan	responsibility
lob-zur tsogpa	slob-zur tshogs-pa	alumni associations
lung-pa	lung-pa	region or village in Tibet
lung-ta	rlung-rta	luck
mang-mö thag-chö	mang-mos thag-gcod	referendum
mang-po	mang-po	many
mangtso	mang-gtso/dmangs-gtso	democracy
mi kyuma	mi dkyus-ma	regular people
mi-ser	mi-ser	citizen (connotes tenant laborer)
mi-tempo	mi-brtan-po	unstable people
mi-tsang	mi-tshang	household
monlam gyab	smon-lam-rgyab	praying to gods
nga-wang	mnga'-'bangs	citizen (connotes landholder)
nyam-nyong	nyams-myong	experience
nyingje	snying-rje	compassion
p'agpa	'phags-pa	enlightened beings

Phonetic Approximation	Transliteration	Translation
p'agpa shing-kun	'phags-pa shing-kun	Swayambhu
pö chi-way mi	bod-spyi-wa'i mi	someone who represents all Tibetans
pö rang-wang den-pai ley-gul	bod rang-dbang bden-pa'i las-'gul	Tibetan Freedom Movement Offices
Po Thang Gonpo	pho-thang rgon-po	Tibetan god of the Tundikhel
pö-ba	bod-pa	Tibetan
pö-bay chi-tsog	bod-pa'i spyi-tshogs	Tibetan society
pö-gi pa-wo	bod-kyi dpa'-bo	Tibetan heroes
pö-mi rig-pa	bod-mi'i-rigs-pa	people who are ethnically Tibetan
Potala	po-ta-la	Dalai Lama's winter palace in Tibet
pu-ti kha-yi drang-tsi dag	spu-gri'i kha-yi sbrang-rtsi bldag	licking honey off the edge of a razor
rang thag rang chö	rang-thag rang-gcod	self-determination
rang-khong le-che-wa	rang-khongs las-byed-wa	local-level staff member
rangzen	rang-btsan	independence
rangzen lagteb	rang-btsan lag-deb	Tibetan identity booklets
rong-pa	rong-pa	"valley-people;" refers to Nepali people
rü	rus	bone, signifies the patriline
sa-mig	sa-dmigs	appointed position
sa-nay	sa-gnas	district
sang-pül	bsangs-phul	to burn incense in offering to the gods
sem	sems	the mind
sem-la nü-pa che-gi-yö-ray	sems-la nus-pa sprad-kyi-yod-red	power that is given in the mind
sempa chung	sems-pa chung	emotional
sha-trag	sha-khrag	flesh and blood, signifies the matriline
shing-nag gi tim	shing-nags-kyi-khrims	the law of the jungle
shonnu tsogpa	gzhon-nu tshogs-pa	Tibetan Youth Congress
shung	gzhung	government
shung-kö le-che-wa	gzhung-bskos las-byed-wa	officially appointed staff member
si-chu dro-tsog	srid-byus gros-tshogs	Tibetan assembly (in Tibet under the PRC)
so-day; so-nam	bsod-sde; bsod-nams	merit
so-nam sag	bsod-nams bsags	to do good deeds
ta-mag; ta-mang	rta-dmag; rta-mang	Tamang people in Nepal
terkha	gter-kha	precious things buried in the earth
tong	mthong	respect; reputation; how others view a person

Phonetic Approximation	Transliteration	Translation
thu-mi	'thus-mi	representative, delegate
tsampa	rtsam-pa	ground barley flour
tsen-nag	tshan-nag	black mark, scar
tsog-pa	btsog-pa	dirty
tung-kar du-chen	khrungs-skar dus-chen	the Dalai Lama's birthday celebration
u-pa	dbus-pa	central Tibetan (e.g., from Lhasa)
wang-thang	dbang-thang	personal influence related to wealth
Yabshi	yab-gzhis	honorific title for the family of the Dalai Lamas
yang-shor	g.yang-shor	risk your prosperity
yul-jong gi kö-pa pun-sum-tsog	yul-ljongs-kyi-bkod-pa-phun-sum-tshogs	perfect ecosystem
yulmi	yul-mi	citizen (connotes native)
zay-cha-dö	bzas-dpya-'dod	voluntary non-eating tax
zhen-pa	zhen-pa	political loyalty
zigpo	rdzig-po	handsome
nga-tso pö-rig pun-da	nga-tsho bod-rigs spun-dag	we are all Tibetan peoples
sha-trag chik-gi-pö-rig	sha-khrag gcig-gi-bod-rigs	Tibetans of one flesh and blood
chol-ka sum-gi-pö-rig	chol-kha gsum-gyi-bod-rigs	Tibetans of all three regions
chö-lug nga'i-pö-rig	chos-lugs lnga'i-bod-rigs	Tibetans of all five religions
dok-tsa chig-dril nang-nay	rdog-rtsa gcig-sgril nang-nas	united as one
de-nay pö-la lo-dro	de-nas bod-la log-'gro	we will return to Tibet
do-may ta-i chol-ka	mdo-smad rta'i chol-kha	Amdo is the region of horses
u-tsang chö-ki chol-ka	dbus-gtsang chos-kyi-chol-kha	Utsang is the region of religion
do-dö mi-i chol-ka	mdo-stod mi'i-chol-kha	Kham is the region of people

References

Adams, Vincanne. 1996. *Tigers of the Snow and Other Virtual Sherpas.* Princeton: Princeton University Press.

Anderson, Benedict. 1983. *Imagined Communities.* New York: Verso.

Andrugtsang, Gompo Tashi. 1973. *Four Rivers, Six Ranges: Reminiscences of the Resistance Movement in Tibet.* Dharamsala: Information and Publicity Office of His Holiness the Dalai Lama.

Appadurai, Arjun. 1996. *Modernity at Large: Cultural Dimensions of Globalization.* Minneapolis: University of Minnesota Press.

———. 1986. "Introduction: Commodities and the Politics of Value." In Arjun Appadurai, ed., *The Social Life of Things: Commodities in Cultural Perspective.* Cambridge: Cambridge University Press.

Avedon, John F. 1984. *In Exile from the Land of Snows.* London: Michael Joseph.

Aziz, Barbara. 1978. "Social Cohesion and Reciprocation in a Tibetan Community in Nepal." In Bhabagrahi Misra and James Preston, eds., *Community, Self, and Identity.* The Hague: Mouton.

Baitenmann, Helga. 1990. "NGO's and the Afghan War: The Politicisation of Humanitarian Aid." *Third World Quarterly* 12 (1): 62–85.

Baral, Lok Raj. 1994. "Bhutanese Refugees and National Security." Paper presented at the International Seminar on Refugees and Internal Security in South Asia. Colombo, Sri Lanka, July 10–11.

Barth, Fredrik. 1969. *Ethnic Groups and Boundaries.* Boston: Little, Brown.

Bass, Catriona. 1998. *Education in Tibet: Policy and Practice since 1950.* London: Zed Books.

Beiner, Ronald. 1995. "Why Citizenship Constitutes a Theoretical Problem in the Last Decade of the Twentieth Century." In Ronald Beiner, ed., *Theorizing Citizenship.* Albany: State University of New York Press.

Benson, Linda. 1990. *The Ili Rebellion: The Moslem Challenge to Chinese Authority in Xinjiang, 1944–1949.* Armonk, NY: M.E. Sharpe.

Bharati, Agehananda. 1979. "Tibetan Buddhism in America: The Late Seventies." *The Tibet Journal* 6 (1): 3–11.

Bhasin, Avatar Singh. 1994. *Nepal's Relations with India and China: Documents 1947–1992.* Delhi: Siba Exim Private Limited.

Bhattacharjea, Ajit. 1994. *Tibetans in Exile: The Democratic Vision.* New Delhi: Tibetan Parliamentary and Policy Research Centre.

Bhawa, Ugen Norbu. 1994. "Nepal Carpet Manufacturers Under Pressure." *Tibetan Review* 29 (10): 8–9.

Bishop, Peter. 1989. *The Myth of Shangri-La: Tibet, Travel Writing and the Western Creation of Sacred Landscape*. Berkeley: University of California Press.

Boli, John. 1987. "Human Rights or State Expansion? Cross-National Definitions of Constitutional Rights, 1870–1970." In George M. Thomas et al., eds., *Institutional Structure: Constituting State, Society, and the Individual*. London: Sage Publications.

Bonacich, Edna. 1973. "A Theory of Middleman Minorities." *American Sociological Review* 38: 583–594.

Bond, George D. 1988. "The Arahant: Sainthood in Theravada Buddhism." In Richard Kieckhefer and George D. Bond, eds., *Sainthood: Its Manifestations in World Religions*. Berkeley: University of California Press.

Brubaker, William Rogers. 1989. "Introduction." In *Immigration and the Politics of Citizenship in Europe and North America*. Lanham, MD: University Press of America.

Cassese, Antonio. 1995. *Self-Determination of Peoples: A Legal Reappraisal*. Cambridge: Cambridge University Press.

Central Bureau of Statistics. 1995. *Population Monograph of Nepal*. Kathmandu: National Planning Secretariat.

Chambers, Robert. 1986. "Hidden Losers: The Impact of Rural Refugees and Rural Programs on Poorer Hosts." *International Migration Review* 20 (2): 245–263.

Chhetri, Ram B. 1990. Adaptation of Tibetan Refugees in Pokhara, Nepal: A Study of Persistence and Change. Ph.D. diss. in anthropology at the University of Hawaii.

Cohn, Bernard S. 1981. "Representing Authority in Victorian India." In Eric Hobsbawm and Terence Ranger, eds., *The Invention of Tradition*. Cambridge: Cambridge University Press.

Coleman, Graham. 1993. *A Handbook of Tibetan Culture*. London: Orient Foundation.

Coutin, Susan Bibler. 1993. *The Culture of Protest: Religious Activism and the U.S. Sanctuary Movement*. Boulder, CO: Westview Press.

Cunningham, Hilary. 1995. *God and Caeser at the Rio Grande: Sanctuary and the Politics of Religion*. Minneapolis: University of Minnesota Press.

Dagyab Rinpoche, L. S. 1992. "Problems in the Development of Tibetan Buddhism in the West." *Tibetan Review* 27 (10): 15–17.

Dahal, Dev Raj. 1995. "Geopolitics of Nepal: Survival Strategies of a Small State." Paper presented at a seminar on the political economy of small states, organized by the Nepal Foundation for Advanced Studies, Kathmandu, Nepal, March 7–8.

Dalai Lama of Tibet. 1990. *Freedom in Exile: The Autobiography of the Dalai Lama*. New York: HarperCollins Publishers.

———. 1983 (1962). *My Land and My People*. New York: Potala Corporation.

Department of Information and International Relations (DIIR). 1995. *Tibetan Women: Peace, Development and Equality*. Dharamsala: DIIR.

———. 1991. "An Interview with Kyabjey Sakya Trinzin." *Chö-Yang*. Dharamsala: DIIR.

———. 1988. *Where Did Tibet's Forests Go?* Dharamsala: DIIR.

Devoe, Dorsh Marie. 1983. *Survival of a Refugee Culture: The Longterm Gift Exchange Between Tibetan Refugees and Donors in India*. Ph.D. diss. in social welfare at the University of California at Berkeley.

Dixit, Kanak Mani. 1994. "House of Cards: Fearing for Bhutan." *Himal* 7 (4): 11–26.

Donnelly, Jack. 1995. "State Sovereignty and International Intervention: The Case of Human Rights." In Gene M. Lyons and Michael Mastanduno, eds., *Beyond Westphalia? State Sovereignty and International Intervention*. Baltimore, MD: The Johns Hopkins University Press.

Dorjee, Nawang. 1992. "An Assessment of the Exile Situation." *Tibetan Review* 27 (2): 11–14.

Douglas, Mary. 1966. *Purity and Danger*. London: Routledge and Kegan Paul.

Dowman, Keith. 1992. "Himalayan Intrigue: The Search for the New Karmapa." *Tricycle: The Buddhist Review* (Winter): 29–34.

———. 1993. "Responses and Rejoinders." *Tricycle: The Buddhist Review* (Spring): 7–8.

Duara, Prasenjit. 1995. *Rescuing History from the Nation: Questioning Narratives of Modern China*. Chicago: University of Chicago Press.

Esping-Andersen, Gøsta. 1990. *The Three Worlds of Welfare Capitalism.* Oxford: Polity.

Federation of Nepalese Chambers of Commerce and Industry (FNCCI). 1995. *Nepal and the World: A Statistical Profile.* Kathmandu: Federation of Nepalese Chambers of Commerce and Industry.

Fermi, Laura. 1968. *Illustrious Immigrants: The Intellectual Migration from Europe, 1930–1941.* Chicago: University of Chicago Press.

Fields, Rick. 1981. *How the Swans Came to the Lake: A Narrative History of Buddhism in America.* Boston: Shambhala Publications.

Fink, Mariann. 1991. "The Tibetan Environment Prior to the Chinese Invasion." *Chö-Yang.* Dharamsala, India: Department of Religion and Cultural Affairs.

Forbes, Ann Armbrecht. 1989. *Settlements of Hope.* Cambridge, MA: Cultural Survival.

Fowler, Michael Ross, and Julie Marie Bunck. 1995. *Law, Power, and the Sovereign State: The Evolution and Application of the Concept of Sovereignty.* University Park, PA: Pennsylvania State University Press.

Freeman, Gary P. 1986. "Migration and the Political Economy of the Welfare State." In Martin Heisler and Barbara Heisler, eds., *From Foreign Workers to Settlers? Transnational Migration and the Emergence of New Minorities.* London: Sage Publications.

French, Rebecca. 1991. "The New Snow Lion: The Tibetan Government-in-Exile in India." In Yossi Shain, ed., *Governments-in-Exile in Contemporary World Politics.* New York: Routledge.

Gellner, David. 1986. "Language, Caste, Religion, and Territory." *Archives Europeennes de Sociologie* 27 (1): 102–148.

Giddens, Anthony. 1991. *Modernity and Self-Identity: Self and Society in the Late Modern Age.* Stanford: Stanford University Press.

Gladney, Dru C. 1998. *Ethnic Identity in China: The Making of a Muslim Minority Nationality.* Fort Worth, TX: Harcourt Brace College Publishers.

Glick-Schiller, Nina. 1994. "Introducing Identities: Global Studies in Culture and Power." *Identities* 1 (1): 1–16.

Goffman, Erving. 1959. *The Presentation of Self in Everyday Life.* Garden City, NY: Doubleday and Company.

Goldstein, Melvyn. 1989. *A History of Modern Tibet, 1913–1959.* Berkeley: University of California Press.

———. 1978. "Ethnogenesis and Resource Competition among Tibetan Refugees in South India." In James Fisher, ed., *Himalayan Anthropology: Indo-Tibetan Interface.* The Hague: Mouton.

———. 1973. "The Circulation of Estates in Tibet: Reincarnation, Land, and Politics." *Journal of Asian Studies* 3: 444–455.

———. 1971. "The Balance Between Centralization and Decentralization in the Traditional Tibetan Political System." *Central Asiatic Journal* 15: 170–182.

———. 1968. *An Anthropological Study of the Tibetan Political System.* Ph.D. diss. in anthropology at the University of Washington.

Gombo, Ugen. 1985. *Tibetan Refugees in the Kathmandu Valley: Study in Socio-Cultural Change and Continuity and the Adaptation of a Population in Exile.* Ph.D. diss. in anthropology at State University of New York Stony Brook.

Gómez-Peña, Guillermo. 1988. "Documented/Undocumented." In Rick Simonson and Scott Walker, eds., *Multi-Cultural Literacy: Opening the American Mind.* St. Paul, MN: Graywolf Press.

Goodin, Robert E., Bruce Headey, Ruud Muffels, and Henk-Jan Dirven. 1999. *The Real Worlds of Welfare Capitalism.* Cambridge: Cambridge University Press.

Government of Nepal. 1994. *Refugees in Nepal: A Short Glimpse.* Kathmandu: Ministry of Home Affairs.

———. 1991. *The Constitution of the Kingdom of Nepal 2047 (1990).* Kathmandu: Ministry of Law, Justice and Parliamentary Affairs Law Books Management Board.

———. 1981. *The Constitution of Nepal 2019 (1962)*. Kathmandu: Ministry of Law and Justice Law Books Management Committee.

Guru-Gharana, Kishor Kumar. 1995. "Strategies for Poverty Alleviation in Nepal and the Role of Foreign Aid." Paper presented at a seminar on the political economy of small states, organized by the Nepal Foundation for Advanced Studies, March 7–8, Kathmandu, Nepal.

———. 1994. "Development Cooperation: An Appraisal of the Activities of Donor Agencies in Nepal." In Heinz Bongartz et al., eds., *Foreign Aid and the Role of NGOs in the Development Process of Nepal*. Kathmandu: Nepal Foundation for Advanced Studies.

Gyatso, Sherab. 1993. "Language Books that Scare Children Away." *Tibetan Review* 28 (9): 16.

Habermas, Jürgen. 1995. "Citizenship and National Identity: Some Reflections on the Future of Europe." In Ronald Beiner, ed., *Theorizing Citizenship*. Albany: State University of New York Press.

———. 1987. "Lifeworld and System: A Critique of Functionalist Reason." In *The Theory of Communicative Action*. Boston: Beacon Press.

Hagen, Toni. 1994. *Building Bridges to the Third World: Memories of Nepal, 1950–1992*. Delhi: Book Faith India.

Hammar, Tomas. 1990. *Democracy and the Nation State*. Aldershot, England: Avebury.

———. 1989. "State, Nation, and Dual Citizenship." In William Rogers Brubaker, ed., *Immigration and the Politics of Citizenship in Europe and North America*. Lanham, MD: University Press of America.

Hancock, Graham. 1989. *Lords of Poverty: The Free-Wheeling Lifestyles, Power, Prestige, and Corruption of the Multimillion Dollar Aid Business*. London: Macmillan.

Handelman, Don, and Elliott Leyton. 1978. *Bureaucracy and World View*. Toronto: Memorial University of Newfoundland.

Hannerz, Ulf. 1992. *Cultural Complexity: Studies in the Social Organization of Meaning*. New York: Columbia University Press.

———. 1987. "The World in Creolisation." *Africa* 57: 546–559.

Harrell-Bond, Barbara E. 1986. *Imposing Aid: Emergency Assistance to Refugees*. Oxford: Oxford University Press.

Harrer, Heinrich. 1983. *Return to Tibet*. New York: Penguin Books.

Harris, David C. 1987. *Justifying State Welfare: The New Rights versus the Old Left*. Oxford: Basil Blackwell.

Harris, Leon. 1979. *Merchant Princes: An Intimate History of Jewish Families Who Built Great Department Stores*. New York: Harper and Row.

Harvey, David. 1990. *The Condition of Postmodernity*. Malden, MA: Blackwell.

Heilbut, Anthony. 1983. *Exiled in Paradise: German Refugee Artists and Intellectuals in America from the 1930s to the Present*. New York: Viking Press.

Hirschman, Albert O. 1970. *Exit, Voice, and Loyalty: Responses to Decline in Firms, Organizations, and States*. Cambridge, MA: Harvard University Press.

Hobsbawm, Eric. 1981. "Introduction: Inventing Traditions." In Eric Hobsbawm and Terence Ranger, eds., *The Invention of Tradition*. Cambridge: Cambridge University Press.

Holborn, Louise. 1975. *Refugees: A Problem of Our Time (The Work of UN High Commissioner for Refugees, 1951–1972)*. Metuchen, NJ: The Scarecrow Press.

Hopkins, Terence K., and Immanuel Wallerstein. 1982. *World Systems Analysis: Theory and Methodology*. London: Sage Publications.

Hornblower, Margot. 1993. "States of Mind." *Time*, February 1.

Huffner, Bryan M. 1992. "The Tibetan Carpet Centre." *The Nepalese Tibetan Carpet*. Kathmandu: Nepal Traveller.

Information Office of the Dalai Lama. 1981. *Tibetans in Exile 1959–1980*. Dharamsala, India: Tibetan Exile Administration.

Jha, Hari Bansh. 1992. *Tibetans in Nepal*. Berkeley: University of California Press.

Jinpa, Tenzin. 1995. "A Tibetan Woman Recounts Beijing Women's Conference Memories." *Tibetan Bulletin* (September–December).

Joshi, H.D. 1983. "A History of the Tibetan Refugees in Nepal." Report prepared for the Swiss Association for Technical Assistance, Kathmandu, Nepal.

Joshi, Bhuwan Lal, and Leo E. Rose. 1966. *Democratic Innovations in Nepal: A Case Study of Political Acculturation.* Berkeley: University of California Press.

Kearney, Michael. 1995. "The Local and the Global: The Anthropology of Globalization and Transnationalism." *Annual Review of Anthropology* 24: 547–565.

Klieger, P. Christiaan. 1992. *Tibetan Nationalism: The Role of Patronage in the Accomplishment of a National Identity.* Berkeley, CA: Folklore Institute.

Knaus, John Kenneth. 1999. *Orphans of the Cold War: America and the Tibetan Struggle for Survival.* New York: PublicAffairs.

Kunz, Egon F. 1973. "The Refugee in Flight: Kinetic Models and Forms of Displacement." *International Migration Review* 7: 125–146.

Lévi, Sylvain. 1909. *Le Népal: Étude Historique d'un Royaume Hindou.* 3 vols. Paris: Leroux.

Levine, Nancy. 1988. *Dynamics of Polyandry: Kinship, Domesticity, and Population on the Tibetan Border.* Chicago: University of Chicago Press.

Lewis, Murial. 1975. "Letter from America: Coming of the Tibetans." *Tibetan Review* 10 (3): 22–23.

Lipman, Jonathan N. 1998. *Familiar Strangers: A History of Muslims in Northwest China.* Seattle: University of Washington Press.

Lyons, Gene M., and Michael Mastanduno. 1995. "Introduction: International Intervention, State Sovereignty, and the Future of International Society." In Gene M. Lyons and Michael Mastanduno, eds., *Beyond Westphalia? State Sovereignty and International Intervention.* Baltimore, MD: The Johns Hopkins University Press.

Malkki, Liisa H. 1995a. "Refugees and Exile: From 'Refugee Studies' to the National Order of Things." *Annual Review of Anthropology* 24: 495–523.

———. 1995b. *Purity and Exile: Violence, Memory, and National Cosmology among Hutu Refugees in Tanzania.* Chicago: University of Chicago Press.

———. 1994. "Citizens of Humanity: Internationalism and the Imagined Community of Nations." *Diaspora: A Journal of Transnational Studies* 3 (1): 41–68.

———. 1989. *Purity and Exile: Transformations in Historical-National Consciousness among Hutu Refugees in Tanzania.* Ph.D. diss. in anthropology at Harvard University.

Mann, Michael. 1987. "Ruling Class Strategies and Citizenship." *Sociology* 21: 339–354.

Marshall, T.H. 1965. *Class, Citizenship, and Social Development.* New York: Doubleday.

———. 1950. *Citizenship and Social Class and Other Essays.* Cambridge: Cambridge University Press.

McCarthy, Robert E. 1997. *Tears of the Lotus: Accounts of Tibetan Resistance to the Chinese Invasion, 1950–1962.* Jefferson, NC: McFarland and Company.

McLean, Sheila Avrin. 1983. "International Institutional Mechanisms for Refugees." In Mary M. Kritz, ed., *U.S. Immigration and Refugee Policy: Global and Domestic Issues.* Lexington, MA: Lexington Books.

Messerschmidt, Donald A. 1978. "Dhikurs: Rotating Credit Associations in Nepal." In James Fisher, ed., *Himalayan Anthropology.* The Hague: Mouton.

Meyer, John W., John Boli, and George M. Thomas. 1987. "Ontology and Rationalization in the Western Cultural Account." In George M. Thomas et al., eds., *Institutional Structure: Constituting State, Society, and the Individual.* London: Sage Publications.

Miller, Beatrice. 1978. "Tibetan Culture and Personality: Refugee Responses to a Tibetan Culture-Bound TAT." In James Fisher, ed., *Himalayan Anthropology.* The Hague: Mouton.

———. 1956. "Ganye and Kidu: Two Formalized Systems of Mutual Aid among the Tibetans." *Southwestern Journal of Anthropology* 12 (2): 157–170.

Nash, June. 1981. "Ethnographic Aspects of the World Capitalist System." *Annual Review of Anthropology* 10: 393–423.

Nepali, Gopal Singh. 1965. *The Newars: An Ethno-Sociological Study of a Himalayan Community*. Bombay: United Asia Publications.

Norbu, Dawa. 1994. "Refugees from Tibet: Structural Causes of Successful Resettlement." Paper presented at the Fourth International Research and Advisory Panel, Refugee Studies Programme, Oxford University.

Norbu, Jamyang. 1990. "Opening of the Political Eye: Tibet's Long Search for Democracy." *Tibetan Review* 25 (11): 13–17.

Norbu, Thubten Jigme. 1990. "I Am Proven Right about Taiwan." *Tibetan Review* 25 (2): 10–11.

———. 1960. *Tibet Is My Country*. London: Hart-Davis.

Nowak, Margaret. 1984. *Tibetan Refugees: Youth and the New Generation of Meaning*. New Brunswick, NJ: Rutgers University Press.

Offe, Claus. 1972. "Advanced Capitalism and the Welfare State." *Politics and Society* 2: 479–488.

Ong, Aihwa. 1999. *Flexible Citizenship: The Cultural Logics of Transnationality*. Durham, NC: Duke University Press.

Onuf, Nicholas. 1995. "Intervention for the Common Good." In Gene M. Lyons and Michael Mastanduno, eds., *Beyond Westphalia? State Sovereignty and International Intervention*. Baltimore, MD: The Johns Hopkins University Press.

Petech, Luciano. 1988. "The Dalai Lamas and Regents of Tibet." *Selected Papers on Asian History*. Roma: Instituto Italiano Per Il Medio Ed Estremo Oriente.

Philpott, Daniel. 1997. "Ideas and the Evolution of Sovereignty." In Sohail H. Hashmi, ed., *State Sovereignty: Change and Persistence in International Relations*. University Park, PA: The Pennsylvania State University Press.

Pradhan, Gouri. 1993. *Misery behind the Looms: Child Labourers in the Carpet Factories in Nepal*. Kathmandu: Child Workers in Nepal Concerned Centre.

Prebish, Charles S. 1979. *American Buddhism*. Belmont, CA: Duxbury Press.

Ramirez, Francisco O. 1987. "Institutional Analysis." In George M. Thomas et al., eds., *Institutional Structure: Constituting State, Society, and the Individual*. London: Sage Publications.

Ray, Reginald A. 1986. "Some Aspects of the Tulku Tradition in Tibet." *The Tibet Journal* 11 (4): 35–69.

Regmi, Mahesh Chandra. 1965. *Land Tenure and Taxation in Nepal*. Berkeley: University of California Institute of International Studies.

Reynell, Josphine. 1989. *Political Pawns: Refugees on the Thai-Kampuchean Border*. Oxford: Refugee Studies Programme.

Richardson, Hugh. 1984. *Tibet and Its History*. Boston: Shambhala Publications.

Robinson, Richard H., and Willard L. Johnson. 1996. *The Buddhist Religion: A Historical Introduction*. Belmont, CA: Wadsworth Publishing Company.

Rose, Leo E. 1971. *Nepal: Strategy for Survival*. Berkeley: University of California Press.

Rosenau, James N. 1995. "Sovereignty in a Turbulent World." In Gene M. Lyons and Michael Mastanduno, eds., *Beyond Westphalia? State Sovereignty and International Intervention*. Baltimore, MD: The Johns Hopkins University Press.

Saklani, Girija. 1984. *The Uprooted Tibetans in India: A Sociological Study of Continuity and Change*. New Delhi: Cosmo Publishers.

Samdup, Thubten. 1992. "Proceedings of the Second Session of the 11th Parliament." *News Tibet* (May–August).

Schüh, Dieter. 1988. *Das Archiv des Klosters bKra-sis-bsam-gtan-glin von sKyid-gron*. Bonn: VGH Wissenschaftsverlag GmbH.

Scott, James C. 1998. *Seeing Like a State: How Certain Schemes to Improve the Human Condition Have Failed*. New Haven, CT: Yale University Press.

———. 1985. *Weapons of the Weak: Everyday Forms of Peasant Resistance*. New Haven, CT: Yale University Press.

Sen, Amartya. 1981. *Poverty and Famines: An Essay on Entitlement and Deprivation.* Oxford: Clarendon Press.

Sever, Adrian. 1993. *Nepal under the Ranas.* New Delhi: Oxford and IBH Publishing Company.

Shah, Saubhagya. 1993. "Throes of a Fledgling Nation." *Himal* 6 (2): 7–10.

Shakabpa, Tsepon W. D. 1967. *Tibet: A Political History.* New Haven, CT: Yale University Press.

Shakya, Tsering. 1999. *The Dragon in the Land of Snows: A History of Tibet Since 1947.* New York: Columbia University Press.

———. 1992. "Tibet and the Occident: The Myth of Shangri-La." *Tibetan Review* 27 (1): 13–16.

Shain, Yossi. 1989. *The Frontier of Loyalty: Political Exiles in the Age of the Nation-State.* Middletown, CT: Wesleyan University Press.

Shawcross, William. 1984. *The Quality of Mercy: Cambodia, Holocaust and Modern Conscience.* London: Andre Deutsch.

Sheffer, Gabriel. 1993. "Ethnic Diasporas: A Threat to their Hosts?" In Myron Weiner, ed., *International Migration and Security.* Boulder, CO: Westview Press.

Shrestha, Bijaya Bahadur. 1992. "The Nepalese Tibetan Carpet: An Overview of the Industry." *The Nepalese Tibetan Carpet.* Kathmandu: Nepal Traveller.

Slusser, Mary Shepherd. 1982. *Nepal Mandala: A Cultural History of the Kathmandu Valley.* Princeton: Princeton University Press.

Sowell, Thomas. 1996. *Migrations and Cultures: A World View.* New York: Basic Books.

Soysal, Yasemin Nuhoglu. 1994. *Limits of Citizenship: Migrants and Postnational Membership in Europe.* Chicago: University of Chicago Press.

Subba, Phanindra. 1993. *Nepal's Quest for Security.* M.A. thesis submitted to the Department of International Relations, International University of Japan.

"Taiwan and Tibet." 1976. *Tibetan Review* 11 (1): 18.

"Taiwan Plans to Spend U.S. $4 m on Tibetans this Year." 1990. *Tibetan Review* 25 (9): 8.

Takhla, Tenzin Namdak. 1990. "The Taiwan Scandal – Who is to be Blamed?" *Tibetan Review* 25 (2): 8–9.

Taring, Rinchen Dolma. 1970. *Daughter of Tibet.* New Delhi: Allied Publishers.

Thinley, Pema. 1990. "Democracy in the Tibetan Society." *Tibetan Review* 25 (1): 12–15.

Thinley, Tenzin. 1993. "Responses and Rejoinders." *Tricycle: The Buddhist Review* (Spring): 7–8.

Thomas, George M., et al., eds. 1987. *Institutional Structure: Constituting State, Society, and the Individual.* London: Sage Publications.

Thomas, Jr., Lowell. 1950. *Out of This World: A Journey to Lhasa.* New York: Greystone Press.

Tibetan Women's Delegation. 1996. *Tibetan Women's Delegation Report on the United Nations Fourth Conference on Women.* Dharamsala, India: Tibetan Women's Delegation.

Trade Promotion Centre. 1992. "The Carpet Explosion." *The Nepalese Tibetan Carpet.* Kathmandu: Nepal Traveller.

Trevor-Roper, Hugh. 1981. "The Invention of Tradition: The Highland Tradition of Scotland." In Eric Hobsbawm and Terence Ranger, eds., *The Invention of Tradition.* Cambridge: Cambridge University Press.

Tsering, Tashi. 1994. "sman-rta brjes-pa ma-gtogs sman brjes med." *dmangs-gtso* 5 (12): 1–2.

Turner, Victor. 1969. *The Ritual Process: Structure and Anti-Structure.* Ithaca, NY: Cornell University Press.

Uprety, Narayan Prasad, and Yagya Nath Acharya. 1994. *An Outline History of Nepal.* Kathmandu: Ekta Books Distributors.

Uprety, Prem. 1984. *Nepal: A Small Nation in the Vortex of International Conflicts, 1900–1950.* Kathmandu: Pugo Mi.

———. 1980. *Nepal-Tibet Relations, 1850–1930: Years of Hopes, Challenges, and Frustrations.* Kathmandu: Puga Nara.

U.S. Department of State. 1995. *Nepal.* Washington, DC: U.S. Department of State Bureau of Public Affairs.

U.S. Senate Foreign Relations Committee. 1993. "U.S. and Chinese Policies toward Occupied Tibet: Hearing before the Committee on Foreign Relations, United States Senate, One Hundred Second Congress, second session, July 28, 1992." Washington, DC: U.S. Government Printing Office.

van Gennep, Arnold. 1960. *The Rites of Passage.* Chicago: University of Chicago Press.

von Fürer-Haimendorf, Christoph. 1990. *The Renaissance of Tibetan Civilization.* Oracle, AZ: Synergetic Press, Inc.

———. 1975. *Himalayan Traders: Life in Highland Nepal.* London: John Murray.

Wallerstein, Immanuel. 1975. *The Modern World System: Capitalist Agriculture and the Origin of the European World Economy in the Sixteenth Century.* New York: Academic Press.

Walzer, Michael. 1983. *Spheres of Justice: Defense of Pluralism and Equality.* New York: Basic Books.

Wangdi, Tashi. 1996. "Self-Determination and the Tibetan Issue." Dharamsala: Department of Information and International Relations.

Wangmo, Kesang. 1995. "China's Attempt to Pit Sister Against Sister Fails as Tibetan Women Reinforce their Identity in Beijing." *Tibetan Bulletin.* (September–December).

Wangyal, Tsering. 1979. "A Mixed Blessing." *Tibetan Review* 14 (1): 4.

Weber, Max. 1978 (1968). *Economy and Society.* Berkeley: University of California Press.

Weiner, Myron. 1998. "The Clash of Norms: Dilemmas in Refugee Policies." *Journal of Refugee Studies* 11 (4): 433–453.

———. 1996. "Nations Without Borders: The Gifts of Folk Gone Abroad." *Foreign Affairs* 75 (2): 128–134.

———. 1995. *The Global Migration Crisis: Challenge to States and to Human Rights.* New York: HarperCollins College Publishers.

Worcester, Ted. 1992. "A History of the Tibetan Carpet in Nepal." *The Nepalese Tibetan Carpet.* Kathmandu: Nepal Traveller.

Wylie, Turrell V. 1959. "A Standard System of Tibetan Transcription." *Harvard Journal of Asiatic Studies* 22: 261–267.

Yeshe, Pedron, and Jeremy Russell. 1986. "The Re-establishment of the Tibetan Monasteries in Exile." *Chö-Yang.* Dharamsala, India: Department of Religion and Cultural Affairs.

Yeshi, Kim. 1991. "The Tibetan Buddhist View of the Environment." *Chö-Yang.* Dharamsala, India: Department of Religion and Cultural Affairs.

Young, Iris Marion. 1995. "Polity and Group Difference: A Critique of the Ideal of Universal Citizenship." In Ronald Beiner, ed., *Theorizing Citizenship.* Albany: State University of New York Press.

Yuthok, Dorje Yudon. 1990. *House of the Turquoise Roof.* Ithaca, NY: Snow Lion Publications.

Zetter, Roger. 1992. "Refugees and Forced Migrants as Development Resources: The Greek Cypriot Refugees from 1974." *The Cyprus Review* 4 (1): 7–39.

Zolberg, Aristide, Astri Suhrke, and Sergio Aguayo. 1989. *Escape from Violence: Conflict and the Refugee Crisis in the Developing World.* Oxford: Oxford University Press.

Index

accommodation of values
limits, xi, 26–28, 65, 93, 111–117, 197
role in maintaining international assistance, ix–xi, 3, 9–14, 25–28, 50–53, 64–65, 93–94, 103, 105–111, 117–119, 120n5, 173, 180, 194–197
alumni associations, 177, 180, 204
Amdo (Amdowa), 67, 173, 184–185, 191n16, 206
Amnesty International, 21, 92, 98, 100, 110
Anderson, Benedict, 174–176
anti-communism, 9, 64, 66, 140
anticipatory refugees, 171n32
Appadurai, Arjun, 20, 24, 62n39, 197
Assembly of Tibetan People's Deputies, 62n35, 64, 75, 79–80, 90n23, 91n26, 119, 178, 184–185
Association Tibet Libre, xix, 92, 106–108
Atisha School, xxiv, 85–86, 106–113, 154–155, 158–162, 170n17, 171n30
authenticity, 109, 114, 116, 197
authority, x, xiii, 3–4, 13–14, 16–17, 21, 26, 31n18, 76, 83, 89n9, 91n32, 96, 125, 149–167, 168n5, 190n3, 194, 199
Aziz, Barbara, 185

Baba Yeshe, 17, 70–72, 89n9, 156–157, 169n11, 169n12, 169n13
Barth, Fredrik, xiv, 3
bat metaphor, x–xi, 1, 3, 20, 26, 28, 197
Beiner, Ronald, 19
Bhutanese refugees in Nepal, 135, 138, 140, 141–143
Birendra, King of Nepal, 71–72, 121n18, 124, 127–128, 141
Bishop, Peter, 95–96, 120n8
blue books (refugee identity booklets), 124–125, 135, 140–146, 148n24
bodhisattva, 76, 172
Boli, John, 25, 198
Bonacich, Edna, 32n23
Boudha, xii, xxii, 1, 38–39, 69, 72–73, 78, 84, 86, 90n13, 111, 113, 121n26, 129, 149, 153, 160, 170n17, 170n24, 178, 181, 191n11, 203
Britain, 53–54, 63, 88n1, 89n3, 120n6
Brubaker, Rogers, 15, 146n3
Buddhism: Tibetan, xi
authenticity of interpretation, 116–117
imitation of Buddha as practice, 114–115
preservation as a system of knowledge, 10

reinterpretation in the West, 93, 96, 98, 100, 113–115, 121n26, 121n27
sectarian divisions, 173, 183, 185, 191n16
veneration of Buddha as practice, 114
view of the Dalai Lamas, 65, 76

Cabinet of Ministers (kashag), 64–65, 75, 91n28, 157, 170n15, 171n34, 174, 204
Camp Hale, 67–68
carpet factories
factory owners, xii, 1, 20, 28, 186
independently owned, 49–50, 53, 61n35, 185
role in patron client system, 8
Swiss-Tibetan, 6, 29n7, 35, 41–43, 45–58, 60n27, 60n28, 194
symbol of Tibetan success, 4–6
U.S.-Tibetan, 6, 53, 64, 66, 71–73, 194
carpet industry
initial development, 41–53
role in Nepal's economy, 4, 29n8, 54, 131
Tibetan control over, viii, 6, 35, 131, 193
See also child labor
Carpet Trading Company (CTC), xvi, 46–50, 54, 59n14, 60n23, 61n29, 61n30
carpets
modern designs, 52, 62n39
production costs, 52, 55–56, 91n33
sales, 4, 30n9, 54
traditional designs, 52–53, 62n39
weaving process, 42, 52–55, 62n39, 73, 91n33
Cassese, Antonio, 190n3
celebrity support for Tibet
Gere, Richard, 88, 94, 97, 99, 195
Seagal, Stevan, 94, 112, 121n24
Yauch, Adam, 92
Chambers, Robert, 15, 30n10
charisma, 16–17, 150–151, 163–165, 167, 168n4, 168n5, 171n33, 196
charity, 10
Charter for the Tibetan Exiles, 64–65, 75, 83–84, 87, 91n23, 91n32, 130, 147n6, 170n20, 176–177
Chialsa, 40, 43, 60n27, 78, 129
child labor, 56, 62n48, 158
China (PRC)
guerrilla war against, 6, 15, 64, 66–68
incorporation of Tibet into, 38, 63–68, 105, 179